A Shortcut to Understanding Affective Neuroscience

Lucy Biven

Fulton Books
Meadville, PA

Published by Fulton Books 2022

Cover image design by Laura Biven Semmelmann

ISBN 978-1-63860-096-1 (paperback)
ISBN 978-1-63860-097-8 (digital)

Printed in the United States of America

For Barrie.

Contents

Introduction

The origins of this book date back to a 1993 custody case between two couples locked in a legal battle over a two-and-a-half-year-old girl. The child's biological mother gave birth in her mid-twenties and agreed to a private adoption, but before it was final, the prospective parents took the newborn into their home. The biological mother soon regretted her decision, and within a week or two, the baby's father, who had not agreed to the adoption, petitioned for his daughter's return. The custodial couple who wanted to adopt the child refused to comply, igniting protracted legal machinations that culminated in the US Supreme Court. The Court ruled in favor of the biological parents and set a date for the child to move to her new home, which was when I became involved. My job was to devise and implement a plan for the transfer of custody. Psychoanalytic theories of development predicted a dire future for the little girl, but she fared well in her new home. Neuroscience, on the other hand, offered specific and detailed reasons for the happy ending.

A public furor erupted in the wake of the Supreme Court decision. By then the biological parents were married and had a new baby, but they were strangers to their daughter. Many child psychiatrists, psychologists, and psychoanalysts believed that a transfer of custody would inflict permanent emotional damage on the toddler. They stressed the importance of her emotional attachment to her custodial mother—the only mother she had ever known. They said that a separation would cause the child to lose part of her identity and her ability to form wholesome relationships would be forever tainted (Lawrence 1993).

They anticipated that the child would be initially devastated, weeping uncontrollably, lashing out in anger, and cowering in terror by turns. They foresaw regressions typical of childhood trauma: she might lose recently acquired verbal skills, abandon toilet training, or refuse food and reject her cup in favor of the bottle. In time, she might appear to adjust, but any ostensible normality would be a hollow pretense, masking her underlying turmoil and misery (Ingrassia and Springen 1994).

Nineteen experts in child development put their names to an amicus brief sent to the Supreme Court, emphasizing the "serious and irreparable harm from the severing of her family attachments at a crucial stage in her development." They highlighted the prospect of the child facing "a devastating deprivation of 'intangible values' of trust and emotional security for which there are no substitutes, and which can never be restored." They stressed that such "harm to children's mental and emotional development involves injuries that cannot be reversed or remedied" (Finkbiner et al. 1993).

The experts based their predictions largely on the teachings of John Bowlby, who proposed that babies and young children have an innate need to be attached to a primary caregiver—either mother or a mother substitute. Bowlby's attachment theory marked a departure from the prevailing belief that a child becomes attached to mother because she provides food and care (Dollard and Miller 1950). In Bowlby's view, the need for attachment is instinctive and independent of everything else (Bowlby 1969).

Bowlby formulated his ideas about attachment by observing the emotional distress of children who had been temporarily separated from their parents and placed in institutional settings like hospitals or children's homes. These children exhibited a debilitating emotional sequence of protest, despair, and detachment (Bowlby 1951). In support of his attachment theory, Bowlby referred to Rene Spitz's seminal studies of infants raised in orphanages where they received adequate nutrition and physical care but had little opportunity to interact with a maternal figure. These infants failed to thrive, they were prone to infections, and they often died (Spitz 1945 and 1946; Ainsworth 1962). Bowlby cited Lorenz's imprinting studies, where baby geese bonded with Lorenz and followed him about as if he were their mother (Lorenz 1935). He also referred to Harlow's experiments, where baby monkeys demonstrated their need for tactile comfort by preferring a terrycloth dummy without milk to a wire one with milk (Harlow 1958).

Bowlby did not just emphasize the importance of maternal care. He maintained that a child's attachment to her primary caretaker is specific and sacrosanct. In his view, nobody could successfully replace a primary caretaker (Bowlby 1988). If the relationship were disrupted or worse yet severed, especially when a child was between the ages of six months and four years, the child would suffer the emotional trajectory of protest, despair, and detachment and would be at risk of developing life-long antisocial behavior along with problems in forming wholesome relationships (Bowlby 1969).

Many of Bowlby's contemporaries agreed that young children need to be attached to a mother figure. Some, however, questioned his belief that a primary caretaker is irreplaceable. Anna Freud believed that the affectionate care of a surrogate mother would mitigate or eliminate a child's emotional suffering and prevent long-term emotional damage. James Robertson, who had worked closely with Bowlby in the early years of his career, agreed with Anna Freud (Van Der Horst and Van Der Veer 2009).

Robertson and his wife, Joyce, filmed documentary studies of toddlers and young children who were separated from their mothers for a week or two and left in Mrs. Robertson's care. Before the separation, Joyce Robertson paid visits to the family home, making friends with the child and eventually taking over some maternal duties like feeding and bathing. During mother's absence, all the children bonded well with Mrs. Robertson and none suffered the distress that Bowlby had observed in institutionalized children (Robertson and Robertson 1967, 1968, 1971).

The Robertsons' protocol applied only to temporary mother/child separations, but it was the best plan available, so it was the one that we used in the child custody case. Following the Robertsons' directives, the custodial parents introduced the child to her biological parents as family friends. The little girl then had twice-weekly, two-hour meetings with her biological parents for three weeks. The custodial parents attended all meetings as did I and, on some occasions, an attorney for the custodial parents.

Things went well from the start. Within a half hour of the first visit, the child was engaged in lively conversation with her biological mother, leaning against her leg and smiling up at her. All the visits went similarly well, and by the end of the three weeks, she viewed her biological parents as she would a favorite aunt and uncle.

Many were incredulous when the child adjusted well in her new home. She expressed moments of confusion, which her parents explained as and when they arose, but she did not display signs of distress or misery and she continued to develop normally. Her vocabulary increased and the toilet training proceeded without interruption. She continued to eat well and drink from a cup. Soon she called her parents Mommy and Daddy and formed fond relationships with her grandparents along with other members of the extended family. She played well with other children and was popular with everyone. In the years that followed, she continued to thrive (Dickerson 2003).

I searched the literature to see if other child psychotherapists had recorded similar good outcomes. The children whom James and Joyce Robertson observed bonded well with Mrs. Robertson, but they were eventually reunited with their mothers. I did not find a case history of a child who moved permanently from one set of parents to another. Virtually all case histories of mother-child separations focused on the deleterious effects that occur when separated children do not have the benefit of good surrogate care (Howard et al. 2011).

I turned to neuroscience for answers and found research supporting Bowlby's view that all young children—indeed all young mammals—crave a close relationship to a nurturing and protective caregiver, typically mother (Panksepp 1998a). But was Bowlby right to claim that the relationship with mother is exclusive? The Robertsons' films suggested that he was not, but Bowlby firmly maintained that an early separation from mother under any circumstances would cause emotional harm (Bowlby 1960; Van Der Horst and Van Der Veer 2009).

Bowlby believed that early separations cause emotional damage because he, like most psychoanalysts of his day, accepted Freud's theory of infantile repression (Bowlby 1960). Freud proposed that infants repress memories, which is why we cannot consciously recall events that happened when we were very young. Freud, however, maintained that repression does not erase early memories but rather relegates them to our unconscious minds where they continue to exist and influence the ways that we think, feel, and behave (Freud 1905). According to Freud, when the orphaned babies in the Spitz studies grew older, they would retain unconscious memories of their motherless desolation. Similarly, the institutionalized toddlers whom Bowlby observed would unconsciously remember feeling abandoned and betrayed by their mothers. The child in the custody dispute would also retain painful unconscious memories about the separation from her custodial mother.

Neuroscientists now know that Freud's theory of infantile repression is incorrect. A structure in the middle of the temporal lobe is called the *hippocampus* because that is the Greek word for seahorse, which this structure resembles. The hippocampus creates enduring personal memories, but it does not begin to function until a child is about four years old (Newcombe et al. 2000; Gleitman et al. 2007). Babies and young children can retain short-term memories, but the neural pathways that encode these memories dissolve after a few weeks or months and the children forget (Fivush and Hamond 1990).

Short- and long-term memories are structurally different. The difference involves the activity of genes within the neurons of the memory pathway. Every cell in an organism, with the exception of germ cells, has the same genes. In different types of cells, some genes are active while others are dormant. For example, some genes are active in kidney cells and others are active in liver cells. Genes make proteins that perform functions, so kidney and liver cells perform different functions. When dormant genes are *expressed* (activated) in a cell, that cell performs functions that it did not perform before (Hoopes 2008).

Long-term memories are created when dormant genes are expressed in the neurons of a memory pathway. These genes produce proteins that keep neurons in the pathway, communicating with one another for a long time—often for a lifetime. When neurons in a memory pathway stay connected, the information that the pathway encodes is retained (Kandel 2006).

Neurons in short-term memory pathways do not undergo gene expression. These neurons have a limited supply of the proteins that keep neurons communicating with one another, but the proteins eventually run out and neurons no longer communicate. When this happens, the memory encoded in the pathway is erased (Kandel 2006). An immature hippocampus cannot make long-term memory pathways, which is why young children can only harbor short-term memories about people, things, and events.

If the child in the custody case had been able to retain enduring memories about her custodial mother, the memories might have been a source of grief. She might have continued to long for her custodial mother or blame the mother for abandoning her. She might have also blamed herself for the abandonment. However, because her hippocampus was immature, she eventually forgot. The memories of the custodial mother were not repressed. The memories no longer existed.

Nevertheless, people can be damaged by infantile experiences that they cannot remember. The babies and toddlers whom Spitz and Bowbly studied could not have remembered anything about the conditions that harmed them, yet harmed they were. If they could not remember, how did their infantile experiences harm them?

Neuroscience offers explanations for unremembered damage, three of which we will briefly discuss. Stressful situations arouse the *sympathetic nervous system* (SNS), which directs an initial fight-or-flight response to danger. The SNS activates the *adrenal glands* that sit on top of the kidneys. One of the hormones secreted by the adrenal glands is *epinephrine* (known also as *adrenaline)*. Epinephrine enters the blood stream, causing increased heart rate, heightened blood pressure, rapid respiration, and the opening of airways in the lungs. Senses like vision and hearing become sharper (Harvard

Medical School 2020). The adrenal gland also secretes *cortisol*, a stress hormone, which makes us alert and causes the liver to produce glucose that can be used as an energy source for skeletal muscles in case a vigorous response to a threat, like attacking or running away, is necessary (Stephens and Wand 2012).

If stressful situations are prolonged, the SNS can have deleterious effects. Chronic SNS activity causes skeletal muscles to become persistently tense in readiness for action. Chronic muscular tension can cause pain and decreased muscle use, which can result in atrophy of skeletal muscles. SNS overarousal is also linked to heart disease, hypertension, inflammation of coronary arteries, and high cholesterol (American Psychological Association, 2018). Most important for our discussion, prolonged arousal of the SNS causes the overproduction of cortisol, which suppresses the immune system, thereby increasing the susceptibility to infection (Dana and Whirledge 2017).

When rat pups are separated from their mothers, they display heightened SNS activity (Loria et al. 2013), indicating that maternal separations are stressful. When one-year-old human infants with insecure attachments to their mothers are left alone in the company of a stranger, they display more SNS arousal than do infants with secure attachments. This indicates that insecure mother-infant bonds also cause stress (Köhler-Dauner et al. 2019).

Stressful situations also activate the *hypothalamic—pituitary—adrenal axis* (HPA axis), which is a second reason for unremembered damage (Drolet et al. 2001). The HPA axis, like the SNS, generates a stress response to a threat. It originates in a part of the hypothalamus (the *paraventricular nucleus*), which secretes two hormones, (*vasopressin and corticotropin-releasing factor* [CRF]). Together, these two hormones stimulate the pituitary gland, which lies just below the hypothalamus, and produces a third hormone (*adrenocorticotropic hormone* [ACTH]), which is released into the bloodstream. This third hormone circulates down to the adrenal gland on top of the kidneys. The HPA axis causes the adrenal gland to secrete *cortisol*, which the adrenal gland also produces as a result of SNS arousal. As we noted above, cortisol provides energy and alertness that help meet a challenge (Stephens and Wand 2012).

When the stressful situation abates, cortisol circulates back to the hypothalamus and to the pituitary gland, instructing them to stop producing stress hormones. Thus, cortisol produces a negative feedback that causes the HPA axis and the stress response to wind down. However, if one cannot escape from or resolve the stressful situation, cortisol feedback is unable to quell the activity of the hypothalamus or the pituitary gland and the HPA axis remains in overdrive (Gjerstad et al. 2015).

In young animals like monkeys and guinea pigs, even brief maternal separations activate the HPA axis (Maken et al. 2016). Chronic HPA axis overarousal produces a host of deleterious effects. It has been linked to childhood anxiety (Dieleman et al. 2015) and depression (Lopez-Duran et al. 2015), to cognitive impairments (Aisa et al. 2007), inflammation in the brain (Cirulli et al. 2009; Harro and Oreland 2001; Miller et al. 2009), destruction of neurons in the hippocampus (Sapolsky 1992; McEwen, and Sapolsky 1995), destruction of muscles and blood vessels (Damasio in Popova 2019), infertility, irritable bowel syndrome, and post-traumatic stress disorder. As we noted above, persistent production of cortisol suppresses the body's immune response and increases the possibility of infection (Dana and Whirledge 2017).

A third cause of unremembered damage concerns the activity of *endogenous opioids* which have the same effect as do opiates like morphine and heroin. In small doses, these chemicals induce feelings of affective comfort. Under normal conditions, the brain's opioid activity depends on social relationships. If we are abandoned, rejected, or defeated, opioid activity in our brains plummets and we feel miserable; but when we are in the company of people we love, our brains are awash with endogenous opioids and we feel a joyful sense of belonging (Panksepp 1998a).

Maternal separations cause a decrease in opioid activity. If rat pups are separated from their mothers and kept in isolation, the number of opioid receptors in their brains decreases (Bernardi et al. 1986) and they continue to be anxious into adulthood (Daniels et al. 2004). When puppies, guinea pigs, and bird chicks are separated from their mothers, they persistently wail; but if small amounts of opiates are infused into their brains, their cries cease, they close their eyes, and they relax (Panksepp 1981). People who suffer from depression, as well those who commit suicide, have depleted opioid levels in their brains (Gross-Isseroff et al. 1998; Zubieta et al. 2003; Kennedy et al. 2006). Drug addicts, who typically suffer from chronic depression and anxiety (Smith 2018), crave the blissful relief that opiates provide (Kosten and George 2002).

Thus, separation from mother increases SNS activity (Kohler-Dauner et al. 2019) and activity of the HPA axis (Ploj et al. 2003; Aisa et al. 2007) as well as causing a decrease in opioid activity (Dimatelis et al. 2012). Probably the orphaned babies in the Spitz studies contracted infections and died because the SNS and HPA axes produced excessive amounts of cortisol which suppressed their immune systems. Diminished opioid activity and activation of the SNS and HPA axis would also explain their joyless demeanor and persistent crying. Similarly, the institutionalized children whom Bowlby observed probably had low opioid activity and hyper HPA and SNS activity, which would explain why they were so miserable and anxious.

In contrast, when Joyce Robertson served as a surrogate mother, the children in her care displayed no significant signs of anxiety or unhappiness, which indicates that their attachment to her protected their brains by keeping opioid levels and HPA/SNS activity within normal limits. The child in the custody dispute also enjoyed continuity of care, and like the Robertson children, she did not suffer. This evidence indicates that Bowlby was right in thinking that young children have an innate need to be attached to a primary caregiver, but he was wrong to believe that children can be attached to only one maternal figure.

To summarize, two areas of brain research explain why the little girl in the custody case adjusted so well to her new home. First, she did not endure emotional pain that might have resulted from long-term memories about her custodial mother because her immature hippocampus could not create those memories. Second, because she enjoyed continuity of care from a devoted maternal figure, SNS, HPA axis, and opioid activity in her brain remained normal. As she forgot her custodial mother, she became ever more closely bonded to her biological mother and emerged from her ordeal unscathed.

It was striking to realize that many child experts misjudged the outcome of this case while neuroscience explained it so convincingly. From then on, I wanted to learn more about the emotional brain.

Most neuroscientists distinguish between *emotion* and *affect* (Paul et al. 2020). They see emotion as a purely physiological response. Some emotional responses like the influx of stress chemicals into the bloodstream cause blushing, sweating, pupil dilation, rapid heartbeat, and so on—reactions that take place inside the body (Purves et al. 2001). Emotion also includes behaviors like smiling, frowning, freezing, approaching, or running away. You can observe and measure emotional responses. Affects, on the other hand, are private conscious experiences that we cannot directly perceive in others. We can only infer the existence of affects by observing behavior or by listening to people when they tell us how they feel (Damasio 2005; Adolphs 2017).

The distinction between emotion and affect, however, is confusing because neuroscientists have different views about both words. Some say that our brains contain genetically hardwired systems, each of which generates a different emotion. They claim that each emotional system consists of identified brain structures that are fueled by specific chemicals and each system generates stereotypical emotional responses that are easy to identify. The fear system, for example, includes pupil dilation, hair standing on end, rapid heartbeat, and freezing (LeDoux 1996; Panksepp 1998a). Others say that emotional systems do not exist and that you cannot assign an emotion to any particular part of the brain. They also claim that emotional responses are ambiguous, so it is often impossible to distinguish one emotional response from another (Barrett 2017a).

Affects pose even more perplexing questions. Most agree that affects are conscious feelings that occur when emotional systems are aroused (Adolphs 2017), but this does not tell us how affects are created. Some researchers say that the cognitive cortex, the outer layer of the brain, creates affects (LeDoux 1996). Others say that affects are feelings of pleasure and pain, created by noncognitive structures that lie deep in the brain (Damasio 1999). Some say that animals like dogs, cats, and rats feel affects just as we do (Panksepp 1998a). Others claim that animals have emotional responses, but they do not experience affective feelings (LeDoux 1996). Some say that homeostatic balance in the body generates positive affect and that homeostatic imbalance signals negative feelings (Damasio 1999). Others say that affective pleasure and pain are independent of homeostasis (Panksepp 1998a).

Research supporting these disparate views is rigorous and persuasive. How can a lay person like me—or you—decide which view is right and which is wrong? It took me more than twenty-five years before I was able to make those decisions, and I wrote this book to provide you with a shortcut to understanding the foundations of affective consciousness.

Each of the first three chapters discusses a different school of thought about emotion and affect. One school espouses a *feedback theory*, which maintains that affects emerge from cognitive parts of the cortex. This feedback theory claims that brain regions beneath the cognitive cortex generate stereotypical emotional responses and feed those responses back to the cognitive cortex, which identifies them as a particular emotion. When this happens, we feel the corresponding affect. For example, if deep layers of my brain caused my heartbeat to accelerate, my hair to stand on end, and I froze in my tracks, these responses would be fed back to my cognitive cortex, which would identify them as fear. Then I would feel frightened (LeDoux 1996).

I call the second school *brainstem theory* because it maintains that all mammalian brains contain genetically programmed emotional systems, located largely in and around the brainstem. Jaak Panksepp has delineated a taxonomy of seven basic emotional systems. In addition to claiming the existence of seven emotional systems, the brainstem school denies that the cognitive cortex creates affects. It proposes instead that affects, like emotional systems, emerge largely from deep noncognitive regions of the brainstem (Panksepp 1998a; Damasio 1999).

A third school, known as the conceptual act theory (CAT), claims that emotional systems do not exist and that emotions do not emanate from any specific brain region. According to this school, affects depend on concepts that we construct largely on the basis of social experience. For example, our brains construct a concept about fear by observing fear in other people and by hearing them speak about fear. This concept enables us to experience fearful affects (Barrett 2017a).

Each school of thought has difficulty making its case, but chapter 4 cites evidence indicating that brainstem theory is the only viable option; emotional brain systems exist and affects emanate largely from subcortical brain stem structures. Since the brains of all mammals have these subcortical structures, all mammals experience the same basic affects.

Chapters 5 and 6 further delve brainstem theory by examining two different hypotheses, one by Antonio Damasio and the other by Jaak Panksepp, explaining how affects might be created. The hypotheses are similar because both agree that affects emanate largely from structures in and around the brainstem. However, they propose different mechanisms about how this happens. The mechanism that Damasio proposes claims that affects depend on bodily homeostasis. In his view, homeostatic balance generates positive affects while imbalance gives rise to negative affects. Panksepp, on the other hand, proposes a mechanism where affects are independent of homeostasis.

Chapter 7 evaluates both hypotheses. Both Damasio and Panksepp assume that consciousness always includes a sense of selfhood. Some evidence, albeit inconclusive, questions this assumption. Each hypothesis also has specific difficulties. Panksepp claims to explain how the brain creates all feelings of pleasure and pain, but he only offers an explanation for the creation of affective pleasure and pain. He does not describe how the brain creates pleasant and painful sensations. Damasio's hypothesis claims that emotional behaviors, like running away, attacking, or approaching, have the purpose of restoring, maintaining, or optimizing homeostasis. This is not always the case. For example, the protective behavior of mothers can undermine the mother's homeostasis.

All the research cited in the first seven chapters implicitly assumes that the brain creates conscious affective feelings, an assumption that brings us face-to-face with the proverbial *hard question* of consciousness, which we discuss in chapter 8. The hard question of consciousness asks how the physical brain creates nonphysical conscious experiences like affects. How do bits of flesh in our heads make us feel happy, lonely, caring, or curious? We will examine evidence indicating that affective consciousness does indeed emanate from the brain, but nobody knows how this happens (Greenfield 2000).

We then discuss an even harder question that neuroscientists often try to avoid, which asks how nonphysical consciousness changes the workings of the physical brain. Robust evidence indicates that conscious ideas have the power to change the brain, but again, no one knows how this is achieved (Gazzaniga 2012). We conclude that although the mechanisms for these mind-body interactions remain a mystery. Experimental evidence indicates that consciousness emanates from the brain, and it also influences the way that the brain functions.

Chapter 9 highlights ways that neuroscience can help mental health professionals. The discussion is piecemeal and far from comprehensive. It is designed to give psychotherapists a peek at some of the ways that neuroscience can enhance our work. Jaak Panksepp has delineated a scientifically robust taxonomy of seven basic emotional systems. Although Panksepp's taxonomy is probably incomplete, it is the most comprehensive one available. It corroborates Bowlby's theory that all young mammals have an innate need to be attached to a caregiver. Panksepp's taxonomy demonstrates that there are two types of anxiety, each emanating from different emotional systems. There are also two pairs of good/depressed feelings, each pair rooted in different emotional systems. His taxonomy demonstrates that the urge to play is fundamental, especially in childhood. It also demonstrates that contrary to some psychoanalytic theories, anger is an unpleasant affect.

Experiments in classical conditioning demonstrate how free associations are created and why they are so important in therapeutic work. Experiments about the extinction of conditioning explain why psychotherapy, even when successful, does not provide a complete cure. We examine evidence explaining psychotherapeutic failure.

Neuroscience also demonstrates that it is not possible for a psychotherapist to be emotionally neutral.

Chapter 10 presents two clinical cases which flesh out ways that neuroscience helped me in treating two boys. One was a depressed adolescent and the other, a nine-year-old with many phobias. In helping these boys, I encouraged the activity of the SEEKING system, one of the seven emotional systems in Panksepp's taxonomy. The SEEKING system engenders a hopeful sense of anticipation, an urge for personal agency, and a willingness to take risks. In an effort to activate their SEEKING systems, I sometimes abandoned the traditional psychotherapeutic role and took on the role of a coach.

Chapter 1

Feedback Theory

Historically, scientists and physicians have adopted a *cortico-centric* view of consciousness, which maintains that the cortex, the outer rim of the brain, creates all forms of consciousness (Kawkabani 2018). The corticocentric view seems sensible because much conscious content consists of thoughts, perceptions, and sensations, which the cortex creates. Affects, however, pose a problem to the corticocentric view: While thoughts, perceptions and sensations usually attend affective feelings, affects possess a unique quality of feeling that is all their own (Ekkekakis 2013).

At the end of the nineteenth century, the American psychologist, William James (1884), and Carl Lange, a Danish physician (1885), independently and almost simultaneously developed a *feedback theory* to explain the creation of affective consciousness. Like many neuroscientists today, James and Lange distinguished between emotion and affect. They proposed that each emotion was akin to an automatic reflex with a specific physiological profile that includes visceral responses, like changes in blood pressure, heart rate, respiration, and digestion along with sweating and pupil dilation. Emotion also includes behaviors like smiling, frowning, shouting, laughing, approaching, attacking, and running away. According to the James-Lange model, a physiological emotional profile of visceral and behavioral change is fed back to the cognitive cortex. The cognitive cortex identifies these visceral and behavioral changes as the profile of a particular emotion. Once we identify the emotional profile, we experience the corresponding affect (LeDoux 1996).

Suppose that you were walking through a rough part of town when you heard the sudden crack of a gunshot. Your body would undergo an immediate and involuntary emotional response. Stress chemicals would pour into your bloodstream, your heart would thud, your breathing would become shallow, and you would grimace, duck down, and freeze. If the gunman were nearby, you would run for your life. But according to the James-Lange theory, you would not yet feel afraid.

The profile of your emotional-physiological reaction would be fed back to your cognitive cortex, which would identify the pattern of your responses as fear. Only then would you feel frightened. According to the James-Lange model, you would not duck for cover because you felt afraid. You would feel afraid because you ducked for cover (LeDoux 1996).

Cannon's Objection

In the 1920s, Walter Cannon criticized the James-Lange feedback model, noting that visceral responses develop slowly while we experience affects right away. Therefore, affects cannot be based on visceral responses (Cannon 1927). Modern feedback theory bypasses Cannon's objection by observing that some emotional behaviors, like freezing, fleeing, smiling, grimacing, and stereotypical body postures, occur immediately. They argue that these immediate responses constitute an emotional profile that the cognitive cortex can identify. In their view, when a person exhibits emotional behavior, the cognitive cortex identifies these behaviors as an expression of a particular emotion and then the person feels the corresponding affect (LeDoux 1999).

Affects as Concepts

When your cognitive brain identifies an emotional profile, it singles out features that are common to that emotion. Fear, for example, includes rapid heartbeat, hair standing on end, grimacing, freezing, etc. When you are in love, your heart might race, and your hair may even stand on end, but you do not freeze, or grimace. Even though some of the same responses may apply to different emotions, each emotion has a distinctive overall profile.

When you single out common elements among different things, you form a concept about those things and assign them to the same category (Murphy 2002). For example, in the course of your life, you acquired a concept about chairs as objects with four legs, a vertical rest for your back, and a horizontal platform on which to sit. You placed all these objects in the same category. Now when you see kitchen chairs, armchairs, deck chairs, or even beanbag chairs, you categorize them all as chairs because you have formed a concept about what chair is.

According to feedback theory, you have also formed a concept about an emotion like fear, which includes responses like rapid heartbeat, hair standing on end, pupil dilation, shallow breathing, freezing, and grimacing. When you exhibit these responses, your cognitive brain identifies them as fear because you have a concept about fear. Concepts are abstract ideas because they are not tethered to any concrete thing, or to any particular instance (Abrams 2012). Your concept of chairs is not about a particular chair, nor is your concept of fear about a single frightening experience.

Concept Formation Is a Sign of Intelligence

Virtually, all modern psychologists maintain that the cardinal feature of intelligence is the capacity for abstract thinking, which involves the ability to identify common features among many different things. When we identify common features among things, we assign those things to the same conceptual category (Purandare 2018). IQ tests, which yield robust results, measure the ability to form concepts (Peterson 2018). Thus, your ability to acquire a concept about an emotional profile is an exercise in intelligent thinking.

The neocortex is the outer layer of the brain that has most recently evolved (Rakic 2009). The frontal region of the neocortex, known as the *prefrontal cortex (PFC)*, is the cognitive part of the brain, and it is most fully developed in primates (Roberts and Clarke 2019). Human beings are the most intelligent of primates because the human PFC has more gray matter than that of other primates (Donahue et al. 2018). The prefrontal cortex carries out executive functions, which include solving novel problems, modifying behavior in the light of new information, generating strategies, and sequencing complex actions (Elliott 2003). The PFC also allows us to retain and manipulate visual images (Lui et al. 2011), and in humans, it enables our sophisticated capacity for language (Frederici et al. 2013).

The dorsal and lateral portions of the prefrontal cortex (dlPFC) generate abstract concepts by identifying common features in a category (Barbey et al. 2012; Zeithamova 2019). Thus, the dorsal and lateral parts of the prefrontal cortex are the seat of highest intelligence. Feedback theory maintains that affects are cognitive concepts about the physiology of emotion (LeDoux 1996), so according to feedback theory, the dorsal and lateral parts of the prefrontal cortex create affects.

Emotions and Affects in Other Animals

Modern feedback theorists maintain that brain regions below the neocortex generate emotional-physiological responses. These brain areas include the *allocortex*, the part of the cortex that evolved before the neocortex. The allocortex occupies only one-tenth of the cerebral cortex, and it is involved with olfaction and survival functions, such as visceral and emotional reactions (Strominger et al., 2012). Below the allcortex lie subcortical regions of the brain, which are involved in a host of functions ranging from emotional regulation to automatic functions, like breathing and heart rate (Samuel 2011; Khan Academy 2013).

Feedback theory maintains that brain regions below the neocortex generate emotional behavior. For example, it identifies the *amygdala* as a source of the fear response (LeDoux 1996). Amygdala is the Greek word for almond, which this small structure resembles in shape. Like most brain structures, the amygdalae are bilateral, and they are situated in deep regions of the temporal lobes just behind the temples (Bourtchouladze 2004).

The amygdalae inaugurate a fear response by responding to threatening stimuli (Phelps et al. 2001) and by sending information downward to the hypothalamus and then further down to the periaqueductal gray (PAG), which is located in the upper brainstem. These structures generate emotional fear responses that we all recognize. For example, lateral parts of the hypothalamus generate changes in blood pressure (LeDoux 2000) while the PAG causes people and animals to freeze (Watson et al. 2016; Roelofs 2017). All mammalian brains contain these structures (Panksepp 1998a); therefore, if any mammal, like a dog, cat, or rat, is exposed to a loud noise, or an electric shock, it displays an emotional-physiological fear response (Panksepp 1998a; Rosen 2004; Chen et al. 2006).

According to feedback theory, these animals have an emotional-physiological fear response, but they do not feel affectively frightened because their prefrontal cortices are poorly developed and cannot generate concepts about the physiology of fear, or about any other emotional response. Only a few intelligent species, like our own, are capable of concept formation, and only these animals are affective creatures (LeDoux 1996).

Feedback theorists maintain that most animals run away from danger without feeling afraid, copulate without lust, and feel no affection when they nurture their young (Tinbergen 1951; Rolls 2005; Damasio 1999; LeDoux 1996). They acknowledge that less-intelligent animals might feel something, but because their prefrontal cortices are so different from ours, we might not recognize their feelings as affects (LeDoux 2011).

Affects and Language

You and I use words to describe concepts. If I had never seen a chair, you could describe features common to all chairs (legs, seat, and back) as well as its use. Your description would allow me to acquire a concept about chairs. From then on, I would be able to identify all types of chairs, and I would be able to distinguish them from tables, beds, dogs, cats, pianos, houses, and everything else (Gottfredson 1997; Sternberg 2003).

Similarly, feedback theory claims that if I had never experienced fear, you could tell me about the common physiological manifestations of fear, like a churning stomach, hair standing on end, freezing in one's tracks, grimacing, etc. You might also describe conditions of danger when fear is aroused, like the sudden crack of a gunshot. Your description would allow me to acquire a concept about fear and know how it feels. From then on, I would be able to distinguish fear from all other affects.

Four Areas of Research Opposing Feedback Theory

1. The prefrontal cortex and emotional arousal.

    As we just noted, dorsal and lateral portions of the prefrontal cortex carry out the highest cognitive functions of concept formation (Miller et al. 2002). During periods of heightened emotional arousal when people are highly stressed, or ecstatically happy, there is reduced neural activity in these prefrontal areas (Arnsten 2009). Conversely, when people are engaged in cognitive activities and emotional arousal is at a low ebb, for example when doing a crossword puzzle, prefrontal regions are active (Elliott 2003).

    If the intelligent capacity for concept formation generated affects, cognitive cortical areas would be aroused when affects run high, and they would be quiescent when we are unemotional (Goel and Dolan 2003; Liotti and Panksepp 2004; Northoff et al. 2009). The fact that the cognitive cortex is inactive during periods of affective arousal and active during unemotional states indicates that the cognitive cortex does not generate affects.

2. The opiate effect.

    When opiates are infused throughout the brain, people report blissful states of relaxation, and animals appear to have similar experiences. Animals will also return to places where they received these opiate infusions, indicating that opiates make them feel good. However, only when opiates are infused into the brain regions below the neocortex will animals return to places where the infusion took place (Olmstead and Franklin 1997). The fact that opioid activity in these brain regions assuages pain and generates pleasure (van Steenbergen et al. 2019) suggests that sub-neocortical brain regions generate feelings of affective pleasure and that the neocortex does not.

3. Affects emerge before concepts.

Neuroimaging technology that measures the timing of mental processes demonstrates that it takes seven hundred to eight hundred milliseconds to process a concept while it takes five hundred milliseconds to generate affective feelings (Damasio 2010). If cognitive concepts generated affects, affects could not emerge before conceptualization.

4. Split-brain patients.

In the 1960s before the advent of effective drugs to combat epilepsy, surgeons treated intractable forms of the disease by severing the *corpus callosum* and *anterior commissure,* the bands of nerve fibers connecting the two cortical hemispheres. This surgery prohibited the spread of epileptic seizures from one hemisphere to the other (Gazzaniga 1995).

People who underwent this procedure were known as *split-brain* patients because their cortical hemispheres could not communicate with each other. Split-brain patients offered a unique opportunity to study each cortical hemisphere separately (Gazzaniga 1995). Researchers discovered a host of differences, one of which was their different capacities for language. The left hemisphere can voice its thoughts and perceptions while the right cannot. If you show an object to only the right hemisphere (left eye) of a split-brain patient, he can recognize what it is. For example, he can point to a similar object with his left hand, but he cannot name it. The left hemisphere, however, can describe objects (Gazzaniga 2000; 2012).

If affects were generated at the level of the cerebral cortex, severing the corpus callosum and anterior commissure would disrupt affects, rendering their verbalization disjointed in some ways. Split-brain patients would be able to speak about affects processed by the left hemisphere, but if the right hemisphere were involved, they would have difficulty in stating their feelings. Nevertheless, split-brain patients speak about their feelings with ease, which suggests that the neocortex does not create affects (Panksepp 1998a).

These considerations, demonstrating that cognitive concepts do not generate affects, undermine a central tenet of feedback theory, thereby questioning its validity.

Chapter 2

Brainstem Theory

Emotional Systems

Jaak Panksepp delineated seven genetically programed emotional systems that are found in all mammalian brains. Panksepp used simple descriptive words to designate these systems, but he wrote the words in capital letters to highlight the fact that emotional systems are physical entities rather than metaphorical descriptions. Each system consists of identifiable brain structures, and each is fueled by specific brain chemicals. These systems, which we will describe more fully in chapter 6, are SEEKING (enthused curiosity), FEAR (typically of physical danger or death), RAGE (in the face of threat or frustration), LUST (the sexual urge), GRIEF (misery in the face of social isolation), CARE (the urge to nurture), and PLAY (friendly competition) (Panksepp 1998a).

Anthropological Evidence

Panksepp cites anthropological research as proof that emotional systems exist. This research, consisting of nearly two hundred studies, demonstrates that people from different cultures can accurately label the emotional meaning of facial expressions (Ekman 2014). Especially persuasive are studies that focused on members of Stone Age societies in New Guinea that are cut off from the outside world, thereby obviating influence from other cultures. These subjects were able to match a word with an expressive face (Ekman and Friesen 1971). The fact that people from different cultures identify emotion on the basis of facial expression suggests that facial expressions and corresponding emotions are universal. If human emotions are universal, this indicates that they are hardwired in the human brain (Panksepp 1998a)

Emotional Systems Are Ancient

Panksepp's seven emotional systems are found in the upper brainstem and in midline parts of the cortex. The brain evolved from the bottom up and from midline to more lateral areas, meaning that subcortical structures evolved before the cortex and that midline parts of the cortex evolved before its lateral parts. The position of emotional systems indicates that they evolved a long time ago. As animal brains have evolved, these ancient emotional systems have been retained across species, and all mammalian brains contain the seven basic emotional systems. The brains of many other vertebrates contain some of these systems. Birds, for example, have GRIEF systems, and baby birds cry in distress when separated from their mothers (Panksepp 1998a).

In contrast, more recently evolved parts of the cortex differ dramatically from one species to another, which is why mammalian species have different perceptual acuities and levels of intelligence. Emotionally, however, we are all cousins (Panksepp 1998a; Damasio 1999).

The Creation of Affects

According to brainstem theory, affect-generating structures, like emotional systems, are located largely in subcortical regions of the brain. Since these regions are so similar in all mammalian brains, brainstem theorists claim that all mammals are affective creatures (Panksepp 1998a; Damasio 1999).

Research Indicating that Affects Emanate from Subcortical Brain Regions

In the middle of the last century, Giuseppi Moruzzi and Horace W. Magoun conducted seminal experiments, which challenged the traditional corticocentric view that the cortex creates consciousness. They destroyed a cat's cortex but left its brainstem intact and discovered that the cat remained awake (Moruzzi and Magoun 1949). These results were replicated in human beings undergoing brain surgery (Penfield and Jasper 1954). The reverse, however, did not hold true. When the cat's brainstem was destroyed and the cortex was left intact, cats fell into a permanently comatose vegetative state. People who suffer the same brain damage as a result of injury, or illness also become irrevocably comatose (Cochrane and Williams 2015).

The Reticular Activating System (RAS)

Embedded in the brainstem is a loosely knit conglomeration of cell bodies and neuronal fibers known as the *reticular activating system (RAS)*. Moruzzi and Magoun discovered that the RAS generates wakefulness in the absence of the cortex (Watt and Pincus 2004). Even when the cortex is intact, it cannot wake up—we cannot think, or perceive—without input from the RAS (Yeo et al. 2013).

Motivated Consciousness

When Moruzzi and Magoun demonstrated that the RAS generates wakefulness, researchers wondered if this meant that the RAS creates consciousness. They reckoned, however, that there is more to consciousness than just being awake. Following an epileptic absence seizure, for example, people are sometimes in a wakeful state of automatism. A person in this condition is aware of her surroundings. Her movements are coherent. She might perform simple acts, like drinking from a cup of coffee that is in her line of vision. She might walk about, and she would not bump into furniture. But she would probably fail to answer if you called her name, and she would not be meaningfully interactive with her environment (Bailey and Davis 1942; 1943; Damasio 1999).

If there is more to consciousness than being awake, what are its other characteristics? Researchers looked to animal experiments, which destroyed brain structures at increasingly deeper levels. The lower the level of destruction, the more completely was motivated, purposeful behavior obliterated (Panksepp 1998b; Watt and Pincus 2004; Merker 2007; Panksepp and Trevarthen 2009). It seemed that deep brain structures, especially those in and around the brainstem, generated not just wakefulness but motivation, which appeared to be a cardinal feature of consciousness.

Noncognitive Motivation

Most of us believe that we are motivated by thoughts. I send my sister flowers for her birthday because I know she will be touched that I remembered. However, the research just cited indicates that motivation emanates from deep subcortical brain structures that are devoid of ideation. What kind of motivation is provided by deep brain structures?

A clue is found in pain research, which demonstrates that painful stimuli are processed along two separate pathways. The *sensory-discriminative* pathway encodes the nature of pain: whether it is sharp, dull, throbbing, or scratchy, its location in or on the body as well as how intense it is. This pathway is located quite high in the brain, coursing through the somatosensory thalamus as well as the primary and secondary somatosensory cortices. In spite of the fact that the sensory-discriminative pathway provides detailed information about pain, it does not include any suffering (Auvray et al. 2010).

The second pain pathway involves deeper structures, like the medial thalamus and the amygdala (Auvray et al. 2010) as well as structures in and around the brainstem (Anaesthetist.com 2006). It is called the *affective-motivational* pathway, and it generates the ouch factor—the experience of pain and suffering (Melzack and Casey 1968; Auvray et al. 2010).

If I slammed my hand in a car door, the sensory-discriminative pathway in my brain would register that the pain was in my hand that it was due to pressure and that it was intense, but this information would not cause me any distress. The deeper affective-motivational pathway would generate my wretched experience of physical pain.

Additional evidence indicates that the same deep affective-motivational pathways that cause pain and suffering also generate sensory pleasure (Berridge and Kringelbach 2015). Brainstem theorists concluded that consciousness of sensory pleasure and pain emanates largely from subcortical structures and that these pleasure/pain experiences motivate behavior (Damasio 1999).

Affective Pleasure and Pain: Empathy Research

The affective-motivational pathway, despite having the word *affect* as part of its label, generates sensory/physical pain. What about affective pain? Research about empathy demonstrates that many of the brain structures, which cause physical pain and suffering overlap with brain structures that generate empathy with other people who are in physical pain. These overlapping structures include subcortical structures in and around the brainstem (Decety et al. 2008).

If you saw me slam my hand in the car door, you would probably wince, and you might even rub your hand even though it did not hurt. You would do this because many of the brain structures that cause you to empathize with me are the same structures that are active in my brain when I experience physical pain. Empathy is an affective response. When you empathize with my physical pain, you are in affective pain. Since both physical and affective pain emerge from many of the same subcortical regions of the brain, this research indicates that affective pain emerges largely from subcortical brain regions (Decety et al. 2008).

What about affective pleasure? There has been little research about empathy with positive sensory experiences in others. Virtually, all the research about positive empathy focuses on empathy with positive affects that other people experience (Morelli et al. 2014). This research does not tell us if there is an overlap between physical and affective pleasure.

Research on taste, however, offers insight into sensory and affective pleasure. When human babies, or animals taste something sweet, they protrude their tongues in rhythmic fashion. But if they taste something bitter, or sour, they gape and shake their heads (Berridge 2003; Berridge and Kringelback 2008). Researchers maintain that positive physical sensations, like a sweet taste, are attended by a "hedonic gloss" of positive affect (Berridge and Kringelbach 2011). Both pleasurable sensations and the affective "gloss" are generated by the same neural substrates (Kringelbach 2010). These brain regions include the cortex as well as the brainstem and nearby structures (Berridge and Kringelbach 2015). This research demonstrates that the creation of affective pleasure includes subcortical brain structures.

The research cited above convinced brainstem theorists that motivation is a crucial component of consciousness. Motivation takes the form of pleasure and pain, including affective pleasure and pain. Crucially important, conscious feelings of pleasure and pain emanate largely from structures in and around the brainstem.

Further Brainstem Arguments

Rats are unintelligent animals, and their prefrontal cortex is so rudimentary that some researchers deny its existence (Seamans et al. 2008). Even though rat brains are probably incapable of generating cognitive concepts, they approach, or avoid certain stimuli, indicating that they either like, or dislike them (Panksepp 1998a). They also exhibit *place preferences*, a tendency to revisit, or avoid places where they have had positive, or negative experiences, again indicating that they liked and disliked those experiences. They will, for example, revisit places where they had sex but avoid places where they ate tainted food (Tzschentke 2007). According to brainstem theory, these preferences indicate that rats like sex and dislike rotten food.

Since rats are so unintelligent, these affective responses must emanate from noncognitive subcortical structures in rat brains (Panksepp 1998a).

Brainstem theorists also highlight affective behavior in *decorticate* animals that have been surgically deprived of a cortex. These animals also display place preferences, indicating that they, too, have affective experiences. *Hydranencephalic* children are born without a cortex, a condition usually caused by a stroke in utero (Merker 1997, 2004, 2007), yet they appear to be affectively conscious. They laugh when positively engaged, they cry and arch their backs, indicating when they are uncomfortable, and they select favorite toys with which to play (Shewmon et al. 1999). These children are also subject to brief epileptic absence seizures, resulting in the temporary loss of consciousness. Their parents can tell when the children are having a seizure and when they seem to become conscious and are again affectively engaged (Solms 2013). Since animals and children who do not have a cortex, appear to be affectively conscious, brainstem theorists argue that affects emanate from subcortical regions of the brain (Panksepp 1998a).

A Brief Digression: Subcortical Sensory Capacities

You might wonder how a person, or animal without a cortex, which includes the sensory cortices for sight, sound, smell, taste, and touch, can perceive anything. How can a hydranencephalic child have a favorite toy that he cannot perceive? The child's ability to perceive depends on subcortical structures that discern sensory stimuli. Subcortical sensory processing does not generate the experiences of seeing, hearing, touching, tasting, and smelling. Nevertheless, subcortical sensory processing provides information about objects and events in the world (Solms 2013).

Cortically blind people often exhibit *blindsight* and walk around objects in their path, even though they do not see anything (Weiskrantz 1986). They can also discern unseen qualities, like color, shape, motion, the orientation of lines (Weiskrantz et. al. 1974), as well as facial expressions (de Gelder et al. 2000), and expressive bodily postures (de Gelder and Hadjikhani 2006).

Although researchers have yet to trace the neural pathway that accounts for blindsight in primates, studies indicate participation by the *lateral geniculate nucleus*, a part of the thalamus (Schmid et al. 2010), and by the *superior colliculus*, a brainstem structure (Cowey 2004; Pessoa 2005). Both these structures process visual information about light waves. This information would allow for blindsight.

Similarly, if the auditory cortex is damaged, people cannot hear anything, but they often turn their heads in the direction of sounds, a phenomenon known as *deaf hearing* (Garde and Cowley 2000). It is likely that the *medial geniculate nucleus* of the thalamus and the *inferior colliculus* in the brainstem process auditory information about sound waves that contribute to deaf hearing (Aitkin et al. 1978).

Other lines of sensory research have revealed that when patients have suffered bilateral lesions to the somatosensory cortices and have lost the sense of touch, they can process tactile information subcortically, a capacity known as *blind touch*, or *numbsense* (Rossetti et al. 1995). Although there has been less research on the other two senses (smell and taste), it is likely that they, too, can be subcortically processed (Panksepp and Biven 2012).

Therefore, even though decorticate animals and hydranencephalic children cannot see, hear, feel, taste, or smell, subcortical sensory structures in their brains allow them to perceive.

Panksepp's Triangulation

Panksepp proposed a simple triangulated approach for understanding affective consciousness in animals: If you stimulate the same emotional system in the brain of an animal and in the brain of a person and then ask the person how he feels, you can assume that the animal feels the same way. If you electrically stimulated a rat's FEAR system and did the same to my brain, both the rat and I would exhibit fearful responses that you could easily recognize. If I told you that I was scared, you could assume that the rat, too, felt scared (Panksepp 2011b).

Affects and Language

Panksepp proposes that affects are primary experiences akin to seeing a color. Words about primary experiences do not describe anything. They are only labels for that experience. When you see the color red, you might use words like crimson, scarlet, or ruby to characterize your experience. But if I were color-blind, these words would mean nothing to me.

Panksepp claims that our words for affects are also labels. If I had never felt afraid, you might describe fearful behaviors and sensations as well as circumstances like the blast of a gunshot that arouse fear. But I still would not know what fear feels like. Unlike the feedback school, which maintains that affects are generated by cognitive concepts that we can describe in words, brainstem theorists claim that affects are primary experiences that words cannot describe at all. You have to see red to know how it looks, and you have to experience affects to know how they feel (Panksepp 1998a; Panksepp and Biven 2012).

The Gunshot

Think back to the gunshot you heard while walking through town. A brainstem theorist would say that the sound of the shot activated neurons in your emotional FEAR system, which relayed information to affect-generating circuits that are also located in sub-cortical and midline cortical regions of your brain. When this happened, you felt afraid.

Objections to Brainstem Theory

Feedback theorists, who maintain that the cognitive cortex creates affects, would probably accept the validity of empathy research because it was carried out on human beings who are intelligent and capable of experiencing affects. However, all the other experiments concerned people and animals with limited cognitive capacity: unintelligent animals, like rats, human babies with undeveloped cortices, hydranencephalic children who do not have a cortex, and decorticate animals whose cortices have been removed. A feedback theorist would say that these people and animals exhibit emotional responses, but their brains are incapable of creating affects.

Feedback theory would also question research demonstrating that animals exhibit place preferences on the basis of affective response. This research assumes that rats go to places where they had sex because they like sex and that they avoid places where they ate tainted food because they dislike the food. For a feedback theorist, this is an unsubstantiated assumption because the behavior may be automatic and devoid of affect.

They would also object to Panksepp's method of triangulation. If you stimulated the FEAR system in a rat's brain and in my brain, we would both exhibit fearful behavior. However, when brainstem theorists claim that the rat is frightened, they are assuming that the rat's brain is capable of generating affects. In other words, feedback theorists maintain that behavior is not a good indicator of affective experience.

Feedback theorists highlight the disconnect between behavior and affect by citing experiments where heroin addicts vigorously press a button in order to receive very low doses of morphine that do not induce intoxication (LeDoux 2002). This suggests that that affective feelings do not motivate their behavior. This conclusion, however, may not be warranted. Another study indicates that low doses of morphine are effective in treating elderly patients who suffer with chronic pain (Lee et al. 2015). Addicts typically suffer from debilitating mental illnesses; therefore, even though a low dose of morphine does not make them high, it may provide relief from affective pain.

Although the morphine experiments are inconclusive, feedback theorists are right about our inability to know what animals, human babies, and hydranencephalic children feel. They cannot tell us, so we deduce their feelings from their behavior. Panksepp maintains that behavior provides an "overwhelming" weight of "evidence for various types of affective feelings in other mammals" (Panksepp 2011a p. 1793). For feedback theorists, the overwhelming evidence carries no weight at all.

Chapter 3

The Conceptual Act Theory

The Conceptual Act Theory (CAT), devised by Lisa Feldman Barrett and her colleagues, maintains that emotional systems do not exist. This is the basis for CAT's hypothesis about the creation of all conscious experience, including affective consciousness (Barrett 2017a).

Consciousness in General

According to the Conceptual Act Theory, consciousness emerges when a stimulus, or situation elicits bodily sensations, consisting of pleasure, or pain and a level of arousal. These bodily sensations are conscious, but they are meaningless. Usually, we hardly notice them. Physical sensations of pleasure/pain and levels of arousal only become meaningful when we place them in context. In order to place them in context, we need to have concepts, which we obtain from experience (Barrett 2008).

Imagine that you felt a stomach pang. By itself, it means nothing. But suppose that your stomach contracted as you walked into a pastry shop. On the basis of past experience, you have acquired the concept that delicious pastries satisfy hunger. This concept prompts you to interpret your stomach pang as hunger. However, if you were out and about in flu season, you might experience the sensation in your stomach as nausea because past experience has given you a concept about flu symptoms. If you were in a doctor's office awaiting test results, the stomach contraction might feel like anxiety because you have a concept that some illnesses are serious. Your physical sensation is only meaningful when you have a concept that makes sense of it in the context of your current environment (Barrett 2017a).

Affective Consciousness

CAT proposes that affects are facilitated by concepts that our brains construct from repeated social interactions and observations. If a child sees his mother and father get cross, anger becomes a concept that is part of his affective vocabulary. He has also observed the conditions when anger is aroused, and these conditions become part and parcel of his affective concept. He knows, for example, that his parents get angry when he steals pocket money. If a classmate at school steals the boy's pencil, his brain uses his concept of anger to construct an angry response. In other words, anger is not an innate response. The boy learns what anger is—he acquires a concept about it—from social experience. If he had never observed anger, he would not know what anger is, and he would never feel angry (Barrett 2017a).

Affects in Animals and Children

Like feedback theory, CAT maintains that the brains of most animals are not intelligent enough to create affective concepts. The brains of young children are also relatively undeveloped, and their ability to acquire concepts is limited. Therefore, they do not experience a full range of affects as do adults (Barrett 2017a; Wright and Barrett 2017).

The Gunshot

Think again about your walk on the wrong side of the tracks. A CAT theorist would say that the sound of the gunshot causes arousing changes in your body. You are minimally conscious of these changes, and by themselves, they mean nothing. In the past, you have learned from films, TV, newsreels, and newspapers that a gunshot means trouble. If the gunman is nearby, trouble is worse. On the basis of this concept, your physical sensation and your present situation, your brain constructs a fearful affect (Barrett 2017a).

Research Supporting and Opposing the Conceptual Act Theory

CAT cites anthropological, neuroscientific, and behavioral evidence to show that hardwired emotional brain systems do not exist.

1. Anthropological evidence.

    CAT questions the legitimacy of anthropological studies, like the one in New Guinea, that seem to support the existence of hardwired emotional systems. CAT maintains that the methodology of these experiments is flawed because researchers provided words like happy, sad, or disgusted as possible matches for expressive faces. This created a bias that skewed results (Gendron et al. 2018).

    CAT researchers found that when subjects were allowed to make free choices, they were often unable to identify facial expressions. They might, for example, think that a scowl indicates anger when it is really a sign of confusion, or intense concentration (Sarwari 2019). Similarly, smiling does not convey happiness, or pleasure because we sometimes smile when we are embarrassed, or even when we are sad (Barrett 2017a). CAT also maintains that frightened people sometimes laugh, or crack a joke (Barrett 2012), which indicates that there is no reliable profile for fear. The fact that facial expressions do not convey universal emotions indicates that hardwired emotional systems do not exist (Barrett 2006; Gendron et al. 2014).

    Countering this objection is anthropological research in which subjects are given the opportunity to make free choices, thereby avoiding the methodological flaw to which CAT objects. For example, forty subjects in the US and in India correctly identified fourteen facial expressions (Haidt and Keltner 1999). Additionally, people who have been blind from birth spontaneously display a full range of facial expressions (Matsumoto and Willingham 2009). Thus, people from different cultures and blind people display a shared set of facial expressions. This indicates that facial expressions and the emotions that they express are universal and that emotional systems are hardwired into the human brain.

Furthermore, an expression like smiling is a broad brush that encompasses different types of distinguishable smiles. A polite social smile involves the voluntary contraction of the *zygomatic* muscles that raise the corners of the mouth. You and I can muster up this kind of smile, even when we are in a bad mood. A genuine smile, on the other hand, includes the involuntary contraction of the *orbicularis oculi* muscles, which raises the cheeks and produces crow's feet around the eyes. We cannot fake a genuine smile (Durrayappah-Harrison 2010). Social and genuine smiles are different, and you can tell them apart (Jaffe 2010), which indicates that different types of smiles can contribute to different emotional profiles.

Similarly, the tendency to joke and laugh is a commonplace response to threat (Inglis-Arkell 2013). Even fake laughter diminishes fear by reducing stress-inducing cortisol and epinephrine and by raising levels of chemicals, like endorphins and dopamine, that make us feel better (Scott 2020; DeLeo 2018). But nervous laughter comes from the throat and sounds different from an involuntary belly laugh (The Audiopedia 2017). Different kinds of laughter, like different smiles, can contribute to different emotional profiles.

Having said this, most of us would agree that facial expressions and behavior can sometimes be misleading, or insufficient. It is easy to see that an expression of intense concentration might be mistaken for anger. Furthermore, almost half the time, we fail to observe *micro-expressions* that occur fleetingly (Matsumoto and Hwang 2011). However, a cluster of expressive behaviors evident in facial expression, bodily posture, movement, tone of voice, etc., usually generates an identifiable emotional profile (Simon-Thomas 2017). CAT refers to a photo of Serena Williams just after winning a tennis match. A close-up of her face expresses apparent rage, or agony, indicating that facial expression does not reveal true emotion (Barrett 2011). In a photo of Williams's entire body, however, her bent elbow, clenched fist, and assertive body posture express her sense of victory. These considerations indicate that emotional profiles exist.

CAT presents anthropological fieldwork carried out by its own researchers on the !Kung culture in Namibia. They discovered that the !Kung people have no word for fear. They concluded that when a member of the !Kung culture experiences the physiological patterns that you and I do when we are frightened (churning stomach, dilated pupils, freezing, etc.), he does not feel frightened because he has no concept of fear (Barrett 2017a). CAT surmises that if an innate FEAR system existed, the word *fear* would be included in the !Kung vocabulary, and !Kung people would experience fear. The fact that they have no word for fear indicates that they never feel frightened and that there is no innate FEAR system in the human brain (Barrett, 2017a).

The !Kung language, however, includes the word *kua*, which denotes a blend of awe, respect, and fear (Shostak 1983). The !Kung people also practice magical spells and apply healing herbs in order to protect themselves from *gangwasi*—dead relatives who purportedly wish them harm (Peters-Golden 2012). The word *kua* and the impulse for self-protection suggests that the !Kung people experience fear and that an innate FEAR system exists.

CAT's anthropological studies also indicate that the Tahitian culture has no word for grief, or sadness. When Tahitians suffer a loss, they say that they feel physically ill rather than sad, or grief-stricken. In CAT's view, this indicates that Tahitians do not experience grief. However, cultures that know nothing about brain science often believe that affects are embedded in the body and speak about affects in bodily terms. Plato thought that affects emanated from the heart and desire from the liver (Schmitter 2010). Many ancient Greeks believed that affects resided in the chest, or midriff, and Aristotle thought they were lodged in the heart (Crivellato and Ribatti 2007). Even you and I speak about our bodies when we describe affective feelings. We walk on air, our blood boils, we itch to discover, our hearts grow cold, we have butterflies in our stomachs, and we are tickled pink.

When we suffer a loss, we are brokenhearted, sick inside, gutted, and crushed. Our words describe feelings of physical malaise and depletion, words that Tahitians use as well (Wright and Barrett 2017). CAT's argument would be more convincing if Tahitians said that they felt well, or that they felt nothing in the face of loss. Instead, the tendency to refer to bodily illness, and fatigue is a common theme in their language and in ours.

2. Neuroscientific evidence.
   A. Voxel examination.

   CAT examined research about voxels (small units of brain tissue) in regions where emotional systems are claimed to exist and found that no one voxel, or group of voxels is invariably active when a specific emotion is aroused. CAT researchers reasoned that if emotions were hardwired in the brain, specific voxels would be active when particular emotions are aroused. The fact that they are not indicates that emotions are not hardwired into specific brain regions. In Lisa Feldman Barrett's words, CAT'S voxel analysis is "...the final, definitive nail in the coffin for localizing emotions to individual parts of the brain" (Barrett 2017a p. 22).

There is, however, massive redundancy in brain function (Glassman 1987). Even if a particular voxel were genetically consigned to produce a specific emotion, it might not always be active when that emotion is aroused. Other genetically consigned voxels might take on the task. For example, electrical stimulation of almost any part of the dorsolateral periaqueductal gray (dlPAG), located in the upper brainstem, causes rats to freeze and emit twenty-two kilohertz ultrasonic vocalizations (USVs) (Graeff 2004; Wright and Panksepp 2011), both of which are typical responses to threat (Behbehani 1995; Kim et al. 2013). When rats are frightened by stimuli, like loud noises, the dlPAG is also active, and rats emit the same ultrasonic vocalizations (Watson et al. 2016). A fear-conditioned rat exhibits the same behavioral responses to conditioned stimuli, and its dlPAG becomes active (Kim et al. 2010). When human brains receive electrical stimulation to the dlPAG, people report intense feelings of fear, agitation, and impending doom (Nashold et al. 1969; Young and Rinaldi 1997). Given the enormous redundancy in brain function, you would not expect every voxel in the dlPAG to be active every time that fear is aroused. However, the fact that many parts of the dlPAG produce fear indicates that many of its voxels are genetically dedicated to the generation of fear and that a FEAR system exists.

Voxel analysis is also limited because each voxel contains about a half-million neurons, and the analysis of whole voxels tells you nothing about the activity of individual neurons within (Uttal 2011; Koch in Paulson 2012). Recent research reveals that individual neurons are genetically consigned to generate specific emotional responses.

Each amygdala has about thirteen *nuclei*, or sections (Bailey 2018). A group of these nuclei is known as the *basolateral complex* (Maren 2001). Research on rats demonstrates that one set of neurons in the rat's basolateral complex is genetically programmed to encode memories of pleasurable events. Another set encodes memories of frightening events. These sets of neurons inhibit each other. Researchers reckon that if there is an imbalance in their populations in the human brain and fear neurons outnumber pleasure neurons, this might result in disorders, like depression, or PTSD, in people (Kim et al. 2016).

If one subjected the basolateral complex of the amygdala to a voxel analysis, it might show that whole voxels are inactive when rats exhibit fear and pleasure, even if a few individual neurons with voxels were active. The fact that individual neurons are genetically assigned to encode pleasure, or fear memories bolsters the brainstem school's view that emotional systems are genetically hardwired into the brain down to the level of individual neurons. This research undermines CAT's claims that voxel analysis disproves the existence of hardwired emotional substrates in the brain.

B.   The amygdala.

In the middle of the last century, the amygdala became known as a fear center when Heinrich Kluver and Paul Bucy removed bilateral amygdalae in the brains of rhesus monkeys (Kluver and Bucy 1939). The monkeys developed what is now known as the *Kluver-Bucy Syndrome*, and among their symptoms was an absence of fear. They were, for example, unafraid of snakes as are monkeys whose brains are intact (Kalin et al. 2004).

In the 1980s, LeDoux conducted seminal experiments demonstrating the crucial role of the amygdala in fear conditioning (LeDoux 1996). Amygdalectomized monkeys, for example, cannot be conditioned to fear a conditioned stimulus (Antoniadis et al. 2009). These elegant experiments catapulted the amygdala to neuroscientific rock-star status as part of an innate fear center (Morris et al. 1996; Williams et al. 2004).

CAT makes four points indicating that the amygdala is not part of an innate fear system: The amygdala is not always involved in the generation of fear, the amygdala can inhibit fear, the amygdala generates emotions other than fear, and the amygdala responds to novelty rather than threat (Barrett 2017a).

a.   The amygdala is not always involved in fear.

CAT cites research indicating that the amygdala does not always participate in unconditioned fear, like the fear of loud noises, or of spiders and snakes. Neuroimaging studies reveal that when people are frightened by these kinds of stimuli, the amygdala is inactive more than half the time (Barrett 2017a).

CAT also cites experiments where subjects breathed air that was loaded with CO_2. The experiments were not life-threatening, but they induced the sensation of suffocation. Participants in these experiments were control subjects with normal brains and three patients suffering from Urbach-Wiethe disease, a rare genetic disorder, which destroys the amygdalae. Urbach-Wiethe patients are normally intelligent and display a full range of emotions with the exception of fear. They cannot be conditioned to fear a conditioned stimulus, nor are they are afraid of stimuli that usually cause an unconditioned fear response. For example, they are unperturbed by fearful, or aggressive facial expressions, or by insects, like spiders, which they placidly allow to crawl on their hands (Trimble et al. 1997; Siebert et al. 2003; Feinstein et al. 2013). They can also watch scary movies and visit a house of horrors at an amusement park with perfect calm (Feinstein et al. 2013). Contrary to expectation, when the Urbach-Wiethe patients breathed in the air loaded with CO_2, they exhibited fear. CAT researchers concluded that because the amygdala is often inactive in fear arousal and because Urbach-Wiethe patients exhibit fear, the amygdala is not part of a FEAR system (Barrett 2017a).

Brainstem theorists maintain, however, that the amygdala is the highest of three structures in a hardwired FEAR system, which also includes, in descending order, portions of the hypothalamus and of the periaqueductal gray (PAG). In the hierarchical FEAR system, deeper structures are more important in generating fear than are structures located higher in the brain. The PAG is more important than the hypothalamus, which is more important than the amygdala (Panksepp 1998a).

In accordance with this hierarchical arrangement is research suggesting that the amygdala plays a role in generating fear when a threat poses no dire physical danger. This would explain why Urbach-Wiethe patients are not frightened by stimuli like scary music (Gosselin et al. 2007). However, when a stimulus poses a threat to life and limb, other structures in the FEAR system, namely the hypothalamus and the PAG, are more important in generating fear. According to this view, the hypothalamus and the PAG, rather than the amygdala, would respond to a variety of life-threatening situations, including the threat of suffocation. Thus, nonparticipation of the amygdala would not rule out the existence of a FEAR system, nor would it prove that the amygdala is not part of that system (Panksepp 1998a).

b. The amygdala can inhibit FEAR.

A surprising outcome of the CO_2 experiments was that the Urbach-Wiethe patients exhibited a greater degree of panic than did normal subjects. Why were these patients more frightened than people whose brains were intact? Researchers hypothesized that when normal people breathe the CO_2 air, their amygdalae inhibit fear. Urbach-Wiethe patients do not have functioning amygdalae to perform this function. This would explain why they were more panicky than normal subjects (Feinstein et al. 2013). CAT researchers suggest that because the amygdala has the capacity to inhibit fear, it is not part of a fear-generating system (Barratt 2017a).

A look into the way that the amygdala achieves inhibition offers a different explanation for this unexpected result. We noted above that the amygdala contains about thirteen nuclei. One of these, the *central nucleus*, plays a crucial role in generating both conditioned and unconditioned fear (Kalin et al. 2004). The central nucleus of the amygdala inaugurates fear by sending information to the hypothalamus and the PAG, which generate fear responses, like a spike in blood pressure, dilated pupils, rapid heart rate, etc. (LeDoux 1996).

The central nucleus uses the neurotransmitter *gamma-aminobutyric acid (GABA)* to send information. GABA is an inhibitory neurotransmitter, and when it projects to other structures, like the hypothalamus and the PAG, it causes them to become inactive. At first glance, it seems that the central nucleus would inhibit rather than inaugurate a fear response. Indeed, the central nucleus of the amygdala can inhibit the PAG's ability to generate a freeze response (Babaev et al. 2018).

However, when the central nucleus is itself inhibited, it can activate the hypothalamus and PAG. Researchers hypothesize that external stimuli, like a sudden loud noise, or a painful shock, inhibit the ability of the central nucleus to inhibit, thereby enabling it to inaugurate a fear response (LeDoux 2008). They proposed that when a threat like CO_2 inhalation occurs inside the body, the threat does not inhibit the central nucleus, and instead of participating in creating fear, the central nucleus inhibits fear.

According to this hypothesis, when normal subjects breathe the CO_2 air, the central nucleus inhibits deeper structures in the FEAR system, and their panic is modulated. Urbach-Wiethe patients exhibit more panic because they do not have functioning amygdalae to dampen down the fear response (Feinstein et al. 2013). This, however, does not disprove that the amygdala is part of a FEAR system. It only indicates that when a threat emanates from within the body, the central nucleus of the amygdala inhibits fear rather than generating it. Therefore, the amygdala can still be seen as part of a FEAR system.

c.   The amygdala generates emotions other than fear.

CAT maintains that the amygdala participates in the generation of anger, disgust, sadness, and happiness as well as fear. For example, the amygdala is active when animals learn to associate a conditioned stimulus (like a tone) with positive experiences, like eating tasty food (LeDoux 2016). On the basis of this research, CAT proposed that it is incorrect to see the amygdala as part of a FEAR system (Barrett 2017a).

However, the amygdala is not a unitary structure. The two amygdalae on either side of the brain do not function identically. The left is activated in positive emotions, but both sides participate in negative emotions (Hamann et al. 2002). Furthermore, the thirteen nuclei of each amygdala perform different functions, and each nucleus is functionally subdivided even further (Bailey 2018). Different nuclei (or different parts of the same nucleus) participate in generating different emotions, both positive and negative (Rolls 2000; LeDoux 2016). For example, lateral portions of the amygdala's central nucleus produce low levels of sustained anxiety while medial parts generate a rapid fear response (Walker and Davis 2008; Keifer et al. 2015). Embedded in this fast-responding medial part of the central nucleus are circuits that respond to positive stimuli (Kim et al. 2016). This research demonstrates that while some parts of the amygdala produce emotions other than fear, other parts do generate fear, and one can regard them as participants in an innate FEAR system.

d. The amygdala responds to novelty.

Urbach-Wiethe patients typically fail to look into the eyes of threatening, or fearful faces. If, however, they are instructed to do so, they feel afraid (Adolphs 2008). CAT researchers suggest that instead of generating fear, the amygdala directs attention to particular stimuli and that fear is generated elsewhere in the brain (Williams et al. 2004). Since novel situations and stimuli capture attention (Velasco et al. 1972), CAT maintains that the amygdala responds to novelty rather than to threat (Barrett 2006).

Research demonstrates that both the amygdala and hippocampus are sensitive to novelty. However, two types of novelty can be distinguished: stimuli that are ordinary but novel in the current context and stimuli that are altogether unusual. Ordinary novel stimuli can be things that you happen to be seeing for the first time in a while, like a photo of a monkey in a dinner jacket. Unusual novel stimuli are things that you hardly ever see, like a monkey sitting at your dinner table. The amygdala, rather than the hippocampus, responds to unusual novel stimuli (Blackford et al. 2010). Anything very unusual might be a threat, suggesting that the amygdala is part of a FEAR system.

Additionally, novel environments and stimuli frequently induce low levels of fearful behavior and visceral response (Oostra and Nelson 2006). When rats, or people listened to innocuous auditory tones played at unpredictable (hence novel) intervals, their amygdalae became active, and they exhibited apprehensive behavior (Herry et al. 2007). If the amygdala responds to novelty, it may also be responding to threat, indicating that it is part of an innate FEAR system.

3. Schadenfreude.

CAT maintains that the brain does not have innate systems that generate any emotion, including anger and aggression. Instead, anger is a concept that we learn from experience. In CAT's view, schadenfreude (pleasure in the pain of others) is a sophisticated concept that young children have not learned (Wright and Barrett 2017).

CAT claims that the immature human brain can create a novel affect—one that it has not learned from social experience—if it combines two affective concepts that it does have. Consider again the boy whose pencil was stolen. Suppose that he sees his offending classmate slip and hurt himself on the playground. The lad might feel a malicious delight if he combines his concept of pleasure and his concept of pain in others. Then he would experience schadenfreude, even though he had no prior concept about it and had never felt it before (Wright and Barrett 2017).

Other areas of research, however, reveal that schadenfreude is a universal human response (Shrand 2017) that begins in toddlerhood (Engelhaupt 2014). If schadenfreude is not an inherent response, why do the brains of young toddlers regularly stitch together the two existing concepts of pleasure and pain in others? CAT has no answer to this question (Wright and Barrett, 2017). The universal and early appearance of schadenfreude indicates that it is an expression of a RAGE system and that it is an inherent response to an enemy, or rival.

The Mental Inference Fallacy

CAT argues that brainstem theorists have fallen prey to "the mental inference fallacy" (2017b), a tendency for scientists to misinterpret data in ways that support a preconceived belief. CAT claims that brainstem theorists harbor a preconceived belief that emotional systems exist and therefore misinterpret anthropological, neuroscientific, and behavioral data in ways that support their belief (Barrett 2017a).

Brainstem theorists could respond by saying that the mental inference fallacy is a two-way street and claim that CAT researchers harbor a preconceived belief that emotional systems do not exist. They could argue that anthropological investigation, neuroscientific evidence (about voxels and amygdalar function), and the existence of schadenfreude in toddlers indicate that CAT has failed to disprove the existence of hardwired emotional brain systems. Therefore, CAT's claim that emotional systems do not exist is open to question.

Chapter 4

A Case for Brainstem Theory: Animal Behavior and Affect

Which school is right? Feedback theory rests on the belief that cognitive concepts create affects, yet persuasive research indicates that they do not. Brainstem theory depends on the unproven assumption that animals feel affects when they exhibit emotional behavior. CAT denies the existence of emotional systems, but it cites unconvincing anthropological, neuroscientific, and behavioral evidence to support its claim. At first glance, it seems that we have reached a stalemate, but this chapter makes a case for brainstem theory.

Brainstem theory claims that when animals exhibit emotional behavior, they have affective feelings. When a mother cat licks her kittens, she harbors protective maternal feelings. When dogs copulate, they feel lustful. When animals fight, they are enraged. But animals cannot tell us how they feel. How can we be sure they are affective creatures? That is the question that we address in this chapter.

Self-Stimulation and Reward

In the middle of the last century, James Olds and Peter Milner discovered that animals would *self-stimulate* particular subcortical brain structures. Self-stimulation occurs when an electrode is placed in a part of an animal's brain. The animal then learns an *instrumental behavior*, like pressing a lever, in order to electrically stimulate that brain region. In this case, the electrode was placed in the *lateral hypo-*

thalamus and in the *medial forebrain bundle*, neural fibers that pass through the lateral hypothalamus (Olds 1977).

Milner and Olds found that animals would press levers in a frenzied manner to the point of exhaustion, or even death in order to self-stimulate the lateral hypothalamus/medial forebrain bundle. Animals work for rewards, and the fact that animals work for stimulation of this brain region indicates that the stimulation is rewarding. Thus, Olds and Milner called the lateral hypothalamus/medial forebrain bundle a *reward system* (Olds and Milner 1954).

Behaviorism and the Elusive Nature of a Reward

At the time of Olds and Milner's discovery in the 1950s, *behaviorism* dominated academic psychology. The behaviorists conducted impressive experiments about the predictable ways that people and animals react to the scheduling of rewards. Suppose that you trained a rat to press a lever in order to get food. If you delivered food pellets after the rat pressed a lever a fixed number of times, rat would press the lever as fast as it could, eat the food, and relax for a moment before again pressing the lever very quickly. If you delivered food pellets after an unpredictable number of lever pressings, the rat would still work quickly but at a slower and steadier pace. If you gave the food pellets at fixed intervals of time, regardless of the number of times the rat pressed the lever, the rat would press the lever slowly just after eating the food and increase the pace until the next bit of food was delivered as if anticipating its arrival. If food were delivered after various unpredictable time spans, animals would press the lever slowly and steadily. Gambling casinos use this kind of research to design the delivery of small payouts at intervals that efficiently relieve you of your hard-earned cash (Panksepp 1998a).

The behaviorists, however, had difficulty defining the meaning of the word reward—a difficulty that was rooted in their refusal to consider questions of motivation. In their view, motivation refers to a mental state that is scientifically irrelevant because it cannot be observed, or measured (McLeod 2017). Consequently, the behaviorists defined reward purely in terms of stimulus and behavior: A reward was a stimulus for which an animal would work. They noted that rewards *reinforce* behavior, meaning that animals will continue to work for more rewards (Skinner 1953).

The behavioral definition, however, failed to explain why hungry, or thirsty animals are more eager to work for rewards, like food and water, than are sated animals. It did not account for the fact that animals will not work to obtain objects, like paper clips. The behaviorists could only conclude that food was more rewarding for hungry animals than for stated ones and that food was rewarding while paper clips were not. The behavioral definition of reward was purely descriptive and led to a circular argument: Rewards reinforce behavior because they are rewarding. This does not tell you anything about the nature of a reward (Tonneau 2008).

Homeostatic Rewards

Neuroscientists tried to resolve the problem by defining the word reward in homeostatic terms. Homeostasis concerns the internal state of the body, and it includes factors like temperature, blood pressure, levels of sugar, oxygen, and calcium as well as circadian rhythms within the body. All these homeostatic factors must exist in a relatively balanced state in order to insure good health and survival (Guyton and Hall 2006). Most neuroscientists equate homeostasis with pleasure and homeostatic imbalance with pain (Cabanac 1979; Craig 2003; Kringelbach et al. 2003; Paulus 2007). Even feedback theorists, who do not believe that other animals experience pleasure or pain, usually see reward and punishment in homeostatic terms (Leknes and Tracey 2008).

Neuroscientists seemed to have provided a definition of reward: Anything that maintains, or restores homeostasis is rewarding. Anything that destabilizes homeostasis is punishing. They also seemed to have solved the problem of motivation. If you are hungry, thirsty, too hot, or too cold, homeostasis is imbalanced, and you are motivated to restore homeostasis by eating, drinking, or finding shelter. Paper clips have no homeostatic value; therefore, food and drink are rewarding, and paper clips are not.

Researchers discovered that if they stimulated the lateral hypothalamus/medial forebrain bundle of an animal that did not have access to a lever but did have access to food, the animal would eat voraciously (Stuber and Wise 2016). If water was available, the animal would compulsively drink (Morgenson and Kucharczyk 1978). They proposed that the lateral hypothalamus/medial forebrain bundle was a neural correlate for various rewarding consummatory activities that restore, or maintain homeostasis (Panksepp 1998a). They predicted that if you moved an electrode around these brain regions, you could induce an animal to consume in various different ways. Stimulation of one part would cause an animal to eat, another part would induce the urge to drink, yet another to find shelter, and so on (Valenstein et al. 1970).

These experiments, however, did not yield the predicted results. Animals did not consume in different ways when different parts of the lateral hypothalamus/medial forebrain bundle were stimulated. Instead, stimulation of any part of this brain region induced animals to persist in anything that they happened to be doing, and they would do so at a fevered pace. If they were eating, they would continue to eat ravenously. If they were drinking, they would continue to drink as if they were parched (Valenstein et al. 1970). If an animal had been eating voraciously and the food was removed and replaced with water, the animal would drink as if it were very thirsty. If the food was later reintroduced, the animal would continue to drink (Panksepp 1998a).

Also, perplexing was the fact that stimulation of the lateral hypothalamus/medial forebrain bundle caused animals to do things that had nothing to do with homeostasis. For example, they would compulsively gnaw wood, excitedly preen by carrying their tails around, nibble on feces, or gather up their young (Panksepp 1998a). It did not seem to matter what they did. What seemed to matter was their fevered enthusiasm. Stimulation of the lateral hypothalamus/medial forebrain bundle generated excited, obsessive behavior that sometimes had nothing to do with homeostasis (Valenstein et al. 1970).

Another discovery made things even more confusing. Under normal conditions, when animals are in a state of homeostatic imbalance, when they are hungry, thirsty, cold, or hot, the lateral hypothalamus/medial forebrain bundle is active. *Interoceptor* neurons, which detect homeostatic imbalances, like depletion of water, low nutritional energy, and thermal issues, unconditionally arouse the lateral hypothalamus/medial forebrain bundle (Panksepp 1998a; Ceunen et al. 2016). However, as soon as people and animals begin to eat, or drink, as soon as they find shelter, these brain structures close down. In other words, the lateral hypothalamus/medial forebrain bundle is not the neural correlate of consumption and the restoration of homeostatic balance. It is the neural correlate of homeostatic imbalance—states like hunger, thirst, and hyperthermia, or hypothermia (Panksepp 1998a). But stimulation of this brain region is rewarding. How can homeostatic imbalance be rewarding?

Kent Berridge observed that motivated behavior has two phases: an appetitive phase that occurs before animals consume and a consummatory phase when they eat, or drink. He proposed that stimuli, like food, have "incentive salience," which means that people and animals want them. During the appetitive phase, resources with incentive salience arouse a sense of *wanting* them before we consume them. Berridge proposed that when we consume resources with incentive salience, we *like* them. In his view, wanting and liking are the two components of reward (Berridge 2009).

Berridge's claim, however, does not fit with the idea that homeostatic balance is rewarding and imbalance is punishing. Arousal of the lateral hypothalamus/medial forebrain bundle correlates with the wanting/appetitive phase when an animal's body is in a state of homeostatic imbalance—typically when it is hungry, or thirsty. If homeostatic balance is rewarding, how can the wanting phase be a component of reward?

We are left with a conundrum. Activity in the lateral hypothalamus/medial forebrain bundle occurs when people and animals are in a state of homeostatic imbalance. Nevertheless, animals work hard to achieve stimulation of this brain region. What sort of reward does it provide? One cannot suppose that homeostatic imbalance is rewarding. If it were, people and animals would strive to be hungry, thirsty, cold, or hot. But people and animals almost always try to restore homeostasis: They eat when they are hungry, drink when they are thirsty, and look for shelter in bad weather. Furthermore, any species that strove for homeostatic imbalance would surely die out.

Can one credibly argue that no motive, or reward is involved in the arousal of these brain structures? When animals press levers to achieve stimulation of the lateral hypothalamus/medial forebrain bundle, is their behavior instinctive? This, too, is an unsatisfactory explanation because animals learn instrumental behaviors, like pressing a lever, in order to obtain rewards (or avoid punishment). Learned behavior is not instinctive (Gillaspy 2015). Animals will not learn to press a lever in order to obtain paper clips, but they will learn in exchange for tasty treats and for stimulation of the lateral hypothalamus/medial forebrain bundle. Some sort of reward motivates them to learn.

Affective Reward

In sum, we know that rewards afforded by the lateral hypothalamus/medial forebrain bundle are neither consummatory, nor homeostatic because these structures shut down when animals consume and restore homeostasis (Bozarth 1994). We know these structures are aroused during periods of homeostatic imbalance, but we cannot believe that homeostatic imbalance is rewarding because animals consume when they experience homeostatic need. We cannot entertain the idea that stimulation of the lateral hypothalamus/medial forebrain bundle provides no reward because animals learn instrumental behaviors in order to receive stimulation. Animals only learn instrumental behaviors in order to receive a reward, or avoid punishment (Cherry 2019).

The only option that explains this behavior is that stimulation of the lateral hypothalamus/medial forebrain bundle generates an affective reward. What else could it be? The process of elimination precludes other explanations (Panksepp and Biven 2012).

The Affective Rewards of Dopamine

Neuroscientists now know that the lateral hypothalamus/ medial forebrain bundle is part of a system known as the *mesolimbic pathway*. The deepest structure in this pathway is the *ventral tegmental area (VTA)* located in the upper brainstem. Above the VTA is the lateral hypothalamus, just above it the *nucleus accumbens*, and further above medial areas of the cortex. These structures are connected by the fibers of the medial forebrain bundle (Panksepp 1998a; Panksepp and Bernatzky 2002).

The VTA produces the brain chemical *dopamine*, which largely fuels the mesolimbic pathway. All animals ever tested become readily addicted to drugs, like cocaine and methamphetamine, which prolong dopamine activity at synapses along the mesolimbic pathway and keep it in an active state. When animals take these drugs, they exhibit the same enthused frenetic behavior that Olds and Milner observed when they applied electrical stimulation (Panksepp 1998a).

When the mesolimbic pathway is electrically stimulated in the human brain, or when people take cocaine, or meth, they do not describe the relaxed sense of satisfaction and contentment after a good meal, a deep drink on a hot day, or the glow following sexual consummation. Rather, they report a high-hearted sense of anticipation when they are looking forward to those rewards. This enthused sense of anticipation is attended by feelings of personal agency—the sense that they can make things happen in the world (Panksepp and Biven 2012).

Subjective experience supports these results. We all know that states of hunger, thirst, cold, or heat are unpleasant (Young 1959; Kelly and Berridge 2002). Yet even when we are in a state of unsatisfied craving, we often experience anticipatory pleasures with which we are all familiar. Before Sunday lunch, we relish the scent of a roast cooking in the oven, even though we are experiencing pangs of hunger. The anticipation of meeting a lover can be almost as keen as the reunion itself. Conversely, after successfully completing work on a long project, our sense of satisfaction is sometimes mixed with a depressing letdown because we no longer enjoy the enthusiasm of working toward a goal.

The SEEKING System

Panksepp renamed this rewarding dopamine/mesolimbic pathway the SEEKING system because when animals are given free arousal of the mesolimbic pathway—when they do not have to work in order to obtain electrical stimulation and when they are not provided with food, or drink—they immediately explore their environments with purpose and enthusiasm. Rats sniff vigorously, which they typically do when they are looking for something—when they are seeking (Panksepp 1998a).

Panksepp proposed that SEEKING arousal provides an affective reward characterized by euphoric anticipation, curiosity, a sense of personal agency, and a willingness to take risks. Once we accept that SEEKING arousal provides an affective rather than a homeostatic reward, the experimental evidence delineated above makes sense. In particular, it explains that Berridge's wanting phase is rewarding because it arouses affects of enthused anticipation, even during periods of homeostatic imbalance.

The SEEKING system, however, has a downside, most notably its link to schizophrenia. Dopamine binds with five different receptors known as D1, D2, D3, D4, and D5. People suffering from schizophrenia have an unusually large number of D2 receptors, and all antipsychotic medications block activity at D2 receptors. If people take drugs, like cocaine, or methamphetamine that stimulate dopamine activity, they, too, can develop schizophrenic-like symptoms. Less egregious overarousal of the SEEKING system can generate compulsive behaviors, like the ones observed under laboratory conditions. Overarousal of the SEEKING system can cause people to gamble, overeat, chain-smoke, or engage in sexual promiscuity. On the other end of the scale, a dearth of dopamine causes depressive lethargy (Panksepp 1998a).

The Distinctive Nature of SEEKING Arousal

The SEEKING system is not the only reward system in the brain. Olds and Milner discovered that animals would also work for stimulation of the *septal* area, which is located in the middle of the brain just above the hypothalamus (Olds and Milner 1954). The septal area generates sexual responses in both people and animals (Heath 1975). Animals, however, do not work in a frenetic manner for septal stimulation. Rather, they press levers methodically without signs of agitation (Panksepp and Biven 2012).

In contrast, when animals work for stimulation of the SEEKING system, they do so in a frenzied manner. Rats sometimes peer around the lever that they press as if curious about it. Why the difference? Very probably the animal's hyperactive behavior reflects the qualities of energy, purpose, and curiosity that are typical of SEEKING arousal. Arousal of the septal area might be equally, or more rewarding, but it does not generate the heightened activity that one sees in stimulation of the SEEKING system (Panksepp and Biven 2012).

The LUST System and Homeostasis

We have argued that the rewards of SEEKING arousal are non-homeostatic; therefore, the SEEKING system generates an affective reward. We can make a similar case for the LUST system because rats will work to achieve stimulation of the septum (Olds and Milner 1954; Panksepp 1998a). LUST arousal is not essential for homeostatic regulation and survival. Neutered and spayed dogs usually live longer than those that are intact (Abrams 2013) and celibate people generally live longer than those who are sexually active (Reid 2017).

Furthermore, animals engage in sexual behavior, even when homeostasis is imbalanced. Research studying sexual behavior of rats divided them into three groups. A control group was given a nutritious diet. A second group had a diet with a normal number of calories but low levels of protein. A third group ate a diet low in calories but with a normal amount of protein. Rats on the low-calorie diet had sex less often than the control group, but surprisingly, rats in the protein-restricted diet had sex 14 percent more often than the control group (De Souza Santos et al. 2004). If it is legitimate to assume that rats in the control group had better general homeostasis than rats in the low-protein group, then positive sexual affects leading to copulation did not correlate with homeostasis. Indeed, the expenditure of energy entailed in copulation would further destabilize homeostasis. Since the rewards of LUST arousal can be independent of homeostasis, we can conclude that LUST, like the SEEKING system, provides an affective reward.

Affects Have Subcortical Origins

How do we know that rewarding SEEKING and LUST affects emanate from subcortical structures? In order to prove that they do, one would need to show that decorticate animals will learn instrumental behaviors (like pressing a lever) and work for electrical stimulation of the SEEKING or LUST system. Although it is difficult to teach instrumental behavior to decorticate animals, they are able to learn, albeit very slowly. For example, decorticate rats can be taught to manipulate a chain in order to obtain food (Oakley, 1980).

One can imagine experiments where decorticate animals learn instrumental behaviors and work to achieve stimulation of the SEEKING and LUST systems. Such experiments would demonstrate that affective feelings of enthused anticipation and sexual desire have subcortical origins. Once we established that subcortical structures are capable of generating affects commensurate with SEEKING and LUST, we could assume, at least provisionally, that they generate the full range of affects that correspond to other emotional systems (GRIEF, RAGE, FEAR, CARE, and PLAY). To my knowledge, however, no such experiments have been conducted.

Nevertheless, research that we have already examined indicates that subcortical structures generate affects. Moruzzi and Magoun's experiments on cats demonstrate that consciousness depends on the RAS. Arguments against feedback theory discussed in chapter 1 indicate that affects do not emanate from the cognitive cortex. Other experiments show that as ever deeper brain structures are destroyed, the more completely is motivated behavior obliterated (Panksepp, 1998b; Watt and Pincus, 2004; Merker, 2007; Panksepp and Trevarthen, 2009). Further studies demonstrate that motivation takes the form of pleasure and pain. Research about pain reveals that the suffering involved in pain emanates from subcortical structures that include the brainstem (Auvray et al. 2010). Similar research demonstrates that the experience of pleasure also has subcortical roots (Berridge and Kringelbach 2015). Empathy research demonstrates that physical and affective pain have overlapping subcortical roots (Decety et al. 2008). Other areas of research indicate that physical and affective pleasure also have overlapping subcortical roots (Berridge and Kringelbach 2011). This evidence indicates that structures in and around the brainstem play a crucial role in generating affective consciousness.

All Mammals Are Affective Creatures

Since subcortical regions of all mammalian brains are very similar, this indicates that other mammals, even those that are very unintelligent, are affective creatures. Therefore, when brainstem theorists say that all mammals can feel curious, lustful, lonely, joyful, frightened, angry, playful, and tenderly protective, we have good reason to believe them.

Summary

The purpose of this chapter was to substantiate the brainstem school's assumption that emotional behavior reflects affective experience. We began with experiments by Olds and Milner, who concluded that the lateral hypothalamus/medial forebrain bundle is rewarding because animals will work for its arousal. Behaviorists were unable to define the meaning of reward, so neuroscientists defined it in terms of homeostasis. In their view, anything that restores homeostasis is rewarding, and anything that disrupts it is punishing. However, stimulation of the lateral hypothalamus/medial forebrain bundle occurs during periods of homeostatic imbalance, so the reward cannot be homeostatic. We concluded that stimulation of this part of the SEEKING system provides an affective reward. We argued that LUST also provides an affective rather than a homeostatic reward.

On the basis of other research, we concluded that subcortical structures in and around the brainstem generate a full range of affective experience. Since all mammalian brains have the same subcortical structures, we concluded that all mammals experience affects just as we do.

The next two chapters look further into the brainstem school by examining two hypotheses, one devised by Antonio Damasio and the other by Jaak Panksepp. These hypotheses propose how the brain creates affective consciousness.

Chapter 5

Damasio's Hypothesis

The Somatic Marker Hypothesis

Damasio's interest in affective consciousness began when he and his colleagues conducted experiments with people who had sustained damage to the *ventromedial prefrontal cortex (vmPFC)*, which is located in the frontal lobes at the bottom of the cerebral hemispheres, just above the eye sockets. The ventromedial prefrontal cortex is involved in the evaluation of stimuli and in the modulation of emotional response (Delgado et al. 2016). When people have sustained damage to the vmPFC, they are intellectually intact and can, for example, carry out logic problems normally. Nevertheless, they are unable to make sound decisions (Damasio 1996).

Patients with ventromedial damage along with normal control subjects were asked to play a computerized gambling game where subjects could choose cards from four decks, each of which contained cards telling the participant that s/he has gained, or lost virtual money. Two of the decks were stacked to yield high gains but higher losses, resulting in greater losses in the long run. The other two decks yielded modest gains and losses, but gains were higher overall (Bechara 2015).

As play continued, normal subjects carried out unconscious cognitive processes, even before they were aware, which decks were good and which were bad. The vmPFC in a normal patient would evaluate these unconscious cognitive processes, and if they played a bad deck, it would inaugurate bodily responses, like sweating (Dunn et al. 2006).

The brains of patients with ventromedial damage could also carry out unconscious cognitive processes about the decks of cards. Like normal subjects, they knew which decks yielded overall gains and losses. However, their damaged vmPFCs could not evaluate this knowledge and hence did not produce bodily responses, like sweating. (Bechara et al. 1997).

Damasio and his colleagues called these physical signals *somatic markers*, and without them, the ventromedial patients made bad decisions (Bechara et al. 2005 p. 159). Even after they were consciously aware of which decks of cards would make more money, they were unable to experience physiological responses in anticipation of their proposed actions. As a result, they tended to play the high-loss decks (Bechara et al. 1994.) Damasio concluded that the somatic marker, rather than reason, provides a gut-level conscious feeling that guides sound decisions (Damasio et al. 1996). In the years that followed, he devised a hypothesis to explain the role that the body plays in affective consciousness.

Homeostasis

As we noted earlier, homeostasis, which Damasio sometimes calls "the machinery of life regulation" (Damasio 2003 p. 111), involves many physical systems in the body that work cooperatively in order to insure good health and survival of the individual (Cannon 1932; Damasio 2010). Like many neuroscientists, Damasio believes that feelings, like hunger, thirst, desire, malaise, and enthusiasm, reflect homeostatic vicissitudes (Damasio 2020). Basically, homeostatic balance feels good, and imbalance feels bad. Since feelings of pleasure and pain provide motivation that is an essential feature of consciousness, Damasio concluded that homeostasis is a somatic marker that is fundamental to consciousness (Parvizi and Damasio 2001).

Brain Structures that Monitor Homeostasis

In order to understand consciousness better, Damasio wanted to discover, which brain structures monitor, maintain and restore homeostasis (Damasio 1999). At first, he thought that the *insular cortex,* which lies high in the brain, between the temporal, parietal, and frontal lobes, might be the crucial homeostatic structure because it plays a role in a variety of conscious experiences, like chronic pain (Kupers et al. 2000), responses to heat and cold (Craig et al. 2000; Brooks et al. 2002), taste and the regulation of eating (Frank et al. 2013), physical and moral disgust (Wicker et al. 2003; Wright et al. 2004; Sanfey et al. 2003; Phan et al. 2002), and feelings of well-being (Craig 2002).

He discovered, however, that patients with *simplex encephalitis* (a viral infection of the central nervous system) who had sustained complete destruction of the insular cortex exhibited and reported a full range of conscious pleasure/pain experiences. He concluded that the insula participates in, but is not essential for, homeostatic regulation and is not essential for the creation of consciousness (Damasio et al. 2012).

He noted that two upper brainstem structures, the *tractus solitarius* and the *parabrachial nucleus,* both receive information from the viscera about pleasure and pain (Kringelbach and Berridge 2009; Bernard et al. 1989). Furthermore, when the brain is intact, these structures relay visceral information to the insula, which provides a further differentiation (Damasio 2010). He hypothesized that these upper brainstem structures along with some others regulate homeostasis. The other structures include the *periaqueductal gray (PAG),* also in the upper brainstem, which generates pleasure and pain (Tershner and Helmstetter 2000; Panksepp 1998a; Jenck et al. 1995), and the *hypothalamus,* which lies just above the brainstem and helps to regulate homeostasis (Sargis 2015). In Damasio's view, these structures in and around the upper brainstem process information and regulate homeostasis (Damasio 2010).

Homeostasis and the Protoself

In addition to linking consciousness to homeostasis, Damasio links consciousness to sense of self. In his view, "There is no consciousness that is not self-consciousness" (Damasio 1999 p. 20). He noted that homeostasis must be balanced within narrow parameters in order to sustain life. For example, if our body temperature rises by only a few degrees, we become ill and might die (Cannon 1932; Bernard 1974; Oza 2014). The self is also stable. You do not wake up in the morning thinking that you are someone else. You retain a continuous sense of who you are. Damasio, therefore, hypothesized that the subcortical structures, which regulate homeostatic stability *(tractus solitarius, parabrachial nucleus, PAG, and hypothalamus)* are substrates of a stable self. He calls these structures the *protoself* (Parvizi and Damasio 2001).

Damasio devised a hypothesis whereby all consciousness experience emerges in two stages, or *orders*, the first of which is *core consciousness*. He proposed that certain stimuli unconditionally cause homeostatic changes. Subcortical protoself structures represent these changes as neural maps of the homeostatic body (Damasio 1999 p. 72). The protoself is not initially conscious but its homeostatic maps are precursors of feelings, which means that the protoself has the potential to experience conscious feelings of pleasure and pain (Damasio 1999 p. 51).

The Mind

As the protoself is creating homeostatic maps, the sensory structures in the cortex create other maps representing stimuli that we see, touch, hear, smell, and taste along with sensations within the body. Damasio calls these sensory structures the *mind* (Damasio 1994 p. 94). Unlike protoself maps, mind maps represent purely objective information with no implications of pleasure, or pain (Damasio 2010; Solms 2013).

Core Consciousness

As consciousness dawns, protoself maps and mind maps combine, causing three things to happen. First, the protoself becomes conscious and generates "felt body images," which are feelings of pleasure, or pain that reflect homeostatic balance, or imbalance (Damasio 2010, 190). Second, the protoself experiences a "feeling of knowing...that our organism has been changed by an object" (Damasio 1999 pp. 168–9). In other words, the protoself knows that a particular stimulus has caused the good, or bad feeling. Third, the protoself becomes a protagonist with a sense of self (Damasio 1999). These three events, a feeling of pleasure, or pain, knowing what has caused the feeling, and a sense of self, constitute core consciousness, which is the first order of consciousness (Damasio 1994; 2010).

Two Examples of Core Consciousness

Suppose that I decide to go to the beach on a hot summer day. When I reach the shore, a cooling breeze wafts my way. My protoself unconsciously maps homeostatic changes caused by the breeze, namely the restoration of thermal homeostasis. At the same time, my mind maps objective features of the breeze: its strength, fragrance, direction, etc. My protoself and mind maps combine, and my protoself becomes conscious of the pleasant cooling of my body. It also has the feeling of knowing that the breeze has made me feel good. At the same time, my protoself acquires a sense of self (Damasio 1994). Thus, it is I—my self—who knows that I feel good and knows that the breeze has made me feel good (Damasio et al. 2000; Lenzen 2005).

But if a bee stings me, its venom destroys nearby cells, and my immune system responds by releasing histamines, which cause local swelling (Noori 2016). My protoself unconsciously maps the homeostatic imbalance caused by the bee's venom and by my immune response. At the same time, my mind map notes that the bee had landed on my arm and stung me before it flew off. When my protoself and mind maps combine, my protoself experiences pain in my arm. It also has the feeling of knowing that the bee has caused the pain, and it is I (my self) who knows and feels this.

Other Animals

Damasio proposes that core consciousness has no memory and occurs as disjointed moment-to-moment pulse-like representations. Without memory, neither consciousness of pleasure and pain, the feeling of knowing, nor a sense of self can be sustained over time. Damasio maintains that many other animals are capable of core consciousness, and they, like us, experience feelings of pleasure and pain, a sense of knowing what has caused the pleasure/pain and a sense of self. But their brains are incapable of creating connected memories of ongoing events. As a result, experiences of core consciousness are episodic and brief. These animals live in the present, and they do not experience a narrative stream of consciousness (Damasio 2010).

An Example of Core Consciousness in Animals

Suppose that I brought my dog along for the outing at the beach. Like me, my dog would enjoy the cool breeze. He, too, would know that the breeze made him feel good, and he, too, would have a sense that he—his self—was the one that felt good.

Suppose that an hour later, a bee stung my dog. He would feel pain, he would know that the bee had caused the pain, and he would have a sense of self that felt pain. Although my dog's brain is capable of these experiences of core consciousness, he would not remember them as features of the outing to the beach because his brain is incapable of creating a narrative.

Extended Consciousness and Autobiographical Self

When memory and sophisticated cognition are added to core consciousness, as they are in human brains, the disjointed pulses of consciousness connect up and collectively represent *extended consciousness* over time. As a result, we humans, and perhaps some other intelligent animals, experience our lives as a narrative, and we have a sustained sense of *autobiographical self* (Damasio 1999 p. 197). Extended consciousness is the second order of consciousness (Damasio 1999).

An example of Extended Consciousness and Autobiographical Self

Suppose that I went to the beach with a group of friends for a picnic. When we arrived, I basked in the refreshing breeze, and I would remember the experience. If a bee flew by a stung me a few minutes later, I would remember that too. Later that day, you might ask me about the picnic, and I would tell you about both experiences. I might also say that we ate sandwiches, drank beer, swam in the ocean, and built sandcastles. This continuous narrative of events would be my extended consciousness about the picnic, and it would be part of my autobiographical self—part of my personal experience.

The Creation of Affective Consciousness

Affects, which Damasio often calls "feeling[s] of an emotion" (Damasio 1999 p. 60), are created by the following three steps. First, an emotional system is automatically aroused by an "emotionally competent stimulus" (Damasio 2003 p. 50). A sudden loud noise, for example, might be an emotionally competent stimulus that arouses the FEAR system. Emotional arousal causes a change in homeostasis which the protoself maps. In the second step, the mind maps objective features about the emotionally competent stimulus like the pitch, duration, and timbre of the noise. In the third step, protoself and mind maps combine. The protoself experiences a sense of self that feels the affect. The self also knows that the emotionally competent stimulus has caused the affect (Damasio 1999).

An Example of Affective Arousal

The bee flying around my head at the beach was an emotionally competent stimulus that aroused my FEAR system. My HPA axis and SNS were activated. Stress chemicals poured into my bloodstream, my heart pounded, my blood pressure shot up, and I broke into a cold sweat. My protoself mapped these homeostatic changes while my mind mapped objective features about the bee that was buzzing loudly and swooping near my face. When my protoself and mind maps combined, my protoself felt the negative affect of fear and knew that the bee had caused my fear. My protoself also acquired a sense of self. At the end of this process, I knew that the bee had frightened me (Damasio 1999).

Optimal Homeostasis

Emotions like fear are painful because they cause homeostatic imbalance. Damasio posits that other emotional systems can create optimal homeostatic states that are superior to normal regulation (Damasio 2003). When you meet up with an old friend, for example, your brain secretes endogenous opioids, and you feel wonderful.

Other Animals Experience Affective Core Consciousness

Because most other animals can only experience disjointed core consciousness, their affects are also disjointed. When your dog sees you walk through the door at the end of the day, you are the emotionally competent stimulus that causes the secretion of endogenous opioids and oxytocin in your dog's brain. This optimizes homeostasis and your dog's protoself maps this positive shift. His mind maps his impressions of the way that you look, sound, and smell. When protoself and mind maps combine, your dog's protoself experiences happiness and knows that he (his self) feels happy because you are home.

Your dog may have other affective experiences in the course of the evening. He may feel frustrated as he waits for you to open his tin of food, and later, he might contentedly rest his head on your knee as you stroke his head. His brain, however, is not able to construct an ongoing narrative about this sequence of affective experiences. Your dog lives in the affective present, from moment to moment.

A Variation on the Feedback Model

You may have noticed that Damasio's hypothesis about the creation of affects is a variation on the James-Lange feedback model discussed in chapter 2. According to that model, an emotion is a set of stereotypical visceral and behavioral responses that are fed back to the cognitive cortex, which generates the commensurate affect (LeDoux 1996).

Damasio, too, sees emotion as a set visceral and behavioral responses that disrupt homeostasis. However, James and Lange thought that information about bodily change was fed back to the cognitive cortex. Damasio maintains instead that information about the homeostatic disruption is fed back to protoself structures in the upper brainstem. In his view, brainstem structures, rather than the cognitive cortex, create affects (Damasio 2011).

Emotional Behavior

In addition to generating affects, an emotionally competent stimulus prompts a behavioral response. Damasio likens emotional behavior to the immune system. When an antigen, like a virus, enters your body, your immune system produces antibodies that get rid of the antigen and restore good health. An emotionally competent stimulus enters your body through sensory capacities of sight, sound, smell, taste, and touch. This arouses emotion and destabilizes homeostasis. Your emotional behavior gets rid of the emotionally competent stimulus, and homeostasis is restored (Damasio 2003; 2004). When I see a bee flying around my head, I either throttle the offending creature, or run away. Either action gets rid of the bee and restores homeostasis.

As-If Loops

Damasio uses the term "body loops" to describe core and extended consciousness because the protoself maps homeostatic changes that take place in the body (Damasio 1996 p. 1415). He proposes, however, that even when homeostatic changes do not occur, the protoself can simulate maps of homeostatic change. Damasio calls these simulated states "as-if loops" because the protoself reacts as if it were mapping homeostatic changes in the body (Damasio 1996).

An Example of an As-If Loop

If I were trying to decide whether or not to have a picnic at the beach, my mind would create an imaginary scene where bees are flying all around. My protoself would simulate an as-if map, which mimics homeostatic changes that occur when real bees are flying around my head. When my mind map and my as-if protoself map combine, my protoself experiences trepidation. It also has the feeling of knowing that the very thought of bees causes anxiety and I (my self) have this knowledge. Following this imagined experience, I might opt to eat at a restaurant.

Damasio explains that as-if loops derive their existence from body loops. My protoself would not be able to simulate as-if maps about fear if I had not experienced homeostatic disruption when real bees were nearby. Because as-if loops do not reflect homeostatic changes, the conscious experience that they generate is not as vivid as consciousness generated by body loops. I might feel nervous when I imagine bees flying around my head, but imaginary bees do not frighten me as much as real bees. As-if loops are advantageous because they can be processed quickly, and they do not use as much energy (Damasio 1999).

Damasio notes that the discovery of *mirror neurons* supports his theory of as-if loops. Researchers discovered mirror neurons when they observed the brains of monkeys that witnessed the actions of others. When a monkey saw someone move his hand, neurons in the monkey's brain that cause it to move its own hand became active (Rizzolatti et al. 1996). In other words, the monkey's brain was acting as if it were moving its own hand. Damasio believes that mirror neurons are the "the ultimate as-if body device" (Damasio 2010 p. 103).

Social Behavior

Damasio applies his ideas about homeostasis to social behavior, a topic that we will discuss further in chapter 7. For now, we only note his observation that all living creatures, from bacteria to people, strive for homeostasis, and they all form societies whose members display similar strategies of social cooperation (Damasio 2018).

Summary of Damasio's Hypothesis

Damasio builds his hypothesis on the assumption that homeostasis is the bedrock consciousness. Homeostatic balance generates conscious feelings of pleasure while imbalance signals pain. He proposes the existence of functional entities that he calls the protoself and the mind. The protoself creates maps about the homeostatic body. The mind creates maps about stimuli in the environment and in the body. We become conscious when protoself and mind maps combine. Consciousness involves three processes. First, the protoself feels pleasure, or pain that reflects homeostasis. Second, the protoself knows that a stimulus in the environment has caused the feeling of pleasure, or pain. Third, the protoself acquires a sense of self.

In animal brains, consciousness occurs in disjointed moments of core consciousness. Intelligent human brains, however, have sophisticated memory, which joins up the moments of core consciousness into a coherent narrative and an autobiographical self.

Affective consciousness occurs when an emotionally competent stimulus arouses an emotional system, which disrupts homeostasis in either positive, or negative ways. The protoself maps this disruption while the mind maps features of the competent stimulus. When the maps combine, the protoself has three experiences. It experiences affective pleasure, or pain. It knows that the emotionally competent stimulus has caused the affect, and it has a sense of self. People and animals behave in ways that redress homeostatic disruptions that attend negative emotions. In the case of fear, for example, they typically freeze, or run away.

As-if loops occur when the mind imagines an emotionally competent stimulus rather than experiencing a real one. The protoself simulates a map of homeostatic disruption, which results in an affective experience. Both body loops and as-if loops inaugurate core consciousness, but body loops produce a more vivid conscious experience. As-if loops have the advantage of speed and low energy expenditure.

Finally, groups of living creatures, from bacteria to human beings, exhibit similar social behaviors.

Chapter 6

Panksepp's Hypothesis

One of Panksepp's major contributions to affective neuroscience is his taxonomy of seven basic emotional systems located largely in the brainstem and in midline cortical areas. These emotional systems are virtually identical in all mammalian brains, and some are present in the brains of other vertebrates.

Panksepp's Seven Emotional Systems

1. The SEEKING system has alternately been described as a "foraging/exploration/investigation/curiosity/interest/expectancy" system (Panksepp 1998a p. 145). SEEKING arousal is characterized by a persistent exploratory inquisitiveness and a willingness to take risks (Gottlieb and Oudeyer 2018). It engenders energetic forward locomotion—approach and proactive engagement with the world—as an animal probes into the nooks and crannies of interesting places, objects, and events in ways that are characteristic of its species. Rats, for example, typically sniff vigorously when they explore new environments.

   The SEEKING system holds a special place among emotional systems because to some extent, it supports and attends all the other emotional systems. When in the service of positive emotions, the SEEKING system engenders a sense of purpose accompanied by feelings of interest ranging from enthusiasm to euphoria. For example, when a mother feels the urge to nurture her offspring, the SEEKING system will motivate her to find food and shelter in order to provide this care. The SEEKING system also plays a role in negative emotions—for example, providing part of the impetus that prompts a frightened animal to find safety.

2. The FEAR system generates a negative affective state from which all people and animals wish to escape. It engenders tension in the body and a shivery immobility at milder levels of arousal, which can intensify and burst forth into a dynamic flight pattern with chaotic projectile movement to get out of harm's way.

3. The RAGE system causes animals to propel their bodies toward offending objects, and they bite, scratch, and pound with their extremities. Rage is fundamentally a negative affect, but it can become positive when it results in victory over one's opponents, or in the control and subjugation of others.

4. When animals are in the throes of the LUST system, they exhibit courting behavior that culminates in copulation with a receptive mate. Arousal of LUST can be pleasurable even when ultimate satisfaction is not obtained, but excessive arousal can result in an unpleasant craving tension. LUST is one of the sources of love.

5. When people and animals are aroused by the CARE system, they have the impulse to envelop loved ones with gentle caresses and tender ministrations. It is typified by maternal care, and without this system, looking after the young would be a burden. Instead, nurturing can be profoundly rewarding. In extreme circumstances, CARE arouses the impulse to protect others even at the expense of one's own safety. Mothers will sacrifice their lives in order to protect their young. The CARE system is not limited to mothers, or to women. Public servants, from the military to hospital

staff, willingly risk life, limb, and well-being for the sake of others. CARE is another source of love.

6.   The GRIEF system (which Pankepp sometimes calls the PANIC, or SEPARATION DISTRESS system) might be called the GRIEF/SOCIAL BONDING system because it generates good and bad feelings (Toronchuk and Ellis 2012). The bad feelings are a panicky misery that people and animals experience when they are socially isolated, or rejected. The negative side of GRIEF can produce a deep psychic wound. When young children and young animals are in the throes of GRIEF, their misery reaches a panicky level, and they cry insistently, urgently trying to reunite with their caretakers—usually their mothers. If reunion is not achieved, the baby, or young child gradually begins to display sorrowful and despairing bodily postures that reflect the brain cascade from panic into a persistent depression.

The GRIEF system also produces feelings of joyful contentment when people and animals benefit from the affectionate support of family and friends. This sense of social belonging engenders a sense of well-being. The positive side of GRIEF is yet another source of love.

Thus, positive social bonds are cemented from two directions. The positive side of GRIEF feels good, and the negative side, which feels terrible, is assuaged by close and supportive relationships. Close and positive social relationships are especially important early in life when young children and animals need the protection of their parents in order to survive. By staying close to their parents, children and other young mammals feel contented and secure. By staying close, they also avoid the anxiety and misery caused by separation.

7.   The PLAY system is expressed in bouncy and bounding lightness of movement where participants often poke—or rib—each other in rapidly alternating patterns. At times, PLAY resembles aggression, especially when PLAY takes the form of wrestling. But closer inspection of the behavior

reveals that the movements of rough-and-tumble PLAY are different from aggression. Furthermore, both participants enjoy the activity. When children, or animals play, they usually take turns at assuming dominant and submissive roles. In controlled experiments, researchers found that one animal gradually begins to win over the other (becoming the top dog, so to speak), but the play continues as long as the loser still has a chance to end up on top 30 percent of the time. When both the top dog and the underdog accept this kind of handicapping, the participants continue to have fun and enjoy this social activity. If the top dog wants to win all the time, the behavior approaches bullying. Even rats clearly indicate where they stand in playful activity with their emotional vocalizations: When they are denied the chance to win, their happy laughter-type sounds cease, and emotional complaints begin. The PLAY system probably helps young animals to learn basic skills. For example, a kitten chasing a ball, or yarn is also developing skills that will eventually enable it to catch mice. Additionally, PLAY provides an arena for learning about social roles (Bekoff and Byers 1998; Brosnan 2006; Keltner et al. 2006). The PLAY system is one of the main sources of friendship (Panksepp 1998a; Pankespp and Biven 2012).

Three Types of Affects

Panksepp states that affects encompass all conscious experiences of pleasure and pain, which he places into three categories: emotional affects, homeostatic affects, and sensory affects. Emotional affects occur when one or more of the emotional systems described above is aroused. For example, arousal of the PLAY system generates joy, the negative side of GRIEF generates sorrow, RAGE generates anger, and so on.

Homeostatic affects are feelings like hunger, thirst, satiation, urges to urinate, defecate, etc. Sensory affects occur in response to stimuli outside and inside the body. This includes sweet and sour tastes, good and bad odors, the experience of rough, or smooth textures, pain associated with tissue damage, etc. (Panksepp and Biven 2012).

The Self

Panksepp proposes the existence of a SELF, which is an acronym for "simple ego-type life form" (Panksepp 1998a p. 309). He proposes that the SELF creates emotional, homeostatic, and sensory affects, which is to say all conscious feelings of pleasure and pain. He uses upper case lettering for the SELF just as he does for the seven emotional systems because he reasons that the SELF, like the emotional systems, includes ancient brainstem structures that are homologous in all mammalian brains and probably in the brains of other vertebrates as well as in some invertebrates. He, like Damasio, states that all conscious affective experiences include an inherent sense of selfhood—a sense of "I-ness" (Pankespp 1998a p. 309).

Panksepp's SELF is similar but not identical to Damasio's protoself. The SELF and protoself are similar because both are relatively stable. However, the pleasure or pain that the protoself experiences depends on bodily homeostasis. The SELF, on the other hand, is independent of bodily homeostasis. Panksepp proposes that the SELF has its own internal homeostatic parameters, and its resting state is represented by a steady set point that is all its own (Panksepp 1998a). This is an important distinction between Panksepp and Damasio to which we will return in the next chapter.

The Creation of Emotional Affects

Panksepp maintains that each emotional system generates commensurate affects in the following way. Certain stimuli inherently arouse emotional systems. Each emotional system consists of assemblies of individual neurons, which exhibit large-scale rhythmic oscillatory patterns of firing where neurons in the assembly fire synchronously. Panksepp proposes that each emotional system generates large-scale synchronous oscillations whose rhythm serves as its signature. The signature neural rhythm of the FEAR system might be a tight staccato, or shivery cadence; the signature rhythm of the CARE system might be slow and gentle; PLAY might be a buoyant, skipping tempo; the negative side of GRIEF might be like convulsive sobs, or a high-pitched wail; etc. (Panksepp 1998a).

Panksepp hypothesizes that affects are created when signature oscillatory rhythms of emotional systems reverberate within the neurons of the SELF, causing the SELF neurons to oscillate in the same rhythm. When this happens, the SELF generates affects and emotional behaviors. The RAGE system, for example, might generate a pounding rhythm, which reverberates in the SELF. The SELF then produces a violent affective state and also directs the limbs to strike out. Thus, both emotional affects and emotional behaviors literally resemble the large-scale oscillatory rhythms of emotional systems (Panksepp 1998a).

Pankespp suggests that stimuli in the environment that mimic an emotional signature can also reverberate in the SELF and inaugurate an affective and behavioral response. He was especially interested in musical rhythms that are similar to the neural oscillations of a particular emotional system. Rock music, for example, might mimic rhythms of the LUST system, causing the SELF to create LUSTful affects and to direct behaviors, like pelvic thrusts in dance (Panksepp 1995;1998a).

An Example of the Creation of Affect

People and animals have innate responses to a few sensory stimuli. The smell of cat fur arouses a rat's FEAR system. If you place a pinch of cat fur in the cage of a rat that has been raised in captivity and has never been exposed to a cat, the rat will become wary and its movements will be constricted. It will go off its food and off sex. Neither the sight of a cat, nor the sound of its purr, nor meow frightens rats. It is the smell of the cat fur that arouses their FEAR systems (Panksepp 1998a).

According to Panksepp, a rat becomes frightened in the following way. When the rat smells the cat, the rat's FEAR system generates a signature oscillatory rhythm that might have a spooky high-pitched, tremulous dynamic. This oscillatory rhythm reverberates in the SELF, which produces a quivering tense affective state and tenuous bodily behaviors (Panksepp 1998a).

The SELF as a Motor Function

Nearly all neuroscientists see consciousness as a sensory function and tend to think of motor systems as outputs that implement the dictates of sensory processing (Panksepp 1998b p. 578). According to this view, fearful affects are encoded by sensory systems, and motor systems carry out commands to freeze, or flee. Motor systems add nothing to the fearful affect (LeDoux 1996). Panksepp proposes an alternative view, whereby the SELF consists of motor systems that generate both affects and emotional behaviors (Panksepp 1998a).

Justification of the Self-Motor Model

Panksepp notes that sensory systems inform motor systems about the way to direct behavior. Sensory systems would have served no purpose if they had evolved before motor systems. Therefore, motor systems must have evolved first. Ancient motor systems, operating without benefit of sensory input, must have directed simple coherent behaviors like obtaining nutrients by continually undulating and filtering water. The subsequent evolution of sensory systems allowed for more adaptive behaviors. With this reasoning in mind, Panksepp proposed that a motor SELF, which produced simple adaptive affects and emotional behaviors, evolved before sensory capacities. For this reason, he sees the SELF as a motor function (Panksepp 1998a).

Panksepp further supports the notion of SELF-motor structures by noting that many of our sensory cortical capacities can be destroyed without alterations to our sense of self. If my visual cortex were damaged, I would be blind, but my sense self—my sense of who I am—would remain unchanged. Since selfhood is part of consciousness, this suggests that consciousness is not a sensory/cortical capacity (Panksepp 1998a).

Even at the high level of the neocortex, motor structures appear to support a sense of self more than sensory structures. For example, damage to the motor cortex is more disruptive to the personality than damage to the sensory cortices. Cortical motor damage compromises functions, like attention, motor planning, imagination, and higher social emotions, like guilt shame and empathy (Panksepp and Biven 2012).

Although Panksepp does not cite them, recent discoveries about fear conditioning offer provisional support for his claim that motor systems have affective capacities. In these experiments, an animal, usually a rat, is classically conditioned by subjecting it to an electric shock to its foot and simultaneously exposing it to an innocuous stimulus, like an auditory tone. There have been two phases in research about fear conditioning, the second of which is ongoing.

Initial experiments, conducted by Joseph LeDoux, revealed that fear conditioning creates circuitry in the amygdala. As we noted above, the amygdala consists of thirteen nuclei. Two of these are the *lateral nucleus* and the *central nucleus*. The lateral nucleus is a gateway for incoming sensory information to the amygdala. If an unconditioned rat receives an electric shock, neural pathways encoding information about the shock reach the lateral nucleus of the amygdala and elicit a strong response. The shock-information then travels to the central nucleus of the amygdala, which inaugurates the fear response by sending information down to various structures, like the hypothalamus and the periaqueductal gray (PAG). The hypothalamus and the PAG generate motor responses typical of fear, like hypertension and freezing (Duvarci et al. 2011). The electrical shock is an unconditioned stimulus because it always arouses fear.

In contrast, when an unconditioned rat hears an innocuous tone, that information, too, is sent to the lateral nucleus, but it elicits only a weak neuronal response, and the lateral nucleus does not send information about the tone to the central nucleus. Thus, the tone is the conditioned stimulus because it does not evoke fear (LeDoux 1996).

LeDoux's initial conditioning experiments revealed that when the shock and tone are administered at the same time, neural pathways encoding both the shock and the tone converge on the same cells in the lateral nucleus of the rat's amygdala. When this happens, the neural pathway encoding the shock (the unconditioned stimulus) changes the neural pathway encoding the tone (the conditioned stimulus) (LeDoux 2014).

The change entails the *expression* (activation) of dormant genes. As we noted above, genes produce proteins that perform functions. Newly expressed genes in the tone-pathway produce proteins that strengthen the synaptic bonds between neurons in the pathway. In its strengthened condition, the tone-encoding pathway gains access to the central nucleus of the amygdala, which initiates the fear response (Johansen et al. 2011). This is how the rat acquires a fear response to the tone. This change in the tone-encoding pathway is an example of *synaptic plasticity* where synapses between neurons become stronger, or weaker in response to increases, or decreases in activity (Hughes 1958).

Conditioning is a fundamental way that people and animals learn and remember (Bouton 2020). We tend to think that learning and memory concern ideas. At school, you learned that the Battle of Hastings happened in 1066, and you remember that date. Rats, however, are unintelligent and probably cannot acquire, or remember ideas. Furthermore, even decorticate rats can be conditioned, so conditioning is not about the acquisition of an idea. Instead, conditioning entails the acquisition of an emotional response. The rat acquires (learns to have) and retains (remembers) a fear response to the tone. Thus, conditioning is a learning and memory process, but it is not about learned and remembered ideas. Conditioning causes us to learn and remember an emotional response to a particular stimulus (LeDoux 1996).

When LeDoux conducted his initial experiments, he believed that all the conditioning mechanisms took place in the lateral nucleus of the amygdala. It was there that the tone and shock pathways converged. It was there that gene expression and synaptic plasticity occurred. It was there that the learning and memory pathways were created. He believed that the central nucleus of the amygdala played no role in conditioning but was instead a passive recipient of learning and memory that had occurred in the lateral nucleus. The central nucleus was seen purely an output that sent information to deeper structures, like the hypothalamus and the PAG, that generated visceral and behavioral fear responses (LeDoux 1996; Wilensky et al. 2006).

Further research, however, demonstrated that LeDoux's early experiments did not reveal the full picture about conditioning. His discoveries about the mechanisms of synaptic plasticity in the lateral nucleus have stood the test of time, but subsequent research has shown that other facets are involved. One of these concerns the role of the central nucleus, which is not simply an output structure. Instead, synaptic plasticity takes place in the central nucleus, and this, too, is an essential component of the conditioning process (Paré et al. 2004; Samson and Paré 2005; Wilensky et al. 2006; Zimmerman et al. 2007).

The central nucleus is part of the brain's motor apparatus because it inaugurates emotional responses, like freezing and rapid heart rate. Yet we now know that the central nucleus participates in learning and remembering a conditioned response. LeDoux is a feedback theorist, and he does not believe that animals, like rats, have affective feelings as we do. From his point of view, the research about conditioning applies only to learning and remembering an emotional response. However, the revelation that the central nucleus plays an active role in emotional learning and memory demonstrates that the motor apparatus of the brain is not just the passive servant of sensory systems. This suggests that motor structure, like the central nucleus, may play an active role in the acquisition (learning) and retention (memory) of an affective response.

Possible Self Structures

When Panksepp hypothesizes about possible SELF substrates, he suggests three brainstem structures, all of which have important motor functions. The first are deep layers of the superior colliculi. The upper layers of the superior colliculi contain sensory maps that are almost exclusively dedicated to visual processing. In chapter 2, we noted that these layers probably participate in blindsight. Deeper layers process sensory information from multiple modalities (vision, hearing, touch, etc.), and some neurons are dedicated to motor functions (Gandhi and Katnani 2011), causing people and animals to orient their bodies to significant stimuli (Sparks 1988). Because the deep layers of the superior colliculi respond to multiple sensory modalities and because they participate in motor orientation, they qualify as possible SELF substrates (Panksepp 1998a).

Another viable candidate is the *periaqueductal gray* (PAG), which contains neurons arranged in columns, each corresponding to different emotional systems, like FEAR, RAGE, CARE, GRIEF, etc. (Depaulis and Bandler 1991; Holstege et al. 1996; Bandler and Keay 1996; Panksepp 1998a; Bartels and Zeki, 2004; Satputea et al. 2013). We have noted above that the PAG generates a freeze response to danger (Babaev et al. 2018), but the PAG also directs a wide range of motor functions (Koutsikou et al. 2015). The periaqueductal gray also qualifies as a possible SELF structure because it lies at the hub of all seven emotional systems and receives input from them all (Panksepp and Northoff 2009).

The *mesencephalic locomotor region*, located in the upper brainstem, is a third SELF candidate because it generates a primitive intentionality—a readiness for action, which typically attends affective arousal (Panksepp 1998a). Research in the 1960s revealed that this region controls walking and running (Shik et al. 1966). Subsequent studies revealed that the mesencephalic locomotor regions control forward locomotion in vertebrate species (Ryczko and Dubuc 2013). It is also involved in automatic behaviors, like respiration and in oral behavior (Arciniegas 2013) as well as in the refractory period following ejaculation in male animals (van Furth et al. 1995). Additionally, many neurons embedded in the mesencephalic locomotor region respond to pain by facilitating bodily arousal and attention (Redgrave et al. 1996).

The Extended SELF System

Panksepp maintains that higher brain regions also participate in the generation of emotional affects and behaviors. He refers to these higher structures as the "extended SELF system" (Panksepp 1998 b p. 571 p). For example, the *anterior cingulate cortex* located in medial parts of the cortex (Stevens et al. 2001) integrates sensory, motor, cognitive, and emotional information (Bush et al. 2000) and is active when isolated young animals cry for their mothers (Landa et al. 2012). Similarly, the anterior part of the insular cortex (the structure, which Damasio initially thought was the protoself), which lies deep between the frontal and parietal lobes of the cortex, plays a role in positive social interactions, like fairness and cooperation (Lamm and Singer 2010).

Panksepp reasons that the epicenter SELF structures are more important than higher extended SELF structures because greater electrical stimulation is needed to create neural activity in the anterior cingulate and insular cortex than is needed to produce activity in the periaqueductal gray. Furthermore, lesions to the periaqueductal gray of cats and monkeys extinguish their ability to respond to emotional stimuli, or to exhibit intentional behavior. Damage to affect-generating areas higher in the brain, like the anterior cingulate and insular cortices, does not have such severe consequences. Panksepp concludes that although higher brain extended SELF structures participate in emotional arousal, they are not as important as the structures that comprise the epicenter of the SELF. (Panksepp 1998a; 1998b).

Attractor Landscapes

Panksepp borrows the term *attractor* from chaos theory to explain how higher regions, like the cingulate cortex and the anterior insula, become involved in the generation of affects and emotional behaviors. Attractors, as the term suggests, exert something akin to a gravitational pull. Imagine that a marble is balanced on the rim of a bowl, and you push it into the bowl. The marble will circle the sides of a bowl and settle at the bottom. The bottom of the bowl can be seen as an attractor because all the time that the marble circles the bowl, gravity pulls it toward the bottom (Williams and Arrigo 2002). The behavior of the marble is predictable, and the attractor at the bottom of the bowl is a fixed point. Constituents in chaotic systems do not behave in predictable ways, nor do they settle on a fixed point. Nevertheless, they gravitate around relatively stable attractors (Muller 2019).

Panksepp writes about *attractor landscapes* of the SELF that act like chaotic attractors by causing neurons in higher brain regions, like the cingulate cortex and the anterior insula, to repetitively fire in ways that are commensurate with signature rhythms as the SELF. In his view, this is how the SELF recruits higher brain regions in the generation of affect (Panksepp 1998a; Panksepp 2005; Ciompi and Panksepp 2005).

Universal and Personal Selfhood

Panksepp proposes that SELF structures are homologous in all mammalian brains. Therefore, the SELF is a universal, or *nomothetic* self, which creates a sense of being a coherent organism that proactively interacts with the world. The nomothetic self generates *anoetic* consciousness of pleasure and pain that is nonreflective and noncognitive. Panksepp believes that all mammals (and possibly all vertebrates as well as some invertebrates) experience a universal nomothetic sense of self along with anoetic consciousness of pleasure and pain (Panksepp and Biven 2012).

Panksepp states that the cognitive cortex participates in the creation of the *idiographic* self—one's personal history and experience. The idiographic self produces *noetic* consciousness that is self-reflective and cognitive. Noetic consciousness and the idiographic self are similar to Damasio's ideas of extended consciousness and the autobiographical self. Panksepp states that it is probable that only human beings are capable of self-reflective noetic consciousness. Furthermore, because we all have different experiences, the idiographic self differs from one person to another (Panksepp and Northoff 2009).

Modest Effects of Bodily Feedback

Although he believes that the SELF produces affects in a way that is independent of homeostasis, Panksepp does not entirely rule out the ability for bodily feedback to influence emotional affects. He concedes that emotional bodily responses can, to some extent, influence the intensity of affects. Presumably, bodily feedback somehow alters rhythms in the SELF, although it is not clear how this might happen. Recent studies, for example, indicate that frowning can lower your mood (Lewis and Bowler 2009). However, the effect of this kind of feedback is, in his view, limited and does not create affects. If you frown when you are in a bad mood, you may feel worse. But if you are feeling happy, conscious frowning will not make you miserable (Panksepp 1998a).

Summary of Panksepp's Hypothesis

Panksepp maintains that all feelings of pleasure and pain are affective, and he puts affects into three categories: emotional, homeostatic, and sensory. He posits that neurons in aroused emotional systems generate signature oscillatory firing rhythms that reverberate in the SELF. When this happens, the SELF generates commensurate affects and emotional behavior. Although SELF structures are located in the brainstem, higher brain regions participate in the generation of affect when the SELF influences their firing patterns. Unlike Damasio's protoself, the SELF is independent of homeostasis.

He also proposes the novel hypothesis that SELF structures have motor rather than sensory functions. By this, he means that motor structures in the brain do not simply carry out orders relayed by the sensory apparatus. Instead, motor structures have the capacity to generate affects.

Chapter 7

Evaluation of Damasio and Panksepp's Hypotheses

Panksepp and Damasio agree that affects emanate largely from structures in and around the brainstem; thus, both oppose the traditional corticocentric view that the cognitive cortex creates consciousness. This is the virtue of their hypotheses. Each hypothesis also has features about which it is currently futile to speculate. For example, they can only make best guesses about possible substrates of the protoself and the SELF. They also propose specific mechanisms to account for the creation of affective consciousness. It is impossible to know if either, or neither of these mechanisms is correct. We will not discuss such imponderable topics. Instead, we will examine some questions, deficits, and errors in each hypothesis.

Consciousness and a Sense of Self

Both Damasio and Panksepp maintain that conscious includes a conscious unified sense of self. There are two objections to this assertion. One, espoused by V. S. Ramachandran, states that a unified sense of self is an illusion because we have different experiences of self (Ramachandran 2009). Ramachandran cites sexual identity, which has several strands, two of which are external anatomy and internal body image. Usually, these two features fuse into a single sense of sexual identity: People with male bodies feel like men, and people with female's bodies feel like women. Thus, sexual identity appears to be unified.

In Ramachandran's view, the two sexual identities are separate, a view supported by neuroscientific evidence. In rat experiments, abnormal timing of hormonal release during pregnancy may result in a mismatch between the gender of the brain and that of the body. A similar problem in utero may account for transsexuality in human beings. A person with a male body might have a female brain, and one with a female body might have a male brain (Panksepp 1998a). Ramachandran concludes that transsexuals have two sexual selves: one male and one female (Ramachandran 2009). Panksepp and Damasio, however, believe that the sense of self is holistic. They would probably say that transgendered people feel like one sex trapped inside the body of another. That would be their unified sense of self.

A second argument maintains that some forms of consciousness do not include any sense of self (Gopnik 2010). Philosophers distinguish between *phenomenal* consciousness that is devoid of self and *self-consciousness*, which includes a sense of self (Block 1995). Critics of Descartes' *cogito ergo sum* refer to this point, noting that Descartes was only entitled to conclude that conscious thinking exists. The assertion that *I* am doing the thinking is an unsubstantiated assumption (Copleston 1963). Proponents of phenomenal consciousness would say that Damasio and Panksepp make the same mistake when they say that consciousness always includes a conscious self.

Subjective reports challenge the idea that self is always part of consciousness. Practitioners of Zen meditation maintain that the most intense states of consciousness occur when a sense of self is absent (Austin 2003). The film critic Roger Ebert described this absence of self in his enraptured review of *Star Wars* when he wrote, "My imagination has forgotten it is actually present in a movie theatre and thinks it is up there on the screen" (Ebert 1977).

Neuroscientific research also indicates that self and consciousness do not always coincide. The neocortex contains two functional global networks. One extrinsic network processes information about the environment while another intrinsic system processes information from within the organism. If human subjects are asked to look at a photograph and report their emotional responses, the intrinsic system is active. But if asked to report quickly and factually about the content of the photograph, reporting, for example, if it is a photo of a monkey, the extrinsic system is active. Both systems generate consciousness, but when extrinsic systems are active, intrinsic self systems are inhibited (Golland et al. 2007). This suggests that when people focus on external stimuli, the sense of self is absent.

Damasio and Panksepp would probably respond by saying that in the brains of Zen practitioners, in Ebert's brain, and in the brains of people who participated in the intrinsic/extrinsic experiment, a noncognitive sense of self underlies these apparently selfless experiences.

A modern theory of conscious known as *Integrated Information Theory (ITT)* maintains that nonliving things can be conscious. ITT claims that consciousness is a property of complex systems, which consist of a group of interacting constituents that exchange information (Tononi 2004). When constituents in a complex system exchange information, it means that each constituent has properties (information) that influence fellow constituents in systematic ways that follow the laws of physics (Lloyd 2019). Integrated information theory hypothesizes that the magnitude of consciousness reflects the degree to which constituents in a complex system exchange of information.

Proponents of ITT propose that consciousness is a fact of nature, like electrical charge, space, time, mass, and energy (Koch 2014). In their view, it makes no sense to ask how an electron creates an electrical charge. Instead, we should accept that electrons simply have a charge. Similarly, we should accept that all complex systems are inherently conscious (Koch 2012b).

ITT uses the symbol φ (phi) to represent the degree to which a complex system exchanges information. Any interconnected system that exchanges information possesses a level of φ, meaning that it is conscious to some degree (Koch 2009). A hydrogen atom with its three interacting quarks is minimally conscious. Your mobile telephone, which contains a fairly large number of interacting parts, is more conscious. The human brain, which contains about eighty-six billion neurons that make synaptic connections measured in the trillions is very conscious (Sukel 2011). However, not every collection of constituents is conscious. A pile of sand composed of many grains is not conscious because grains of sand do not exchange information (Koch 2009).

At first glance, it seems outlandish to believe that inanimate objects, like hydrogen atoms, or mobile phones, are conscious entities. However, proponents of ITT argue that the brain is nothing more than a lump of flesh that functions according to the laws of physics. If a lump of flesh is consciousness, why is it bizarre to believe that other complex systems governed by the same physical laws are also conscious (Greene 2020)?

ITT has enthusiastic supporters (Aaronson 2014) and equally enthusiastic critics (Horgan 2015). One of its drawbacks is that it does not assign a function to consciousness. Thus, consciousness might be an inert feature of complex systems (Koch 2009; Marcus 2013). Integrated information theory is of interest to our conversation because it proposes that consciousness is not limited to life-forms. If inanimate objects can be consciousness, their consciousness may not include a sense of self.

There is no way to disprove that selfhood is part of consciousness, but there is no reason either to assume that it is. The evidence supporting brainstem theory indicates only that noncognitive consciousness generates feelings of pleasure and pain. None of this evidence suggests anything about a self. When Damasio and Panksepp say that affective consciousness always includes a sense of self, they are assuming the existence of a protagonist who has conscious experiences pleasure and pain. At first glance, this might appear to be axiomatic, but there are credible arguments to the contrary.

A Deficit in Panksepp's Hypothesis

Panksepp uses the word affect when speaking about three types of pleasure/pain experiences: homeostatic, sensory, and emotional. This broad use of affect is confusing because you and I usually use the word sensation when we speak about the experiences that Panksepp calls homeostatic and sensory affects. We say that experiences like hunger, or a bee sting are sensations, and we reserve the word affect for experiences like joy and sorrow—the experiences that Panksepp calls emotional affects.

Panksepp's terminology, however, is not just confusing. It also reveals a deficit in his hypothesis, which only accounts for the creation of emotional affects. He maintains that emotional affects are created when emotional systems generate signature large-scale oscillatory rhythms. These rhythms reverberate in the SELF, which generates commensurate affects and emotional behaviors. If this mechanism also accounts for the creation of homeostatic and sensory affects, homeostatic and sensory systems would also create signature oscillatory rhythms reverberated in the SELF. However, Panksepp does not explain how this might happen.

With regard to homeostatic affects, he acknowledges that "we know little about the neural systems that subserve such feelings" (Panksepp 1998a p. 166). For example, neuroscientists do not yet know the exact structures, or chemical processes that govern hunger and satiation (Pankespp 1998a). Similarly, they do not fully understand sensory affects. Pain remains an unsolved riddle. Many forms of pain are assuaged by opiates like morphine, but some forms of pain are opiate resistant (McCormick and Schreiner 2001; Jamero et al. 2011) and elude medical redress (Nelson 2013). Panksepp does not explain how these unknown structures and chemical interactions influence the SELF in the creation of homeostatic and sensory affects.

Panksepp is also inconsistent when writing about sensory and homeostatic affects. Some research indicates that sensory affects are independent of homeostasis. Animals readily work in exchange for tasty treats, but it is difficult to induce them to work for the direct infusion of food into their stomachs, even though the infusion of nutrients restores homeostasis more quickly than eating (Panksepp 1998a). This indicates that the sensory taste of the food is more rewarding than the restoration of homeostasis, an observation that suggests a disconnect between sensory affects and homeostasis. He states, however, that a positive sensory experience, like a pleasing taste, "is nature's way of telling the brain that it is experiencing stimuli that are useful—events that support the organism's survival by helping to rectify biological imbalances" (Panksepp 1998a p. 182).

This suggests that sensory affects exist in order to restore homeostasis and that there is a close tie between sensory affects and homeostasis.

Panksepp also maintains that homeostatic affects are independent of homeostasis. He partially substantiates this claim by citing research about hunger. People and animals feel very hungry when their blood sugar drops, but this happens before energy levels have reached a dangerously low ebb. Instead of reflecting a serious homeostatic imbalance, extreme hunger serves as a signal to replenish energy before a homeostatic emergency occurs (Panksepp 1998a). By the same token, we feel very thirsty before our bodies are dehydrated (Gizowski and Bourque 2017). This research indicates that homeostatic affects, like hunger and thirst, do not directly reflect homeostatic vicissitudes. However, their link to homeostasis exists.

In sum, Panksepp's hypothesis claims that the SELF creates all three types of affective experiences, but it only accounts for the creation of emotional affects.

Damasio: Homeostasis and Emotional Behavior

Damasio states that emotionally competent stimuli arouse emotional systems, thereby destabilizing homeostasis. He likens the stimulus to an antigen, like a virus, and he compares emotional behavior to the immune system. Just as the immune system gets rid of an antigen and restores health, emotional behavior gets rid of a destabilizing stimulus and restores homeostasis (Damasio 2003; 2004).

The Triple Win of Emotional Behavior

Damasio's hypothesis maintains that emotional behavior provides a triple win. First, it restores, or optimizes homeostasis that is disrupted by emotional arousal. When a bee was flying around my head at the beach, it was an emotionally competent stimulus that aroused my FEAR system and disrupted homeostasis. My SNS and HPA axis were activated resulting in an influx of epinephrine and cortisol. I ran away from the bee (my emotional behavior), and once at a safe distance, my SNS and HPA axis wound down and homeostasis was restored. That was the first win. I also felt affectively better because I was no longer afraid. That was the second win. By running away, I also protected homeostasis by avoiding the disruption that a bee sting would have caused. That was the third win. In Damasio's words, "Emotions contribute to the survival and well being of individuals…by providing organisms with a swift, automated means to circumvent dangers and take advantage of opportunities" (Damasio 2011).

Many instances demonstrate that emotional behavior provides a triple win. Social isolation is an emotionally competent stimulus that arouses the GRIEF system, especially in young children and animals. GRIEF arousal includes activation of the HPA axis and the SNS as well as opioid depletion (Panksepp 1998a). When young children and animals are isolated, they exhibit emotional behavior of crying out, and this alerts parents to come to their rescue. With the arrival of parents, the youngster's GRIEF system winds down and homeostasis is restored. Youngsters feel comforted, and with their parents nearby, they are physically protected.

RAGE can also generate behavior that provides a triple win. RAGE arousal involves the activity of the *neuropeptide* (small protein) *substance P* and the stress hormone *norepinephrine* (Katsouni al. 2009; Terbeck et al. 2016). Animals are usually enraged by threatening intrusions, or by frustrations (Panksepp 1998a). If one animal tries to steal food from another, the thief arouses the owner's RAGE system. The owner of the food exhibits threating emotional behavior, like the baring of teeth and growling, and the thief retreats. Levels of substance P and norepinephrine subside, and homeostasis is restored. The owner calms down, and his food supply is safe. Human life is usually less dramatic, but we, too, endure challenging moments. If someone tried to cut ahead of you in a queue at the movies, he would arouse your RAGE system. You would tell him off (your emotional behavior), and when he backed away shamefaced, the chemicals that aroused your RAGE system would diminish, and you would feel better. You would also safeguard your place in line.

One also sees the triple-win scenario with sanguine emotions. Remember that GRIEF has a positive as well as a negative side. The positive side ascends when we are in the company of people who love and support us. Under these happy conditions, homeostasis is optimized by the secretion of chemicals like endogenous opioids and oxytocin (Panksepp 1998a). We engage with people who love us and the optimizing homeostatic effect continues. As a result, we continue to feel good. Engagement with people who love us is beneficial to homeostasis because they take care of us and protect us.

Limitations of the Triple Win: Emotional Behaviors that Are of No Homeostatic Consequence

Sometimes emotional behavior makes us feel good but has no effect on well-being, or survival. Panksepp notes that the LUST system generates sexual behaviors that are of no homeostatic consequence. "Obviously, sex is not essential for the bodily survival of any individual member of a species, 'merely' for the survival of the species itself." (Panksepp 1998a p. 228). Sexual behaviors, from courting to copulation, feel good but do nothing to enhance homeostasis, or survival. As we noted above, neutered and spayed dogs as well as celibate people generally live longer than those who are sexually active (Abrams 2013; Reid 2017).

Damasio claims to overcome the hurdle of sexuality by saying that the "deeper goal" of both reproduction and homeostasis is "the same" (Damasio 2010 p. 55). But this is not true. The deeper goals are different. Panksepp was right to point out that the goal of homeostasis is survival of the individual while the goal of sexuality is survival of the species. Nevertheless, many researchers place LUST on a par with homeostasis, claiming that emotional behavior either supports homeostasis, or enhances reproductive success (Schore 2001; Solms 2013; Nummenmaa et al. 2013). However, even if one includes sexuality and homeostasis in the same arena, other emotional behaviors undermine homeostasis.

More Limitations of the Triple Win: Emotional Behaviors that Undermine Homeostasis

In chapter 4, we saw that under laboratory conditions, hungry and thirsty animals ignore food and water in favor of pressing a lever that electrically stimulates their SEEKING systems (Panksepp 1998a). If an animal is given one meal per day at the same time that it is given the opportunity to stimulate its SEEKING system, it will opt for electrical stimulation rather than food (Ikemoto 2010). We concluded that while food provides a homeostatic reward, arousal of the SEEKING system provides a superior affective reward. Thus, the animal's behavior (pressing a lever) undermines homeostasis. Like these laboratory animals, human addicts also ignore homeostatic needs and spend money on drugs rather than on food (Santolaria-Fernández et al. 1995).

It might seem that these anti-homeostatic behaviors are specific to laboratory conditions, or addictive pathology. However, the SEEKING system induces us to take risks, which we do in everyday life, even though any risk can have bad consequences. We take risks when we choose a career, when we get married, have children, buy a house, engage in sports, or cross the street.

Considered risk-taking is a sign of good mental health. Life is interesting and exciting when we take risks. When a risk has a good outcome, we become more confident. If risk results in failure, it gives us an opportunity to correct our mistakes (Derrow 2019). Risk-taking is also essential to social progress. In Mark Zuckerberg's view, the most egregious risk in business is the refusal to take risks (Zuckerberg 2017).

The Wright Brothers, for example, were not daredevils. Because they knew the dangers involved, they rarely flew together. Yet they repeatedly risked their lives because of their burning desire—a manifestation of their SEEKING systems—to conquer flight. Orville and Wilbur Wright's SEEKING systems benefited mankind but did not enhance the homeostasis of either brother. In 1908, Orville's plane crashed from an altitude of 125 feet, killing his passenger and causing a hip injury that led to medical complications for the rest of his life

(Akpan 2015). When Orville was recovering from his injuries, a friend asked if he had lost his nerve. Orville replied, "Oh, do you mean will I be *afraid* to fly again? The only thing I'm afraid of is that I can't get well soon enough to finish those tests next year." (Kelly 1989, italics his). Risk-taking often feels good and does good, but it is not always good for us.

Arousal of the CARE system can also engender behavior that undermines homeostasis. CARE arousal involves brain chemicals like oxytocin and endogenous opioids that generate positive urges to nurture and protect others. When a mother's CARE system is aroused, she will deprive herself of food in order to nourish her young. She will also put her own survival in peril, perhaps by drawing the attention of a predator away from her brood. The CARE system is not limited to mothers, or to women (Panksepp 1998a). Soldiers, firefighters, police officers, and health professionals behave in altruistic ways, risking life, limb, and well-being in order to protect others.

Emotional systems are not usually aroused in isolation. Probably, the Wright Brothers were sometimes frightened as are mothers and public servants who put themselves in danger. However, if the aim of emotional behavior were to protect homeostasis of the individual, FEAR would dominate. The Wright Brothers would have stayed planted on the earth, mothers would leave their young to perish, and public servants would not come to our rescue.

These observations demonstrate that there is sometimes a disconnect between emotional behavior and homeostasis. Sexual behavior generated by the LUST system makes us feels good but has no effect on well-being and survival. Arousal of the SEEKING and CARE systems also make us feel good, but they sometimes induce us to behave in ways that endanger survival. This indicates that Damasio has made a mistake—Damasio's error as it were. Emotional behavior does not always restore, or optimize homeostasis.

Social Behavior and the Homeostatic Imperative

Damasio's error is evident in his account of social behavior. He states that all living creatures are bound by the "imperative requirements of homeostasis" to thrive and survive as individuals (Damasio 2017 p. 235). At the same time, living creatures from bacteria to human beings display similar cooperative social behaviors. He indicates that cooperative behaviors are compatible with the homeostatic imperative and cites an example of pushy upstart bacteria that try to take over those that are more established. The rivals reach a compromise when the upstarts become a satellite of the more established bacteria, a solution that benefits the homeostatic needs of each. Damasio states, "The successful option was shaped by the imperative requirements of homeostasis" (Damasio 2018 p. 235). He continues that the homeostatic imperative prompts living organisms to exhibit social cooperation across virtually all species. "The marvel is that when comparable problem configurations were encountered on other occasions, at other points in the messy evolution of life forms, the same solutions were found" (Damasio 2018 p. 236).

Sometimes social cooperation fits well with the homeostatic imperative. Colonies of bacteria exhibit the phenomenon of *quorum sensing* when individual bacteria secrete chemicals into the surrounding medium. When a bacterial population reaches a critical number, the level of these chemicals in the medium also becomes critical, and the chemicals simultaneously bind with receptors on the surface of all bacterial cells in the colony. This inaugurates synchronous gene expression in all the bacteria (Li and Tian 2012; Solano et al. 2014).

As we noted earlier, gene expression occurs when dormant genes become active and produce proteins. The newly produced proteins perform functions that the cell did not perform before. When quorum sensing occurs in a colony of bacteria, the proteins produced can cause cooperative social behavior. For example, quorum sensing in the bacteria *Pseudomonas aeruginosa,* which causes pneumonia and blood infections, results in the formation of a *biofilm,* whereby cells stick together and increase their virulence (Lee and Zhang 2015). Quorum sensing and gene expression also allows bacteria to recognize kin members that are welcomed into the biofilm and to exclude nonkin bacteria that attempt to exploit it (Kalamara et al. 2018). In this instance, quorum sensing and gene expression results in cooperative behaviors that benefit individual bacteria in the colony.

Damasio states that in bacteria the "obeisance of homeostatic imperatives is strict" (Damasio 2018 p. 21). However, the following examples demonstrate that bacteria sometimes defy the homeostatic imperative. *Bacillus subtilis* is a bacterium found in soil. When food supplies are short, 30 percent of the members in a colony undergo gene expression, which causes them to produce proteins that break apart dead cells, thereby converting them into food for the entire colony.

Gene expression and the production of new proteins is a costly business because it uses energy (Rutherford and Bassler 2012). Thus 30 percent of the bacteria make a sacrifice by expending precious energy for the good of all. During times of famine, their sacrifice is more egregious because some of the *Bacillus subtilis* bacteria cluster into spores where they safely await better times. Spore formation requires energy that the food-producing bacteria provide. Yet none of the food-producing bacteria become part of the spores (Veening et al. 2008). Thus, 30 percent of the bacteria expend energy to feed the entire colony during lean times, and they are likely to perish because they do not become members of the spores that they helped to create.

Some bacteria make the ultimate sacrifice for the good of all by committing suicide. Most bacteria harbor toxin-antitoxin systems in which antitoxins inhibit the activity of toxins that can potentially destroy the bacteria from within. Most of the time, antitoxins keep the cell alive; however, the genes that produce antitoxins are unstable and sometimes fail to function (Van Melderen and Saavedra De Bast 2009). The antitoxins that these genes produce are also unstable and are apt to degrade (Yang and Walsh 2017). If bacterial cells are stressed, for example, in times of famine, antitoxin function can break down, freeing toxins to do their deadly work (Sedwick 2011). Suicide death by a subpopulation in a colony of bacteria can boost the health of the colony. Although the reasons for this are not entirely clear, researchers reckon that suicide deaths may cause the release of toxins that attack competing bacteria, thereby enhancing the survival of their own (Mutschler et al. 2011).

Insects also display social behavior that undermines homeostasis. Damasio notes that the social behavior of wasps fulfills "a particular need—theirs, or the group's, or the queen's." Under these conditions, they "act in a seemingly altruistic manner whenever sacrifice is needed." (Damasio 2018 p. 23). However, if individual insects sacrifice their well-being, or their lives in order to fulfil the needs of the group, or the queen, those insects are not obeying the homeostatic imperative.

These examples demonstrate that Damasio has not reconciled the homeostatic imperative with altruism and self-sacrifice that are integral to cooperative social behavior.

Human Altruism and Self-Sacrifice

Damasio writes that organisms like bacteria and wasps do not have conscious motives. Their behavior is automatic, and they exercise "blind cooperation" when they exhibit altruism and self-sacrifice (Damasio 2018 p. 237). Automatic regulation is efficient, but it is inflexible and sometimes fails to take advantage of opportunities, or avoid misapplication. With the evolution of the nervous system, organisms became capable of experiencing conscious feelings that provide another way to regulate homeostasis.

Damasio explains that feelings are always valanced, which means that they feel either good, or bad. Because feelings of pleasure reflect homeostatic balance and pain reflects imbalance, we care whether or not homeostasis is balanced. Because we care, we behave in ways that make us feel good, and these behaviors benefit homeostasis (Damasio 2018). Damasio states, "*Feelings are informative regulatory interfaces. Their mental aspect, emerging as it does in consciousness, turns the owner of the respective organism into a potential agent of its own regulation*" (Damasio and Damasio 2016, italics theirs).

Damasio notes that animals with feelings exercise both automatic and voluntary behaviors to meet their homeostatic needs. For example, the *anterior preoptic area* of the hypothalamus has *interoceptor* molecules that detect dehydration in the body. These interoceptors cause the kidneys to excrete less water. In this way, the body automatically retains water, which supports homeostasis (Alcedo et al. 2009; Stratford 2014). The same hypothalamic area has interoceptors that cause the conscious experience of thirst. When we are thirsty, we drink and voluntarily restore homeostasis (Popkin et al. 2010).

In Damasio's view, human voluntary behavior includes the exercise of free will, which he defines as the ability to deliberate before taking action. We exercise free will when we deliberate about whom to marry, or even how to organize the afternoon's activities. Free will, however, is not completely free because it is ultimately tethered to homeostatic goals. We are free to deliberate about how to go about meeting those goals (Damasio and Hutsvedt 2011).

Damasio writes that free will conscripts human capacities of intelligent reasoning, memory, and language in order to optimize homeostasis and achieve well-being. The intelligent exercise of free will has produced cultural achievements, which include, art, science, agriculture, government, morality, justice, religion, finance, and infrastructure. All these social achievements have the goal of optimizing homeostasis and making us feel good (Damasio 2018). For example, like all animals, we need to slake our thirst. However, instead of drinking at a watering hole as other animals do, we have developed a public water supply that reaches almost every home and business.

Damasio explains that free will enables human beings to behave in ways that defy the homeostatic imperative. He notes that simple organisms, like bacteria and insects, strive for profit, which means that they try to take in more energy than they expend, a principle that benefits homeostasis (Keesey and Powley 2008). Profit is biologically good, but biological and cultural good do not necessarily coincide (Damasio 2018). Sometimes cultural good involves the exercise of free will in ways that oppose the homeostatic imperative, and we voluntarily deprive ourselves of biological profit. This exercise of free will includes behaviors that express "compassion, admiration, awe and gratitude." He continues, "Altruism can be deconstructed and taught in families and schools as a deliberate human strategy…altruistic behavior can be encouraged, exercised, trained and practiced in society" (Damasio 2018 p. 237). When we express altruism, we often behave in ways that are "in conflict with or even counter the main homeostatic goals" (Damasio and Damasio 2016). He concludes, "Here lies the great evolutionary novelty of human cultures, the possibility of denying our genetic inheritance and absolute control over our fate, at least temporarily. We can directly and willfully counter our genetic mandate when we refuse to act on our appetite for food or sex, or resist the impulse to punish another, or when we follow an idea that runs counter to natural tendency, such as procreating or depleting natural resources like drunken sailors" (Damasio 2018 p. 229–30).

By seeing voluntary altruism as an "evolutionary novelty of human cultures," Damasio indicates that it is an expression of free will rather than an in instinctive proclivity. Neuroscientific research, however, demonstrates that altruism is also an instinctive expression of the CARE system (Panksepp 1998a). Mother rats will endanger their own lives by attacking predators in order to protect their pups (Rosenblatt et al. 1994). Animals like rats have a minimal thinking cortex and probably do not have the capacity to deliberate, or exercise free will. Furthermore, decorticate female mammals exhibit normal maternal behaviors (Ferris et al. 2019), which indicates that their altruistic behavior is instinctive.

Recent research on mice has identified subcortical neurons that participate in instinctive maternal behaviors. In the female brain, the *anteroventral periventricular nucleus (AVPN)*, a small cluster of neurons in the *preoptic area (POA)* of the hypothalamus, has a multitude of oxytocin receptors while the same region of the male brain has very few. Oxytocin plays a central role in the formation of positive social relationships, including maternal bonding (Panksepp 1998a; Vacek 2002; Odendaal and Meintjes 2003). Oxytocin binds with receptors in the AVPN of the female's hypothalamus, and this generates her urge to nurture and protect her young (Sharma et al. 2019).

Since subcortical brain regions are virtually the same in all mammals, even unintelligent, or decorticate animals that can neither deliberate, nor exercise free will, exhibit altruistic maternal behaviors.

When mammalian mothers feel the positive urge to nurture, this urge, rather than the homeostatic imperative, motivates their behavior. Maternal behavior sometimes endangers the well-being, or life of the mother, which indicates that the mother's feelings are not "informative regulatory interfaces" in the service of homeostasis. Instead, her feelings—the urge to nurture and protect—can prompt her to behave in ways that can endanger her life and defy the homeostatic imperative.

We see that the homeostatic imperative does not always prevail in organisms like bacteria and insects whose behavior is mindless and automatic. Neither does it always prevail in animals that have feelings. Just as bacteria and insects sometimes defy the homeostatic imperative, people and animals also display instinctive behaviors that undermine homeostasis.

Society as a Complex System

An examination of complex systems explains, at least in principle, how opposing tendencies like the homeostatic imperative and altruism contribute to the creation of a cooperative society. Scientists have known about the existence of complex systems since the latter part of the nineteenth century (Jenkins 1997), but it is a new branch of science because it requires a great deal of computation that only became possible when computers were widely available (Vemuri 1978). Complex systems are groups of interacting entities that abound in nature. The science of complex systems applies to disparate disciplines, like meteorology, physics, immunology, engineering, economics, biology, and the social sciences (Stewart 1997).

Complex systems create *emergent properties* that are different than and more than the systems from which they emerge. Envision a group of birds flying together as a complex system. When birds fly together, they flock, which is a property that emerges from the system (group) of birds. In a computer simulation, "birds" interacted in accordance with three rules of behavior: they avoided collisions, they matched the speed of neighbors, and they flew close to each other. By following these three rules, groups of computer birds formed flocks. The formation of a flock is different than and more than a group of birds flying willy-nilly. Similar rules of behavior cause fish to swim in schools and land animals to travel in herds (Reynolds 1987).

Emergent properties have three characteristics. First, they self-organize. When birds flock, no bird leads the way, or directs the activity of others. Instead, the flock formation spontaneously emerges when the birds follow the three rules just mentioned: they avoid collisions, they match the speed of neighbors, and they fly close to each other. Second, you cannot predict what an emergent property will be even if you know a great deal about the complex system from which it emerges. If you knew that birds obeyed these three rules, you would not be able to predict that these rules cause them to flock (Gazzaniga 2012).

The third feature is that emergent properties exert an effect on the systems from which they emerge (Corradini and O'Connor 2010). When birds fly in groups, birds that are sick, or injured will slow down the speed of their neighbors. Strong birds, on the other hand, will step up the pace. If two birds have recently fought over food, one might try to attack the other, causing it to swerve off course in order to avoid a collision. This will exert a ripple effect, causing other birds to swerve off course as well. If each bird were flying alone, it could fly in any direction and at any speed that it could achieve. But when birds flock, the direction and speed of each bird is constricted by the movement of its neighbors. This is how an emergent property, in this case flocking, exerts an effect on the system (the group of birds) from which the property emerged.

Before the discovery of emergence, classical physicists believed that the principle of *reductionism* explained complex systems. Reductionism relies on Newtonian determinism, which states that if you know the position, mass, and velocity of an object at a given point in time, and if you know the forces that impact on that object, you can know the object's position at the next instant, the one after that, and so on, forever. You can use the same laws to reconstruct the position of that object at every moment in the past (Stewart 1997). If, for example, you knew the position, mass, and velocity of a billiard ball, and if you knew the angle and force of the cue that impacts on it, you could predict its position at any moment in the future, and you could reconstruct the same about its past.

Reductionism concerns the activity of a group of interacting entities. According to the principle of reductionism, if you applied the rules of determinism to each constituent in a system of interacting entities, you could predict the activity of the entire system in the future, and you could know how the system behaved in the past. You would know how the billiard game turned out, and you would know the state of play at every moment in the past and in the future. In classical physics, the profound belief in reductionism cannot be overestimated. In 1844, Pierre-Simone Laplace, stated that if one knew all the forces in nature and the position, mass, and velocity of every object, one could, in principle, know everything that would happen and everything that had happened in the universe (Gillispie 1997).

Researchers have since discovered that each constituent in a complex system obeys deterministic rules, but reductionism does not apply to the activity of the system. Complex systems are not simply the sum of each determined interaction. Instead, surprising properties, like flocking, emerge from many interactions (Stewart 1997; Lodge et al. 2003; Sapolsky 2010).

Social cooperation exhibits all three characteristics of an emergent property (Little 2012). First, it self-organizes. We all go about our business in individual ways, and our collective interactions self-organize into cooperative enterprises. Second, you cannot predict events. Even if you knew what every person was doing all the time, you would not be able to predict that these individual activities would create the complex cooperative society in which we live. Third, the emergence of society influences the ways that organisms behave. Once society has emerged, it imposes rules and regulations with which we all comply. Thus, the society that emerges from our interactions exerts an influence over the very interactions that created society in the first place.

Researchers use computer programs, like the one about flocking, to discover which factors contribute to emergent properties (Complexity Labs 2016). A meaningful computer program should identify the inherent characteristics that contribute to an emergent property. However, it is not currently possible to identify the many factors governing human interactions that contribute to a multifaceted emergent property like social cooperation (Friedkin 2015).

When considering behaviors that contribute to social cooperation in all living organisms, one can imagine that the homeostatic imperative is one of them but so, too, must be innate proclivities that are independent of homeostasis. In bacterial colonies, food production and toxin-antitoxin systems can cause individual bacteria to behave in ways that defy homeostasis. In the animal kingdom, the LUST, CARE, and SEEKING systems engender affects that can prompt us to behave in ways that are either indifferent to homeostasis, or undermine it.

Emergent social properties like flocking enhance the well-being of most of the individuals in the system. Flocking provides warmth for individual birds and assists in foraging for food since one bird may spy a food source that feeds other members of the flock. Similarly, a single bird may notice a predator, which the entire flock can avoid. Flocking also facilitates courtship since a male will be seen by a variety of females, and this enhances his chance of reproducing (Maynz 2019).

Traits like the homeostatic imperative along with other innate behaviors like altruism and self-sacrifice, that contribute to the emergence of society, have probably been retained across species because they favor the emergence of cooperative stable societies that enhance the survival and reproduction of most individuals.

Homeostasis and the Creation of Affects

We have seen that emotional behaviors, and their commensurate affects do not always have the goal of restoring, or optimizing homeostasis. We are sometimes motivated to behave in ways that make us feel affectively good, even though the behavior undermines homeostasis. This indicates a disconnect between homeostasis and affects, but how deep is the disconnect? What role, if any, does homeostasis play in the creation of affects?

On this point, Damasio and Panksepp disagree. Damasio maintains that homeostatic vicissitudes determine affects that we experience. According to his hypothesis, the protoself maps homeostasis and on that basis, generates affects. When homeostasis is balanced, or optimal, we feel good, and when it is imbalanced, we feel bad. Panksepp, on the other hand, maintains that the creation of affects is independent of homeostasis. He proposes that aroused emotional systems generate signature neural oscillations that reverberate in the SELF, which generates commensurate affects and emotional behaviors. This process occurs solely in the brain and bypasses bodily homeostasis.

Many researchers accept Damasio's hypothesis that affects reflect homeostasis (Fotopoulou and Tsakiris 2017; Solms 2013; Tyng et al. 2017; Watt 2017). However, we noted above that interoceptor neurons that detect homeostatic imbalances unconditionally arouse the SEEKING system, which generates positive enthused affects (Panksepp 1998a; Ceunen et al. 2016). Even though SEEKING arousal feels good, the good feeling does not always reflect homeostasis. Similarly, the body can be in a state of homeostatic imbalance when LUST is aroused and generates positive sexual feelings.

The relationship between affect and homeostasis, however, is complicated because there are two ways to think about homeostasis. One way concerns the general state of the body. General homeostatic imbalance occurs when, for example, we are tired, sick, hungry, thirsty, cold, or hot. General homeostatic balance, or optimal functioning indicates flourishing good health. The other way to think about homeostasis is to consider changes that occur when an emotional system is aroused. According to Damasio, an emotionally competent stimulus can arouse an emotional system, which impacts on homeostasis. FEAR arousal, for example, causes homeostatic imbalance because it generates an influx of stress hormones while the positive side of GRIEF, which generates oxytocin and endogenous opioids, causes optimal homeostatic balance.

Sometimes general and emotional homeostasis are at odds with each other. When your general homeostasis is imbalanced by hunger, your stomach may be growling, but you can still feel enthused and happy as you are about to win a marathon game of Monopoly. If affects reflect homeostasis, this would mean that the positive homeostatic effects of emotional arousal, in this case, the secretion of dopamine (SEEKING arousal), override the general homeostatic imbalances caused by hunger. Similarly, if I were relaxing after lunch, and a bee suddenly started flying around my head, it would arouse my FEAR system, and stress chemicals would supersede the positive effects of a satisfying meal.

It is credible to believe that the prospect of winning a game can trump the negative effects of hunger and that fear of a bee might supplant my contented state after lunch. But consider more extreme situations where terminal cancer patients who have love and support from friends and family report feeling fulfilled and even happy (Bramlet 2013). How can the positive effects of endogenous opioids and oxytocin (the positive side of GRIEF) create optimal homeostasis in the face of devastating homeostatic imbalances caused by terminal cancer? By the same token, very healthy people can be miserable. Recent studies revealed that high school and college athletes are as likely to experience depression as is the general population (Wolanin et al. 2015). If affects reflect homeostasis, this means that the negative homeostatic effects of cortisol and epinephrine (the negative side of GRIEF) override the positive effects of good health.

It is difficult to believe that emotional homeostasis can rule the day with terminal patients and healthy athletes. After all, the homeostasis of the cancer patients eventually breaks down entirely and they die. Depressed athletes often continue to excel at sports, indicating that their general homeostasis remains optimal. This suggests a disconnect between homeostasis and the creation of affects.

Damaso's hypothesis, which maintains that affects reflect homeostasis, cannot explain such phenomena. Panksepp, however, claims that affects are independent of homeostasis. According to him, it is possible to feel good when one's general health is bad and to feel bad when one is in the prime of life.

These examples, however, only indicate that Damasio's hypothesis is not always right. It may be true that affects reflect homeostasis most of the time. Furthermore, Panksepp offers scant evidence for his hypothesis, and the evidence that he does offer concerns only sensory and homeostatic affects. As we noted above, he highlights a disconnect between sensory affects and homeostasis when he observes that animals work in exchange for tasty food, but they are reluctant to work for food that is directly infused into their stomachs, even though infusion restores homeostasis more quickly than eating (Panksepp 1998a). He also points to a degree of disconnect between homeostasis and homeostatic affects by noting that intense hunger does not reflect extreme homeostatic imbalance (Pankserpp 1998a).

There is almost no evidence (at least none that I have found) supporting Panksepp's claim that emotional affects are always independent of homeostasis. One study concerning depressed patients who are physically ill suggests that negative affects reflect brain dysfunction rather than homeostasis. Diseases like cancer and influenza cause immune cells to produce *cytokines,* small proteins that fight disease but also cause inflammation in surrounding tissue. When an illness is protracted, cytokine-induced inflammation in the brain can result in depression (Simon 2001; Dantzer et al. 2008; Leonard 2010). This indicates that these patients are not depressed because of overall homeostatic imbalance. Their depression is caused by inflammation of the brain. This, however, does not demonstrate that affects are generally independent of homeostasis.

One could make a case for a disconnect between homeostasis and affect by hypothesizing that emotional arousal can generate visceral changes that have little, or no effect on homeostasis. We have seen that chronic arousal of the SNS and the HPA axis can cause bodily harm, but can the same be said about brief periods of emotional arousal? Suppose I was driving when another car sped by and cut me off, nearly causing an accident. My FEAR system would be aroused, stress chemicals would flood my bloodstream, and I would experience moments of intense fear. But I would not become ill. Would the brief influx of stress chemicals reflect a homeostatic imbalance, or would it reflect emotional arousal that is of no homeostatic consequence?

At the end of the day, the relationship between homeostasis and the creation of affects remains a mystery. Damasio's hypothesis as a general rule is undermined by the fact that homeostatic imbalances can unconditionally arouse positive affects generated by the SEEKING system and that LUST arousal can occur during periods of homeostatic imbalance. Panksepp's proposes that homeostasis and affects are independent, but he does not provide evidence to support his hypothesis as a general rule.

Summary

This chapter has touched on the following points. The assertion made by both Damasio and Panksepp that all consciousness includes a sense of self is open to question. Panksepp's hypothesis is incomplete. He provides a mechanism explaining how the SELF creates emotional affects but does not explain how homeostatic and sensory affects are created. Damasio's hypothesis claims that emotional behavior restores, or optimizes homeostasis. Yet sexual behavior has no effect on homeostasis, and some expressions of the SEEKING and CARE systems undermine homeostasis. Damasio's discussion about the ubiquity of cooperative social behavior does not address the fact that cooperative behaviors that involve altruism and self-sacrifice cannot always be reconciled with the homeostatic imperative. Affects do not always reflect homeostasis, but the role that homeostasis plays, or fails to play, in the creation of affects is unclear.

Chapter 8

The Consciousness Conundrum: Hard and Harder Questions about Consciousness

Throughout our discussion, we have ignored two hard mind-body questions. There is an easy question as well, which asks, which brain structures and functions correlate with consciousness. The easy question is not at all easy, but it is at least possible to answer (Chalmers 1995). The first hard question asks how the physical brain creates nonphysical conscious experience. This presents us with a category error—a question of apples and oranges. How does the mass of jellied of tissue between our ears gives rise to nonphysical conscious experiences of seeing colors, tasting flavors, feeling joy and sorrow, anticipating the future, and remembering the past (Freeman 2000)?

How might a traditional scientist address the hard question? She would probably be unwilling to say that brain functions actually cause consciousness to occur. Instead, she would take refuge in the easy question and say that conscious experience corresponds to activity in certain brain substrates and functions, which she would refer to as *neural correlates* of consciousness (Crick and Koch 1990). If she felt particularly forthcoming, she might even say that these neural correlates contribute to consciousness (Rees et al. 2002).

She would prevaricate because traditional science is caught in a bind from which it cannot escape. Science deals with the physical world and has no tools to examine immaterial consciousness. Nevertheless, few people doubt that the brain creates consciousness because various brain lesions result in specific alterations of consciousness and mental capacity. If our auditory cortex is destroyed, we will not be able to hear. If our lateral and dorsal prefrontal cortices are compromised, we will be unintelligent. If our hippocampus is damaged, our brains will not create recollections about the past. If our periaqueductal gray is injured, our emotional and affective capacities will diminish (Damasio 1999; LeDoux 1996; Schiff 2007; Panksepp 1998a).

All traditional scientific attempts to answer the hard question of consciousness fail. Some researchers give up and accept that the hard question cannot be scientifically addressed (McGinn 1989). Others insist that there is no hard question because the idea that consciousness is a unified experience is an illusion (Dennett 2003b; Ramachandran 2009). According to this view, there is no central location of a conscious self in the brain (Rorty 1991). Instead, disparate areas in the brain process a few stimuli as strands of consciousness, and our brains weave these strands into an illusion of unified consciousness (Dennett 2003a). This view, however, does not deny the existence of consciousness. It only denies unified consciousness. We are still left with the hard question of how the brain can create conscious strands.

The only approach that avoids the hard question takes a dualistic position, arguing that the body and the mind occupy separate existential spheres. According to this view, the brain directs bodily functions and behaviors, but it does not generate consciousness. Consciousness is seen as a nonphysical but fundamental feature of nature whose status is different from but equal to that of the physical world (Chalmers 1996). Integrated information theory, which we discussed in the previous chapter takes a quasi-dualistic view by claiming that complex systems are inherently conscious. A similar view is *dual aspect monism*, which maintains that consciousness is an aspect of the physical brain (Panksepp 1998a; Solms and Turnbull 2002; Panksepp and Biven 2012).

Most neuroscientists reject dualism because it circumvents the hard question by placing immaterial consciousness outside the realm of scientific inquiry. These researchers cite lesion experiments, like the ones mentioned above, which indicate that consciousness is a manifestation of brain function (Velmans 1995). These objections, however, again raise the hard question. Because traditional science cannot answer the hard question, it has been largely ignored in neuroscientific circles (Chalmers 1995). Lesion experiments have persuaded almost everyone that the brain creates consciousness, but nobody knows how this happens.

The Harder Question

There is an even harder question—or at least one that is equally difficult—which asks if immaterial consciousness can cause changes in the physical brain. If we posed this question to our traditional scientist, she would probably make a polite excuse and opt out of the conversation (Sperry 1969). The idea that an immaterial entity can change the workings of the physical brain does not sit well with scientists.

Yet there is ample evidence, every bit as convincing as lesion experiments, indicating that consciousness does influence brain function. Neuroscientists have known for some time that learning results in the creation of new neural pathways in the brain. While you are reading this book, the ideas that I am now typing out on my computer are creating new neural pathways in your brain. When we learn about anything, the architecture of our brain changes (Kandel 2006).

We regularly use ideas to change architecture in the brains of other people. If you were having dinner with a friend, you might try to tempt him to go out for a sizzling pizza rather than cold sushi. Your suggestions would hopefully create neural pathways in the parts of his brain that make decisions and direct consequent behavior. Politicians propose ideas to get our votes, and the advertising industry depends on the power of ideas to direct our purchasing habits. All these conscious ideas change our brains, which direct our decisions and behaviors.

Imagine that you received a letter about a big lottery win. There is nothing about squiggles written on a piece of paper that usually impress you. You regularly receive letters in the same format without a flicker of interest. On this occasion, however, you experience a joyful thrill, your heart races, you hyperventilate, jump in the air, shout to your wife, gather your children around, and call your parents. All the while your face is wreathed in smiles. Your brain dictates these behaviors, and it does so in response to the idea of a windfall.

Research on patients undergoing brain surgery also demonstrates the power of ideas on brain function. Patients are often conscious during brain surgery because the brain itself does not feel pain. During some of these operations, surgeons put an electrode on the patient's olfactory bulb without the patient's knowledge. The surgeon asked the patient to think of something nice. Then the surgeon electrically stimulated the olfactory bulb, again without the patient's knowledge. The patient suddenly reported a lovely scent, perhaps a rose. Leaving the electrode in the same place, the surgeon later asked the patient to think of something unpleasant and after again stimulating the olfactory bulb, the patient reported a bad smell (Gazzaniga 2009). The doctor's suggestions influenced the patient's olfactory experience, which indicates that conscious ideas impact the functioning of the brain's olfactory bulb (Gazzaniga 2012).

Reasons Why Neuroscience Ignores the Harder Question

Given this wealth of evidence, demonstrating that ideas influence the workings of the brain, why do neuroscientists shy away from the harder question? It is not just because we are ignorant of the mechanism that would allow conscious thoughts to influence the brain. We do not know the mechanism that causes the brain to create consciousness, but lesion experiments have convinced almost everyone that it does.

There are two possible reasons for skepticism: one experimental and the other historical. Benjamen Libet and his colleagues conducted experiments, which demonstrate that parts of the cortex register decisions before we are conscious of coming to those decisions (Libet et al. 1979). The time lag between brain response and conscious awareness can be up to ten seconds (Brass and Haggard 2008).

At first glance, this seems to suggest that consciousness is something that happens after the brain has made the real decisions. If you applied this reasoning to affective consciousness, you could argue that emotional systems in the brain direct survival-enhancing visceral and behavioral responses, like arousal of the HPA-axis and running away from danger. Affective consciousness would be seen as a side effect. One could conclude that if affects did not exist, emotional systems would direct adaptive responses necessary for survival. If consciousness were an afterthought of brain function, why would anyone believe that it has the power to change the brain?

A chapter in scientific history also explains why neuroscientists tend to deny that consciousness can change the brain. Hippocrates is known as the father of modern medicine because he based his hypotheses on observation rather than on religious mythology (Gill 2019). Scientists cannot determine whether or not myths describe anything real; therefore, they have no place in science (Ayala 2010). Researchers can, however, test the validity of a scientific hypothesis. Problems arise when scientists devise hypotheses that they cannot test. An incorrect, untestable hypothesis may not have religious overtones, but it is nonetheless a myth, which science sometimes accepts as fact. Hippocratic medicine is a case in point.

Hippocrates believed in the principle of *vitalism*, an idea that extends back to ancient Greece (Scott-Phillips 2015) and Egypt (Hountondji 1996). Vitalism maintains that all living creatures are powered by an unseen vital force that distinguishes them from inanimate things (Bechtel and Williamson 1998). The ancient Greeks also believed that there were four basic substances: earth, water, air, and fire. Hippocrates proposed that each of these substances had a corresponding *humor*, or liquid in the body, which he designated to be black bile, phlegm, blood, and yellow bile (Boeree 2002). In his view, the four humors were physical manifestations of unseen vitalistic forces that accounted for health and sickness.

A stable balance of humors indicated that vitalistic forces were balanced and that good health prevailed. People became ill because vitalistic forces and corresponding humors were imbalanced. Accordingly, the medical interventions that Hippocrates advocated were designed to rebalance bodily humors and hence, vitalistic forces (Smith 1979). This included treatments like bloodletting and purges as well as the use of emetics, which modern medicine has since judged to be often useless, or harmful (Wootton 2006). Doctors continued to practice Hippocratic medicine for two thousand years (Garrison 1966).

Vitalism was finally discredited by inventions like the microscope, which allowed researchers to discover that some diseases were caused by microorganisms rather than by imbalances of bodily fluids. By the middle of the eighteenth century, a group of physicians and scientists known as the *Berlin Biophysics Club* rejected Hippocratic vitalism (Greenspan and Baars 2005). They advocated an evidence-based approach to medicine that prevails to this day (Panksepp and Biven 2012).

Left in the wake of vitalism was a deep suspicion of immaterial forces. In psychology, this suspicion led the behaviorists to reject the study of consciousness, or even deny its existence, and focus exclusively on observable behavior (Lashley 1923). It is a mistake, however, to place consciousness in the same category as a scientific myth, like vitalism. Both are immaterial, but vitalism does not exist (Mayr 1988) while consciousness does exist.

As we noted above, when behaviorists rejected the study of motivation and mental life, they created an insoluble problem. The notion of reward is central to their theory, but behaviorists could not define its meaning. Neuroscientists tried to define reward in terms of homeostasis, the physical state of the body. But this, too, was unsuccessful because people and animals will work for rewarding stimulation of the SEEKING system, which is typically aroused during periods of homeostatic imbalance.

Panksepp, proposed that the SEEKING system provides an affective reward. Panksepp and fellow brainstem theorists, like Damasio, maintain that conscious affective experiences of pleasure and pain motivate behavior. Since the brain's decision-making and motor apparatus direct behavior, this means that immaterial conscious affects influence the workings of the brain. This belief is central to brainstem theory.

Brainstem theory allows us to see Libet's decision-making experiments in a new light. These experiments demonstrate that our brains make decisions before we become conscious of them, which suggests that consciousness is unimportant. But consider the following scenario. Suppose that I decide to vote for a presidential candidate. My brain makes the decision before I am conscious of it. However, once my decision becomes conscious, it influences the way that I interpret and react to subsequent events. If my candidate makes a stupid remark, I will be likely to forgive or rationalize it. Conversely, I will probably be inclined to overvalue any of his or her real virtues. I might also try to persuade my friends and family to cast their votes as I do. Although consciousness does not inaugurate my decision, once my decision becomes conscious, it influences the way my brain directs future decisions and behavior. Seen from this vantage, the time lag between decision-making and consciousness does not obviate the importance of consciousness.

In recent years, neuroscientists have begun to take the harder question seriously. In the words of Michael Gazzaniga, "Mental states that emerge from our neural actions do constrain the very brain activity that gave rise to them. Mental states such as beliefs, thoughts and desires all arise from brain activity and in turn can and do influence our decisions to act one way or another" (Gazzaniga 2012 p. 107).

Summary

We do not yet know the mechanisms that would answer the hard and harder questions. We do not know how the brain creates consciousness, or how consciousness influences the brain. Researchers are engaged in heroic efforts to discover these mechanisms, but the mind-body conundrum persists (Gazzaniga 2012; Tononi 2004).

Nevertheless, virtually all neuroscientists believe that the brain creates consciousness, and a great deal of evidence indicates that consciousness influences the workings of the brain. Despite of our present state of ignorance about the interface between consciousness and the brain, there is good reason to believe they are mutually interactive.

Chapter 9

Neuroscience and Mental Health Professions

This chapter discusses some ways that neuroscience can help mental health professionals better to understand human nature and improve our skills. The discussion that follows is somewhat disjointed and far from complete, but hopefully, it will demonstrate the important role that neuroscience can play in improving theory and clinical practice.

Panksepp's Taxonomy of Basic Motives

Freud maintained that libido (LUST) and aggression (RAGE) are the basic drives that motivate our affects, thoughts, and behavior (Mills 2004). Bowlby (1969) added the need for attachment, and Kohut (1971) claimed that we also need affirmation of our worth. Klein focused on the necessity of fusing ambivalent infantile feelings of love and hate (Etherington 2020). These views about basic drives are based on things that people say and do, which are open to interpretation and subject to disagreement (Killingmo 1985). Panksepp's taxonomy is more reliable because it identifies brain structures fueled by specific chemicals that result in stereotypical emotional behaviors. We can observe these phenomena and agree upon their existence. Additionally, his taxonomy provides a wider repertoire of basic motivations than does psychotherapeutic theory.

Panksepp acknowledged that his taxonomy may not be complete. Other emotional systems may eventually be discovered. Paul

Ekman's research about universal facial expressions proposes that disgust is a basic emotion (Ekman 1992). This claim is bolstered by the fact that animals, like rats, express disgust when presented with unpalatable food (Travers and Norgren 1986). Yet a circuit for disgust is yet to be found (Panksepp 1998a).

The urge for power and social dominance also appears to be a primary emotion because almost all animals organize into social hierarchies (Peterson 2019b). Yet neuroscientific research has not identified discreet circuitry, or chemistry for social dominance. Some researchers propose that systems for disgust and social dominance exist and will eventually be discovered (Toronchuk and Ellis 2012). Alternatively, others speculate that these emotional proclivities may result from the interaction of other systems. For example, the urge for social dominance may result from the interaction of SEEKING, RAGE, FEAR, and PLAY systems (Panksepp and Biven 2012; van der Westhuizen and Solms 2015). Although Panksepp's taxonomy does not include disgust and social dominance, both of which appear to be basic emotions, his list is more complete and more scientifically reliable than any other that is currently available (Panksepp 1998a).

Support for Attachment Theory

Panksepp's taxonomy resolves a psychoanalytic disagreement about the status of attachment as a drive (Killingmo 1985). According to Freud's formulation, the libidinal drive is not overtly sexual in early childhood. Instead, libido is gratified by the intake of nutrition and by the pleasures of receiving maternal care (Freud 1926). On this basis, Freud proposed that babies and young children are attached to their mothers because they provide libidinal gratification. Indeed, Freud believed that all positive attachments were based on the satisfaction of libidinal impulses (Bergman 1982).

Psychoanalytic theorists like Suttie (1935), Fairbairn (1952), and, predominantly, Bowlby (1969) disagreed, maintaining that the need for attachment and secure relationships, especially in early childhood, is a drive that is independent of libido (Grossman 1995).

Panksepp's neuroscientific emotional taxonomy supports their assertion that the need for attachment is a non-libidinal expression of the GRIEF system (Panksepp 1992). Similarly, the PLAY and CARE systems generate nonsexual attachments (Panksepp 1998a).

Two Types of Anxiety

Panksepp identified the GRIEF system on the basis of experiments on a wide variety of species, including primates. These experiments revealed that electrical stimulation of specific brain structures caused animals to cry out in distress. These brain structures include the periaqueductal gray (PAG) located in the upper brainstem and extend upward to portions of the hypothalamus, the thalamus, parts of the stria terminalis, located just above the thalamus, and to certain sites in the amygdala. In higher vertebrates and primates, the cingulate cortex, which is located in the middle of the cerebral cortex, is also involved (Damasio et al. 2000; Lorberbaum et al. 2002; Swain et al. 2007). These structures are active in the brains of young animals when they are separated from their mothers and cry. These same structures are also substrates for depression and sadness in human beings (Panksepp 1998a).

Unlike GRIEF, the FEAR system, which extends upward from the PAG to parts of the hypothalamus and the central nucleus of the amygdala, is typically aroused in anticipation of physical injury, or death, but we can be afraid of any impending adverse event, like a final exam, or a tax audit (Panksepp 1998a).

The GRIEF and FEAR systems respond to different medications. GRIEF is mitigated by the antidepressant imipramine. Imipramine also diminishes panic attacks, which suggests that panic attacks are manifestations of GRIEF arousal (Klein 1964; Panksepp 1998a). Imipramine, however, is ineffective in reducing FEAR of danger (Panksepp 1998a). Benzodiazepines, like Valium, assuage the FEAR of danger, but they have only a modest effect in quelling panic attacks. The fact that benzodiazepines lessen anticipatory anxiety and imipramine diminishes panic attacks indicates that one type of anxiety emanates from the FEAR system and the other from GRIEF (Panksepp 1998a).

It is likely that there are different subdivisions in emotional systems. For example, rats are inherently afraid of well-lit open spaces. Researchers test anxiety in rodents using an elevated plus-shaped (+) maze. Two of the platforms of the maze have walls that provide protective enclosure while the other two platforms are open (Pellow et al. 1985). Rats avoid the open arms of the maze and stay in the enclosed arms. When rats are treated with benzodiazepines, they remain in the enclosed arms, indicating that they continue to feel anxious in the open space. When treated with morphine, however, they are willing to venture into the open arms of the maze, which no longer cause anxiety. The fact that different drugs quell different levels of anxiety indicates that there are different neurochemical levels of FEAR (Panksepp 1998a).

Research conducted in the 1960s revealed that GRIEF and FEAR arousal often coincide. When people suffering from panic attacks took imipramine, the number of attacks diminished, but they continued to suffer from anxiety because they continued to anticipate the onset of another attack. This secondary anxiety was a manifestation of the FEAR system, which responds to benzodiazepines. When they took benzodiazepines in addition to imipramine, they felt better (Klein 1964; Panksepp 1998a).

Two Ways to Feel Good and Two Ways to Feel Depressed

Panksepp's taxonomy also highlights two good/bad pairs of affects. One pair emanates from the GRIEF system and the other pair from the SEEKING system. There are two sides to GRIEF. A positive side generates contented feelings of comfort and joy in the supportive company of friends and family. The negative side generates misery, loneliness, and depression when we are abandoned, betrayed, or defeated (Panksepp 1998a).

Brain chemicals like the excitatory neurotransmitter *glutamate* and the stress hormone *corticotropin releasing factor (CRF)* activate the negative side of GRIEF while opioids and oxytocin activate the positive side. Feelings of sadness, depression, and panic attacks are accompanied by low levels of brain opioids (Zubieta et al. 2003; Kennedy et al. 2006). Additionally, the administration of drugs that block opioid receptors increase the incidence of panic attacks (Panksepp 1998a).

The SEEKING system is fueled by dopamine. When our SEEKING systems are active, we feel energized, confident, and purposefully engaged with life. The SEEKING system makes us curious about new experiences, eager to achieve, and prepared to take risks. When this system is chronically under aroused, we feel hopeless and unmotivated. Drugs like cocaine and methamphetamine promote dopamine activity, and recovering addicts typically experience depression when their brains are deprived of dopamine (Hartney 2020).

These chemical differences explain why the good and bad feelings engendered by the GRIEF and SEEKING systems are different. We are comforted when the positive side of GRIEF ascends and its negative side produces a gnawing desire for love and support. SEEKING arousal, on the other hand, causes an energized sense of independence and purpose while under arousal engenders an empty sense of hopelessness (Panksepp 1998a).

The Importance of Play

The urge to PLAY is characterized by joyful friendly competition. There are many forms of human play from formal games to social banter. However, Panksepp proposes that rough-and-tumble play, especially in young children and animals, is the most fundamental type of play that mammals exhibit (Panksepp 1998a).

Rough-and-tumble play appears similar to fighting, but in rats, PLAY and RAGE are distinguishable. When rats fight, they stand on their back legs and box. When one animal gains the upper hand, it pins the other for a sustained period of time. Play, on the other hand, typically starts when one rat jumps on the back of another, and the episode ends when one briefly pins the other. Then a new cycle begins (Panksepp 1998a).

RAGE and PLAY also involve different chemicals. Testosterone promotes fighting but not play while anti-aggressive agents like *fluprazine* reduce fighting but not play. When animals fight, there is a winner and a loser, but when rats play, both participants win and lose by turns. Rats will continue to play if one pins the other 70 percent of the time and the other pins 30 percent of the time. If the ratio is further imbalanced, the more frequent loser declines to play (Panksepp 1998a).

There is still much to learn about the anatomy and chemistry of the PLAY system. In rats, PLAY involves brain structures like the reticular formation of the brainstem and areas of the thalamus. It also involves the release of endogenous opioids. However, researchers have yet to discover details about the neural circuitry and chemistry of PLAY (Panksepp 1998a).

Nevertheless, behavioral evidence indicates that the PLAY system exists. Panksepp devised an experiment to observe the behavior of young animals that had been isolated without any chance to play with others. He reckoned that if the animal spontaneously played when placed with other young animals, this would demonstrate that the urge to play is innate. It is not possible to test this hypothesis with some mammals because social isolation arouses the GRIEF system making them despondent and miserable. For example, when an isolated young monkey is put into the company of its fellows, it initially craves comfort rather than play. Only when it feels socially confident will it play (Panksepp 1998a).

Rats raised in the laboratory, however, have weak GRIEF systems, and they cope relatively well with social isolation. Normally, rats start to play at the age of seventeen days. If a rat is kept in isolation from fifteen to twenty-five days and has no opportunity to play, it will engage in vigorous rough-and-tumble play at the first opportunity when placed with other young rats. This indicates that the impulse to play is not based on past experience. It is an innate proclivity emanating from hardwired brain circuitry (Panksepp 1998a).

The negative side of GRIEF can interfere with the urge to PLAY but so, too, can FEAR and RAGE. When clients, especially children, have no sense of humor, or if they do not like to play, this is not simply a character trait. It is a sign of that negative emotional systems have inhibited their capacity for joy.

Aggression Is Not Pleasurable

Over the years, there has been much disagreement about the role of aggression in psychoanalytic theory (Dennen 2005). Many psychoanalysts believe that aggression, like libido, is a source of instinctual pleasure (Hartmann, Kris, and Loewenstein 1949). Neuroscientific research, however, opposes this view. Animals avoid places where their RAGE systems were electrically aroused, indicating that RAGE arousal is an unpleasant experience, except, of course, when one is about to win the day. However, part of the pleasure in winning is that you no longer need to feel aggrieved and angry (Panksepp 1998a).

RAGE is an inherent emotional and affective capacity that is unconditionally aroused when people and animals feel threatened, or frustrated. We all know the feeling. Does it not rankle to know that Stalin died peacefully, or that only a small number of Nazi war criminals were ever brought to justice (Schubert and Schmidt 2018)? Most of us can put these feelings on the back burner, but if people have endured brutality, or injustice early in childhood, they may be angry all their lives. It may appear that such people enjoy being angry because they are so easily incensed. But the sad truth is that they do not know anything else.

The exception to this rule may be the bully. A recent study on adolescents indicates that the traditional view of the bully as an unhappy person who overcompensates for an underlying feeling of worthlessness is not always correct (Formica 2009). This study indicates that many bullies are happy and generally successful people (Koh and Wong 2015). These happy bullies, however, may not be angry with their victims, or hate them. Rather, they may enjoy the social domination, which would indicate that the source of their happiness and high self-esteem does not emanate from the RAGE system but from some as-yet-undiscovered system that generates a will to social dominance.

The Creation of Free Associations

Freud introduced the method of free association as a therapeutic tool because he found that when clients spoke their minds without censorship, unconscious thoughts and wishes came to the fore. Free associations, like dreams, were "royal road(s) to the unconscious" mind (Freud 1900). Free associations, however, may appear to be a confusing web of disconnected ideas. LeDoux's rat conditioning experiments explain why free associations make sense and why they are so important in psychotherapy.

At birth, people and animals have emotional responses to a small repertoire of stimuli. Rats are innately afraid of the smell of cat fur. They also inherently fear well-lit open spaces. All animals innately fear pain (Panksepp 1998a) and many fear loud noises (Clasen 2017). Most young animals, including human babies, are innately afraid of heights (Gibson and Walk 1960), and many mammals, including humans, have an innate fear of spiders and snakes (Papple 2017).

The other six emotional systems also respond innately to a small number of stimuli. Social isolation arouses GRIEF, certain pheromones arouse LUST, frustrations arouse RAGE, and exposure to very young animals of the same species elicits CARE, even in male adolescents. Danger arouses FEAR. Novel situations can also arouse low levels of FEAR, but they also can arouse the SEEKING system. Rough-and-tumble fun prompts the urge to PLAY (Panksepp 1998a).

Another look at LeDoux's conditioning experiments explains how the small repertoire of stimuli to which an animal inherently reacts expands exponentially. We have already learned that when a rat is simultaneously exposed to an electric shock to its foot and an auditory tone, it learns to fear the tone. Synaptic plasticity takes place in the lateral nucleus of the amygdala. Synaptic plasticity entails the expression of previously dormant genes that produce proteins that strengthen communication between neurons in the tone pathway. In this stronger state, the tone pathway gains access to the central nucleus of the amygdala, which generates the fear response (Johansen et al. 2011). The strong communication between neurons persists, which means that the learning pathway is also a memory pathway. After conditioning, the rat continues to fear the tone (Wilensky et al. 2006).

The rat also comes to fear a variety of *contextual*, or background stimuli. For example, it may fear the sound of the spinning wheel in its cage, the smell of the sawdust, or the sight of the approaching researcher. In contextual conditioning, the basic mechanism of gene expression and synaptic plasticity is the same, but it involves the hippocampus as well as the amygdala (LeDoux 1996).

We noted that the hippocampus is necessary for the creation of long-term memories. In addition to creating memories, the hippocampus integrates spatial stimuli and provides a means of orienting an organism so that it can effectively navigate through space (McNaughton et al. 1996; Lee et al. 2012). When people and animals undergo conditioning experiences, the hippocampus integrates information about contextual stimuli and projects that information to various nuclei of the amygdala (Jordão et al. 2015). Neural pathways encoding information about contextual stimuli undergo synaptic plasticity. Gene expressions results in the production of proteins that strengthen the connections between neurons in the pathways that encode contextual stimuli. The pathways gain access to the central nucleus of the amygdala, and the rat learns to fear contextual stimuli. The strengthened connections between neurons persists over time, and the context-pathways become memory pathways. Thereafter, the rat is afraid of contextual stimuli (LeDoux 2000; Rodrigues et al. 2001; Goosens and Maren 2001).

Conditioning to contextual stimuli is vital to survival. Suppose that an urban rat lived near a house with a pet cat. The rat stays away from the cat because it is innately afraid of the smell. If the cat wore a bell around its neck, the rat would soon learn to fear the sound of the bell. The rat might also learn to fear the sound of the cat's meow, the sight of the cat's toys, and the sound of its owner's voice when he calls the cat in for dinner. By avoiding these stimuli, the rat keeps safely away from the cat.

All these stimuli, the smell of the cat, the sound of its bell, the sight of the cat's toys, and the sound of its owner's voice are associated, but in what way? Ordinarily, we think that associations occur between ideas. We might think that when the rat hears the sound of the bell, it thinks about the smell of the cat and becomes frightened. However, decorticate animals, like rats and dogs, whose entire cortices have been surgically removed can be conditioned even though their brains cannot process ideas (Culler and Mettler 1934; Wirsig and Grill 1982; Kolb and Wishaw 2009). Hydranencephalitic children who are born without a cortex can also be conditioned (Merker 2007). This means that conditioned and contextual stimuli are not associated on the basis of ideas.

For the urban rat, the bell, meow, toys, and the owner's voice are associated because their encoding neural pathways project to the central nucleus of the amygdala, which is part of the rat's FEAR system. These stimuli are associated because they all elicit the same emotional/affective response, namely fear. Unintelligent animals, like rats, probably cannot make ideational associations between stimuli. Probably, the urban rat is just afraid of the bell, the meow, the toys, and the owner's voice. That is enough to keep it alive.

Conditioning and Cognitive Associations

Human beings and probably some other intelligent creatures have thoughts when they are emotionally aroused, and these thoughts become part and parcel of affective experience. For example, when FEAR is aroused, the amygdala is active. Activity in the amygdala mobilizes cortical attention, and we take notice of things around us (Pessoa 2010; Wargo 2010). The cortex sends information about the environment to the hippocampus (Tyng et al. 2017) which is also activated by the amygdala (Abe 2001). As we noted above, the hippocampus integrates information about the environment. Recent research explains that hippocampus immediately projects integrated information to the cognitive prefrontal cortex (Preston and Eichenbaum 2013) which generates thoughts about the environment. Thus, thoughts become part of FEAR arousal. Even when we are not in danger, scary thoughts can frighten us because the prefrontal cortex has neural projections to the amygdala (Ghashghaei et al. 2007).

Think back to the gunshot. Just before the shots rang out, you were casually walking down the street, perhaps musing about a few things that you need to buy. When you heard the shot, you immediately froze, and all thoughts about shopping vanished. You ducked behind some dustbins in an alley next to a Chinese restaurant. While you waited in a state of trepidation, your cortex took notice of the dustbins, and you looked down the street to see if there was any sight of the gunman. Meanwhile, the smell of Chinese food filled your nostrils. Your cortex sent information about these stimuli to your hippocampus. Your amygdala facilitated activity in your hippocampus, which sent integrated information about the environment to your prefrontal cortex which generated cognitive thoughts about the environment.

Later that night when you were safely home, your wife surprised you with a Chinese takeaway meal. She bought your favorite dish, but when you breathed in the aroma of the food, you suddenly felt agitated and had no appetite. The next morning when you went out to empty the trash, you felt anxious when you approached your own dustbins. The following week when you happened to walk down the street where you heard the shot, you felt nervous, even though all about was calm.

You are an intelligent human being with a good memory and you might suppose that the Chinese food, the dustbins, and the city street upset you because they reminded you of the shooting incident that frightened you. But you would be mistaken. Fear conditioning is achieved the same way in both people and other animals—including unintelligent rats and decorticate animals (Goosens and Maren 2001).

The urban rat feared the cat's bell, its meow, the sight of its toys, and the sound of its owner's voice because information about all these stimuli was encoded in neural pathways that projected to the central nucleus of the rat's amygdala. Your brain underwent the same process. Information about the smell of Chinese food, the sight of dustbins, and a city street was encoded in neural pathways that projected to your central nucleus. Because you are intelligent, your amygdala facilitated the creation of thoughts about the unconditioned, conditioned, and contextual stimuli. But any thoughts that you had about the relationships between these stimuli occurred after conditioning had already happened.

Of course, purely cognitive associations exist, and we make them when things are similar, when they occur near each other in time, or space, or when one thing seems to cause another thing to happen. Suppose that after your bad experience, you read in the paper that the street where you were walking was a center for drug traffic. You would make a cognitive connection between the information that you read in the paper and the gunman whom you saw. You might conclude that the gunshot was probably about a drug deal gone bad. On the basis of this cognitive association, you might avoid that part of town.

We have conditioning experiences all the time—for better and for worse. Consider a baby who innately bonds to mother. As time goes by, stimuli like the sound of mother's voice, the smell of her perfume, the food she cooks, and the texture of her clothes all become things, which arouse the baby's love, joy, and longing. On the surface, a voice, the smell of perfume, the taste of food, and the texture of clothing seem to have nothing in common. These associations make sense when we understand that they all elicit the same emotional response, namely a love and longing for mother. When clients come to therapy, they present a jumble of disparate ideas that seem confusing, but they make sense if a therapist can discern the underlying affects that connect them.

A Clinical Example of Free Associations

Sixteen-year-old Gemma suffered a panic attack in a restaurant, and ever since, she had been unable to go out for a meal. In every other way, she seemed normal. She had a circle of good friends, she was a reasonably good student, and she enjoyed sports. There had never been a hint of delinquency, or drug abuse.

The phobia began when she was seated at a restaurant in the middle of a semicircular couch between her grandparents with whom she got on well. Suddenly, she felt trapped. The music playing in the background sounded strident, and the dimmed lighting made everything appear sinister. She abruptly left the table and went outside to wait in the car. After a while, she calmed down, but the thought of going back into the restaurant brought on palpitations, so she stayed in the cold while the others finished eating. She had no idea why she had become so panicky.

Her speech was hesitant, and when I remarked on it, she said that she had trouble speaking her mind. Essays at school posed a particular problem. As soon as she wrote something down, she would second-guess herself, worrying that her teachers would misunderstand and think her stupid, or mean spirited.

She also suffered from insomnia and could only sleep when the bedroom door was locked. On nights when her parents insisted that the door remain unlocked, she would lie awake for hours, staring at the door handle to see if it moved.

She said that her parents were temperamentally different and argued a great deal. Mother had a bad temper and often rowed with Gemma as well. Quarrels would sometimes go on long into the night. On occasion, Mother, unable to sleep, would wake Father, or Gemma in the early hours of the morning to continue venting her spleen.

Gemma earned pocket money by babysitting for neighborhood children whom she had recently taken to the movies to see Walt Disney's *Snow White*. In the scene where Snow White's evil stepmother turns into a hideous witch, Gemma experienced a moment of anxiety similar to the panic that she experienced in the restaurant.

Sometimes when she and her parents were out and about in company, Mother would give Father, or her the evil eye, a portent of a blowup when they got home. Gemma remembered that when she panicked at the restaurant, Mother, seated across, had given her the evil eye.

Gemma spoke of a recent argument with Mother who backed her up against an open window. Just when Mother thought she had her cornered, Gemma stepped out onto the roof, which was slanted and unsafe.

She recalled that when she was little, Mother would shout at her and sometimes resorted to smacking and pinching her.

On several occasions, Mother had threatened Father with a kitchen knife. Both Gemma and her father believed that this was a dramatic display rather than a serious threat. However, shortly before the restaurant panic, Mother had waved the knife in anger, inflicting a cut on his hand.

At first glance, these associations do not seem connected: panic in a restaurant, inability to speak her mind, insomnia with an unlocked door, arguments at home, the witch in *Snow White*, Mother's evil eye, stepping onto the roof, Mother's verbal and physical abuse when Gemma was little, and Mother's knife attack on Father. The associations made sense because fear of Mother was the thread that ran through them all. Gemma could not express her opinions because she felt guilty and nervous about her animosity toward her mother. She could not sleep because she feared that Mother would intrude in one of her nocturnal tempers. She panicked when watching Snow White because the wicked witch reminded her of Mother. She stepped onto the roof to avoid Mother's wrath, and as a child, she feared her mother's abuse. She was frightened when Mother physically attacked Father and drew blood.

It was clear how the restaurant phobia came about. Mother's evil eye was the unconditioned stimulus that aroused Gemma's FEAR system. Her position, wedged between her grandparents, was the conditioned stimulus that made her feel trapped. The music and the poor lighting were contextual stimuli that also filled her with dread.

Gemma's treatment did not have a happy ending, but her life improved. Her level of fear and the fact that Mother had attacked Father with a knife indicated that Gemma might be in physical danger. I suggested calling in social services, but at age sixteen, she was entitled to refuse, which she did, believing that any intervention would only make matters worse.

I spoke to the parents in the hope of securing therapy for Mother, or possibly couples therapy. Father, however, felt that their problems were not serious. My suggestion angered Mother who refused any further discussion with me. Although my talk with Gemma's parents did not have the desired result, I surmise that it did some good because they agreed to let her move into the local YMCA. There, she lived out her final eighteen months of high school before going to college and sharing a flat with friends. She often saw her father, but contact with her mother was sparse.

Gemma was, however, safe at the Y. She said that her first night there was the best night's sleep that she had had in years. She no longer felt guilty about her anger toward her mother, and she was able to express her opinions more easily. After a while, she began to frequent cafés with her friends. Therapy, however, cannot replace parental love and support, which was the part of Gemma's life that could not be fixed. Nevertheless, because she was no longer inhibited, or phobic, she could lead a normal life and find love in the future.

Psychotherapeutic Cure Is Incomplete

If you condition a rat by simultaneously exposing it to an auditory tone and a foot shock, the rat will learn to fear the tone after just one or two exposures. You can extinguish the fear response by repeatedly subjecting the rat to the tone without any accompanying shock (Milad and Quirk 2016). Following extinction, the rat is no longer afraid of the tone. Extinction circuitry occurs in medial parts of the rat's prefrontal cortex and within the amygdala itself. Once created, the extinction pathways inhibit the ability of the central nucleus to generate a fear response, and the rat no longer exhibits fear when exposed to the tone (Sotres-Bayon et al. 2004; Amano et al. 2010). Neuroscientific research about extinction has centered on the FEAR system, but psychiatric studies indicate that the principle of extinction applies to other emotional systems, like GRIEF and RAGE (Denny et al. 2018).

Even when extinction is successful, however, the fear response can be revived. If the animal is returned to the cage where it was conditioned, or if it is subjected to an unexpected shock, it will again fear the tone (Myers and Davis 2007; Chang et al. 2009; Sevenster et al. 2018). This indicates that circuitry created during the conditioning process persists. Instead of erasing the conditioning circuitry, extinction creates new circuitry that competes with the fear-generating pathways. Usually, the extinction circuitry competes successfully, but during periods of stress, it can lose the competition and fear will reemerge (Milad et al. 2006).

Extinction is rarely achieved if administered soon after the conditioning experience, but if a substantial length of time elapses between conditioning and extinction, the results are better. This indicates that conditioning circuitry deteriorates during this interval (Myers and Davis 2007). The atrophy, however, is incomplete, and the potential to fear the conditioned stimulus persists.

Psychotherapeutic cure is very similar to extinction. Suppose that a boy has a tyrannical father whom he hates and resents. The bad relationship with his father has chronically aroused the boy's RAGE system, and he regularly gets into fights with classmates and argues with his teachers. Later in life, quarrels with his boss jeopardize his job. Psychotherapy would help the man to understand that his anger with his boss is really about his father. This would allow him to see his boss as a separate person instead of unconsciously conflating him with his father. In other words, the acquisition of psychotherapeutic insights would be a learning process that extinguishes the man's inappropriate anger, freeing him to have a better life. The RAGE circuitry would deteriorate over time, but it would continue to exist, rendering the man vulnerable to relapses during periods of stress. Psychoanalytic studies corroborate this view about the partial success of treatment. They indicate that even when therapy is successful, a client's problems are weakened rather than eradicated (Pfeffer 1963; Oremland et al. 1975).

Psychotherapeutic Limitations and Failures

LeDoux's research on the FEAR system explains how the cortex inhibits emotional arousal. The central nucleus of the amygdala, which inaugurates the fear response (freezing, hypertension, pupil dilation, etc.), receives information via two pathways, which LeDoux calls the "high and low roads" (LeDoux 1996 p. 161). Both roads start in the thalamus, which is the part of the brain that receives and processes sensory information before sending it on to other brain regions. Part of the thalamus can discriminate between different types of sensory inputs. For example, it can tell the difference between a gunshot and loud rock music. Another part of the thalamus cannot make this kind of distinction and reacts to any loud noise (LeDoux 1996).

The high road begins when the discriminatory part of the thalamus sends information to the cortex for further processing. If the discriminatory thalamus has deemed a noise to be rock music, the cortex can discern if rock music is by The Beatles, or by Kayne West. The cortex then sends information to the central nucleus of the amygdala. The low road takes a more direct route when the nondiscriminatory part of the thalamus sends information directly to the central nucleus of the amygdala. The low road has fewer synapses than the high road, so it reaches the central nucleus a bit faster (LeDoux 1996).

Think back to your walk through the dodgy part of town. Suppose that instead hearing a gunshot, you heard a sudden blast of rock music from a speeding car. The noise would startle you, and you might move to duck into a nearby alley. A moment later, you would recognize the sound as a rock band and go on your way. Undifferentiated information about the loud noise traveled along the low road from your thalamus to the central nucleus of your amygdala, which inaugurated your initial fear response. A moment later, the high road reached your central nucleus with information that the noise was only loud music. The high road inhibited activity in your central nucleus, and you calmed down (Ray Li and Sinha 2009). It is easy to see the adaptive value of these two pathways. If you had heard a gunshot instead of rock music, the low road would have prompted you to duck for cover immediately. If you had waited for the high road to provide information, you would have lost valuable time (LeDoux 1996).

LeDoux' high/low road experiments demonstrate that information provided by the cortex can inhibit emotional expression. Psychotherapy is largely a cognitive process where the cortices of both therapist and client engage in a joint effort to make sense of the client's problems (Neuman 2015). In order to do this, the client needs to engage in rational thinking, a process that entails a degree of emotional control. In order to control one's emotions, the cortex needs to inhibit them—at least temporarily.

People suffering from borderline personality disorder exhibit impulsive behavior and pervasive negative affect, indicating that cortical inhibition of emotion is curtailed. Research on people with borderline personalities revealed a difference in the response of parts of the *orbitofrontal cortex (OFC)*, The OFC is part of the prefrontal cortex and obtained its name because it is located just behind the eyes (Yates 2015). Medial portions of the OFC inhibit negative emotions while lateral portions process sensory information. When people suffering from borderline personality disorders experience negative sensory stimuli, the medial portion of the OFC is relatively inactive while activity in the lateral portions increases. This indicates that people with borderline personality disorders are attuned to negative sensory stimuli and that their ability to inhibit negative emotion is diminished (Silbersweig et al. 2008).

Other areas of research indicate that ineffective functioning of the OFC and the rest of the adjacent prefrontal cortex (PFC) can result in violent behavior due to insufficient emotional inhibition. Two people who had suffered damage to these brain regions in early childhood exhibited antisocial behavior in their twenties. Both had a history of verbal and physical abuse, outbursts of explosive anger, and deficits in moral reasoning (Davidson et al. 2000).

Cortical deficits can result in decreased inhibition of emotion, but excessive emotional arousal can inhibit cortical function (Salzman and Fusi 2010). It is probable that persistent stress causes chronic dysfunction of the prefrontal cortex. High emotion also strengthens primitive responses (low road transmission) causing us to revert to reflexive way of behaving (Arnsten 2018).

Thus, there appears to be a reciprocal relationship between emotional arousal and failures of cortical inhibition. Cortical damage to the PFC can cause uninhibited emotional expression. Conversely, overweening arousal of emotion can damage the inhibitory capacities of the PFC.

Another area of research explains why cortical inhibition some-times fails. LeDoux discovered that there are many more connections from the amygdala to the neocortex than there are in the reverse direction, which means that the amygdala has a robust capacity to arouse fearful thoughts and perceptions in the neocortex, but the neocortex has less ability to inhibit fear (LeDoux 1996). If there is a similar directional inequality between the cortex and other emo-tional systems, it would mean that the cortex is generally limited in its ability to inhibit emotional arousal.

An implicit assumption of psychotherapy is that the revelation of unconscious content will effect a cure (Nagera 2018). As thera-pists, we hope that when clients become conscious of the reasons for their affective pain, they will find ways to feel better and to quell the troublesome affects. However, clients with personality disorders have ineffective cortical inhibition over their emotions (Morris et al. 2012) and tend to be emotionally unstable, impulsive, and often suicidal (Paris 2005). They fail to exhibit a capacity, or willingness to inhibit their feelings, even when unbridled emotional expression only worsens their plight. In these cases, the revelation of the reasons for their painful affects can intensify those affects and decrease a cli-ent's ability to think rationally (Bateman and Fonagy 2010). If the man who argued with his boss had been unable to curb his anger, then the revelation of his anger with father might have exacerbated his anger, making matters worse. Indeed, one study indicates that 20 percent of clients deteriorate during psychotherapy (Lambert 2007).

In neuroscientific terms, this happens when emotional systems overwhelm the rational and strategic capacities of the cognitive cortex.

Emotional Sensitization

Chronic and/or extreme emotional arousal can occur when emotional systems become sensitized by experience. If a rat is repeatedly exposed to a cat, the exposure causes synaptic plasticity and the creation of long-term memory pathways between the central nucleus of the rat's amygdala and its periaqueducal gray (PAG) as well as within the PAG itself (Adamec et al. 2009). The central nucleus of the amygdala and the PAG are structures in the mammalian FEAR system (Panksepp 1998a). Following repeated exposures to a cat, the rat becomes excessively anxious and fearful. The increased strength of neural circuitry indicates that exposure to a predator causes the FEAR system to become sensitized and unusually responsive to a wide range of stimuli.

Recent research indicates another way that FEAR sensitization occurs. When rats are subjected to threat, a particular type of neuron in the central nucleus of the amygdala known as SOM+ neuron (so called because it produces the peptide *somatostatin)* becomes active. When researchers *knocked out* (deleted) a particular gene (called Erbb4) in SOM+ neurons in the central nucleus, the neurons produced excessive amounts of the opioid *dynorphin. Opioids* are opiate-like chemicals made by the brain. Some opioids like endorphins make us feel good (Panksepp 1998a), but dynorphin produces anxiety as well as aversive feelings of disorientation and dissociation (Land et al. 2008; Watt and Panksepp 2009).

SOM+ neurons are also found in the *bed nucleus of the stria terminalis (BNST),* which is located near the amygdala and which has connections to it (Miles and Maren 2019). Many see the BNST as an extension of the amygdala (Lebow and Chen 2016). Normally, the central nucleus inhibits the activity of the BNST, but when genetically altered, SOM+ neurons in the central nucleus produce excessive amounts of dynorphin. The dynorphin excites SOM+ neurons in the

BNST. As a result, the rats became excessively fearful and anxious. This research holds out hope for future antianxiety medications that block dynorphin activity. Important for our discussion is the fact that this same dynorphin-driven anxiety happens in genetically normal rats that have been exposed to excessive threat, resulting in sensitization of their FEAR systems (Ahrens et al. 2018).

Conflict versus Deficit

Classical psychoanalytic theory proposes that the mind is divided into three parts: id, ego, and superego. The contents of the id are sexual and aggressive impulses that are unconscious. The gratification of id impulses would give us great pleasure, but for the most part, they are socially unacceptable and would invite punishment from the world at large. The ego is the rational part of the mind that experiences anxiety and other negative affects when id impulses threaten to emerge into consciousness and push for gratification. When the ego experiences negative affects, it institutes defenses, like repression, or projection, that keep id impulses unconscious. Much ego functioning is also unconscious, and we are usually unaware of our ego defenses (Freud, A. 1936; Brenner 1982).

The superego, which is the moral part of the mind, also inhibits the id by inflicting guilt and shame when we are tempted to gratify id impulses that are depraved, or unjust (Freud, 1926). Classical psychoanalysis maintains that the id continually generates conflicts that the ego and superego try to manage (Thornton 1995). The id, however, does not always get the short straw because the ego fashions acceptable ways to partially gratify id impulses (Brenner 1982).

Consider a little boy in the throes of the Oedipus complex. He wants to marry his mother and get rid of his father, but his ego generates anxiety because he fears his father's retribution. He may defend against his wish to win his mother and defeat his father by becoming immature and babyish as if to reassure everyone, including himself, that he poses no threat. Yet this very defense against oedipal wishes also gratifies them, at least to some extent. As a weak little boy, he coaxes his mother to coddle him and conscripts her attentions at his father's expense. In this way, the boy's ego avoids anxiety because he relinquishes the wish to marry his mother and usurp his father's place. His superego no longer condemns him for his bad sexual and aggressive wishes. Yet his id obtains gratification by getting his mother to pamper him and exclude his father.

Classical theory proposes that the id encompasses our inherited motivations, which are desires that always press for gratification (Freud 1933). For this reason, the id always causes conflict. But conflict need not be a problem if the balance between id inhibition and id gratification is adaptive and satisfying. When the balance is maladaptive, it qualifies as a symptom. In order to unravel a symptom, the client needs to become conscious of id impulses and defenses, which is the aim of classical psychoanalysis (Nagera 2018).

A schism occurred within the psychoanalytic community when therapists like Bowlby, Kohut, and others proposed that an insecure attachment to mother (Fonagy 2001), or insufficient validation of a child's worth (Ronningstam 2016) could create *deficits*, which were injuries to the personality (Glita 2010). Deficits generate affective pain, like anxiety and depression. Instead of seeing affective pain as the ego's response when it conflicts with the id, the deficit model proposes that the pain can be a direct expression of psychic injury.

The deficit model maintains that cure is not necessarily a matter of unveiling unconscious defenses and id impulses. The aim of psychotherapy is to heal the deficit through the therapeutic relationship in which the therapist's expression of empathy is of paramount importance (McLean 2007). It is through the therapeutic relationship that the client achieves personal maturation that corrects the deficit and effects cure (Black 2019). Thus, the deficit model opposes the conflict model, which is the cornerstone of classical psychoanalytic theory (Papiasvili 1995).

Suppose that the clingy boy mentioned above had a mother who did not love him. He would suffer from an attachment disorder and would clamor for love by behaving in immature demanding ways. In this case, the babyish behavior would not reflect a conflict between id, ego, and superego over oedipal wishes. It would be a direct expression of his emotional pain and his craving for love.

Neuroscience supports both the classical and the deficit models. Support for the classical model is found in Panksepp's taxonomy, which demonstrates that human beings, like all mammals, have hardwired emotional LUST and RAGE systems that correspond to the classical id drives of libido and aggression. The neocortex, which is the cognitive part of the brain, roughly corresponds to the ego (Solms and Panksepp 2012) and generally serves to inhibit emotional systems (Liotti and Panksepp 2004). In other words, the neocortex inhibits untoward expression of sex and aggression in accordance with classical theory.

Panksepp's taxonomy also supports the deficit model. Unlike the classical model, which posits the existence of only two drives, libido and aggression, Panksepp's taxonomy paints a more comprehensive picture of our basic motivations. Some emotional systems like LUST, CARE, PLAY, SEEKING, and the positive side of GRIEF yield pleasure, and do not necessarily cause conflict. Other systems like FEAR, RAGE, and the negative side of GRIEF are inherently painful.

As we noted above, neuroscientific research indicates that the FEAR system can become sensitized by experience. Thus, one can see sensitization as an emotional injury, or deficit. Frightening experiences can leave us with chronic fears, post-traumatic stress disorder (PTSD) being a typical example (NIMH 2019). It is worth noting, however, that if all emotional systems can be sensitized, the results can be felicitous. If the positive side of your GRIEF system is sensitized, you will have a happy life. The same claim can be made for the PLAY, SEEKING, and CARE systems. However, sensitization of a negative system is painful, and these are the systems on which psychotherapy focuses.

The conflict/deficit controversy rests largely on the way a therapist deals with the client's *transference*. Transference is a ubiquitous phenomenon whereby we play out childhood conflicts in our relationships with other people. Suppose that the oedipal boy whom we discussed earlier grows up to be a man and has a series of girlfriends with whom he is clingy and covertly hostile, just as he was with his mother when he was a boy. This man has transferred his childhood conflicts about his mother onto his relationships with his girlfriends.

If this man goes into therapy, he will transfer the same conflicts onto the relationship with the therapist and will become demanding and resentful. When transference occurs in the therapeutic relationship, the therapist has the opportunity to understand it and explain it to the client. It is through understanding the transference that unconscious defenses and id impulses become conscious. Thus, the transference is a major vehicle for cure (Brenner 1955; Kernberg 2016).

According to classical theory, the transference develops when therapists adopt a neutral stance. This means that therapists should remain open to everything that the client says without revealing their personal views, feelings, or opinions in the therapeutic conversation (Schafer 1983). Classical theorists maintain that if a therapist fails to remain neutral, his or her views might contaminate the transference, or hinder its development (Sugarman 1995). Those who accept the deficit model, however, maintain that therapists should drop the guise of neutrality and express empathy that heals the deficit (Kaluzeviciute 2020).

Many therapists believe that clients are troubled by both id conflicts and deficits. In their view, a therapist should discriminate between the parts of the client's personality that suffer from deficits and the parts that suffer from conflicts caused by id impulses. Then the therapist should address each issue in different ways. When a therapist addresses conflicts, s/he should remain neutral and interpret the transference. When dealing with deficits, the therapist should display empathy with the client's plight (Killingmo 1989). Thus, a therapist should provide a nuanced balance of neutrality and empathy.

Conflict-oriented therapists argue, however, that it is not possible to combine the two models because if the therapist expresses empathy in an effort to repair the deficit, this will alter the therapist's neutral persona when s/he tries to understand transference manifestations about id-conflicts (Sugarman 1995). In the case of the oedipal man, for example, a warm empathic response might obscure his transferred anger with mother that results from oedipal frustration.

For classical theorists the conflict/deficit model cannot be reconciled in terms of the therapist's technique (Buirski and Haglund 2001).

Neuroscientific evidence, however, indicates that therapists cannot be emotionally neutral, even when they try to be. When people are exposed to novel neutral faces that express no emotion, their amygdalae became active (Balderston et al. 2011). Neutral facial expressions are ambiguous and ambiguity makes us anxious (Cooney et al. 2006). In other words, people feel ill at ease when they think that other people are indifferent to them. From a client's point of view, an emotionally neutral therapist is not neutral at all.

Furthermore, no matter how neutral we might try to be, clients learn a great deal about us from our body language, our tone of voice, our choice of dress, the way that we decorate our offices, and so on (Thompson 2011). Like many psychotherapists, I have observed that a variety of very different clients have made accurate observations about my character. It is unrealistic to believe that clients know little about us. If a therapist tries too hard to be neutral, s/he will probably come across as inauthentic.

Most psychotherapists agree that they should not discuss their own problems, or express personal opinions about issues like politics, or religion. After all, therapy is about the client, not the therapist. Nevertheless, most psychotherapists believe they should be empathic and care about their clients (Gelso and Kanninen 2017). As for the transference, it is remarkably persistent regardless of what the therapist says, or does (Glassman and Anderson 1999). When therapists fail to understand the transference, it is not because the transference has failed to appear. It is usually because the therapist has failed to see and understand it (Kernberg 2016).

A more balanced view maintains that the separation of conflict from deficit is artificial because deficits can intensify conflicts over id impulses (Eagle 1984). A boy who endures an attachment disorder might have fraught oedipal feelings because his oedipal desire for mother is strengthened by his longing for an attachment to her. Furthermore, both id impulses and deficits generate conflict and consequent defenses (Eagle 2011). The man suffering from oedipal conflicts might defend against rejection by choosing to date women who are timid and needy. The man suffering from an attachment disorder might do the same because he also fears rejection for different reasons. If a man suffers from both oedipal conflicts and an attachment disorder, you might see the same defense serving a dual purpose of defending against conflict and deficit.

Neuroscience may not be able to reconcile the conflict/deficit debate, but it does indicate that both conflicts and deficits are compatible with neuroscientific evidence. One cannot credibly adhere to one and disregard the other.

Summary

Panksepp's taxonomy offers a more complete list of human (and animal) motivations. It supports attachment theory about the primary need for nonsexual bonds, especially early in life. It explains that there are two types of anxiety and two types of depression. It highlights the importance of PLAY, especially in childhood. It demonstrates that contrary to classical psychoanalytic theory, the arousal of RAGE is not a pleasant experience.

LeDoux's fear-conditioning experiments show how free associations are created and explains that ideas are associated on the basis of common affective roots. Fear-extinction experiments explain why psychotherapeutic cure is incomplete and other areas of research explain why psychotherapy sometimes fails. Neuroscientific research also demonstrates that clients usually suffer from both psychic conflicts and from deficits. It also explains that it is not possible for a therapist to be emotionally neutral.

The next chapter demonstrates ways that an understanding of neuroscience informed my treatment of two clients. In particular, my understanding of the SEEKING system fashioned a technique that some therapists have begun to exercise, namely the role of the therapist as a coach (Bader 2009).

Chapter 10

Coaching the SEEKING System

As we noted above, therapists tend to focus on classical conflicts and on attachment disorders that have sensitized a client's GRIEF system. Far less attention has been paid to the therapeutic potential of the SEEKING system, which engenders high-hearted anticipation, personal agency, and a willingness to take risks. Many psychotherapists, most notably Melanie Klein, implicitly refer to the SEEKING system when they emphasize a child's need to actively master negative affects like anxiety (Waska 2001), but there is little discussion about the positive enthusiasm, which is a hallmark of SEEKING arousal.

The SEEKING system might be seen as the opposite of GRIEF, which generates our need to be attached to others. Although attachment is of prime importance in leading a good life, independent achievement is also necessary for fulfilment and happiness (Peterson 2019a). This chapter discusses two clinical cases with a particular emphasis on my role as a coach in mobilizing the SEEKING system as an agent of cure. At the time, I did not intend to act like a coach, nor was I aware of taking on that role. Only in retrospect did I realize that this was what I had done. This shift in technique occurred when I was becoming acquainted with Panksepp's ideas, and I doubt I would have taken the tack that I did if I had not known about the SEEKING system.

Qualities of an effective coach include direct communication about a player's weaknesses, encouragement to improve, and setting a personal example (DeHaven 2014). When a therapist acts like a coach, s/he identifies the client's basic problems, which is to say his or her weaknesses. SEEKING arousal also encourages clients to get better by engendering a sense of hopeful anticipation and a proactive approach to their problems. Although therapists should not indulge their vanity by offering themselves up as exemplars, therapists can indicate that they have endured and overcome similar difficulties, or that they know of someone who has done. To this extent, a therapist/coach can serve as a personal example.

Colin

Before seeing seventeen-year-old Colin, I met with his mother who said that her son was capable and intelligent, but in recent years, he had lost motivation for anything worthwhile. He disparaged his teachers and refused to clean his disordered bedroom in which he slept until noon on weekends. He smoked cigarettes and probably cannabis as well. His only real interest was playing guitar in a band with his friends. Yet he rarely practiced and did not play well.

She and her ex-husband divorced when Colin was eight and his brother was five. Father was not a family man and took little interest in the children. He had never attended a sporting event, a musical recital, or a school play, even though Colin had participated in these activities when he was younger. Father lived in London, only an hour away by train. Visits with the children had never been frequent and had gradually trailed off to the odd weekend two or three times a year. Colin and his brother came home from these reunions in bad moods, complaining that they had been bored.

Father briefly remarried but now lived alone. Mother had a supportive circle of friends, but she had not been in a serious relationship since her divorce more than a decade earlier. She and Colin had been close when he was young. They used to talk about films, books, and life in general. In those days, he was polite, and his appearance was neat and tidy. Now he was a grungy goth, answering in monosyllables, and constantly moaning. She realized that he was genuinely depressed, but she was exasperated by his negative attitude.

When we met, Colin avoided eye contact, and his handshake was limp. He was a tall slim lad dressed in black with lank hair, poor posture, and a dejected facial expression. He began by saying that I should not take it personally, but he did not believe in psychotherapy. Probably, I would give him advice, which people do all the time, but nothing helps. I asked why he bothered with me if he had so little confidence. He looked up with an expression of sadness and alarm, saying that he was desperate. I said that in that case, he should give me a chance and not shut me out automatically. He agreed, and on that tenuous basis, we began.

He explained that he had bad relationships with everyone in his family. He hardly saw his father who expressed no interest in him other than disapproval of his poor academic performance and general laziness. When he was younger, he and mother had been close. She used to say that he, unlike father, was sensitive, and she joked that they were like best girlfriends. In those days, he felt superior to other boys because he saw himself as more refined. Even now, he did not feel especially masculine, but it was a trait that he liked in himself because he had always derided loutish macho attitudes and behavior. Now mother criticized him all the time. Even his little brother had no respect for him.

He had similar problems with friends who did not care enough about him, or about anything important. He was always the one who reached out to them, but they did not reach back. It was he who usually arranged band practice, and even so, one of the lads would sometimes fail to show up. He liked girls, but they were not interested in him. For a few weeks, he had a girlfriend, but she offered a lame excuse and broke up with him.

It soon became clear that Colin had a pervasive pattern of passive-aggressive interaction. He would fail to meet his responsibilities, and when others became irritated, he would reproach them for being uncaring and callous. He never studied, but he was offended when his teachers disapproved. He admitted that his bedroom bordered on the unhygienic but argued with his mother when she asked him to clean it. He criticized his friends for their lack of commitment to their band, but he would arrive for practice unprepared. He did not bother to know much about his girlfriend and never took her out, but he accused her of being unfeeling when she broke off the relationship.

Colin tended to wallow in unhappiness, but his real misery was evident in his body language. There was a pathetic expression about his mouth, and when he sat, he seemed to shrink into his chair. However, he was glad that I took an interest in him, and our conversations seemed to relieve his misery, at least temporarily. As time went on, he made eye contact with increasing frequency, and on occasion, he would make a sardonic joke. He said that therapy was his weekly fix, and he rarely arrived late, or missed an appointment.

He was open to my observations, frequently contributing comments of his own. He acknowledged his passive-aggressive ways of interacting. He agreed that he was hurt and angered by Father's indifference and that he rejected schoolwork in an effort to antagonize Father and also get his attention. He saw that his attitude to his father had become a template for relationships with his mother, teachers, friends, and his erstwhile girlfriend. He understood the paradox in his relationship to his mother. Mother saw him as superior to Father because he, Colin, was her sensitive and caring best girlfriend. Thus, he had relinquished his masculinity in order to be close to her. He realized that this role contributed to his rejection of masculinity, which was also a defense against his fear of failure.

Our conversations, however, did not have a therapeutic effect. Instead of highlighting behavior that he should change, our talks accentuated Colin's sense of himself as a victim. He saw his passive-aggressive attitude as an inevitable response to people who were too obtuse to appreciate, or understand him. Father was an unfeeling clot, his mother was self-involved, his brother was a dork, his friends were selfish, his teachers were devoid of imagination, and his girlfriend had a heart of stone. He felt superior to them all and remained obdurate when it came to making practical changes. Any faults that he might have resulted from his depression, which in his view, was an inevitable consequence of his sensitive nature.

In time, the transference emerged, and he expressed the same passive-aggressive attitude toward me that he did toward everyone else. He became increasingly convinced that I could not help him, and we settled into an aimable standoff where I urged him to change, and he refused. He sometimes demanded to know when I would make his life better, and I would smile and shrug, saying that I could not do it alone. For a while, I worried that Colin might abandon therapy, but he was lonely, and I was a friendly face, so he continued attending sessions. It seemed that therapy, like everything in Colin's life, was going nowhere.

At the end of summer, he arrived in a bad state and flung himself into his chair. His eyes were bloodshot, and he fought back tears. "That's it," he said. "Now I have no one." He heard that Lewis, a lad in his band, had been complaining about him in scathing terms, saying that he was a nagging little bitch and a pain in the ass. Nobody defended him, and he was horrified to learn that a couple of the boys had agreed with Lewis. They had all betrayed him, and he could never again have anything to do with them.

He explained that the breach with Lewis began with a conversation early in the summer. The boys in the band wanted summer jobs, and Lewis said that his uncle owned a warehouse where they all could work. The jobs, however, never materialized, and as the weeks went by, Lewis prevaricated, saying that his uncle might have some openings soon. The other boys drifted off and found work elsewhere. Only Colin took Lewis at his word and called him a few times a week all summer, asking when he could begin work.

I shook my head, saying that it was hard to understand him. He was an intelligent person. He understood people. Why hadn't he seen this coming? When Lewis offered the jobs, he probably hoped that his uncle might provide them, but he had made an empty boast, the way that people sometimes do. The other lads understood this and did not press the point, knowing that it would humiliate Lewis. But Colin kept calling him, putting him on the spot, and showing him up as a liar who let him down.

His lips went white, and he breathed heavily for a few moments. He began cursing himself, saying that he was a sniveling fuckwit. Lewis had every right to be angry. For a minute, he was lost in contemplation of his mistake. "But what can I do? I've burned my bridges."

I said that they may not be burned. I advised him to call Lewis and apologize for being a pain in the ass all summer. Colin could tell him the truth. He could say that he heard about Lewis's complaints and realized that he was right. "What if he tells me to go to hell?" I said it was unlikely. He and Lewis had been friends for a long time, and decent people accept a sincere apology. Besides, he was not the first person to be a fuckwit. Lewis was a jerk to promise nonexistent jobs. Everyone is a fuckwit at one time, or another. I joked that, of course, I would not know from personal experience, and he chuckled, which was a good sign. He was not completely immersed in his misery.

I asked why he had not mentioned any of this all summer. He said that he had suspected all along that there was no job. He had never really wanted to work at the warehouse. He would not be as strong as the men who regularly worked there, and he dreaded their derision. I said that probably, he was right about not being as strong. A man's upper body does not fully develop until his midtwenties, and besides, he would not be experienced at the job. But if he had shown a willingness to do his best, the other men would have respected him. He looked surprised. "Would they?" he asked. Again, I shook my head, saying that it did not occur to him that people might think well of him.

I asked why he had continued calling Lewis since the job that he did not want was not even in the offing. He said that he hated the thought of going through interviews and red tape at the local employment office. The people who work there would not care about him. It was easier to call Lewis and pretend that he could get a job without those indignities.

I said that he was struggling with a lot of insecurities about failure and rejection. Perhaps if his father had cared more, if he had given him practical advice and encouragement, he would be more confident. He nodded and looked up. "You know, my father doesn't give a fuck about me. He never did." I said that I did know. It was bad luck. The trouble was that he made his luck worse by punishing other people as if they, too, let him down. It was time for him to man up and start standing on his own two feet. His father may not help him, but other people will do, if only he lets them.

The next week, he said that he felt happy when I told him to man up at the previous session. He never thought of himself as a man, but obviously, I did. After this conversation, Colin promised himself that he would never again demean someone else and himself. He changed. He stood up straight, his facial expression was resolute, and he abandoned his passive-aggressive complaining ways. Lewis accepted his apology, and all his friendships improved. He started to pay attention at school and cleaned up his room. A couple of months later, he fell in love with a girl who fell in love with him.

He got together with his girlfriend when they were both tipsy at a party. She was a classmate whom he did not know well, but she struck up a conversation, and he asked her to dance. Later, when they were talking outside, she said that she had liked him for a while and hoped he thought well of her. He was touched to the core that she valued his good opinion. He walked her home that night and went back to her house the next day. Her parents accepted him and approved of their relationship. From then on, they were inseparable.

Discussion of Colin

As we noted in the last chapter, depression can result from arousal of GRIEF or from under arousal of the SEEKING system. Under arousal of the SEEKING system causes disengagement with the world, but Colin proactively initiated passive/aggressive inter-actions with people. This indicated that his SEEKING system was functional albeit misdirected. On the other hand, he correctly believed that his father did not care about him. Thus, GRIEF arousal was the primary cause of his depression. But Father's indifference was not the only reason for Colin's unhappiness. By seeing Colin as her best girlfriend, Mother undermined his self-confidence as a boy and simultaneously offered him a way to feel defensively superior.

All seven emotional systems participated in Colin's emotional problems. By refusing to even try to succeed at anything, Colin avoided the GRIEF of rejection and failure. Although his SEEKING system was functional, it was compromised because he was unwilling to take any risks that might lead to failure and rejection. Because rejection and failure were so painful, he FEARed them and avoided all challenges, like working at the warehouse, going to the employment office, studying for school, or practicing guitar, where he might not measure up. Colin's LUST system was active insofar as he was attracted to girls, but he thwarted chances of romantic success by adopting a superior persona of androgynous sensitivity. He self-directed the CARE system when he soothed himself with a defensively high self-regard. His passive-aggression involved RAGE when he reproached people who failed to appreciate him. The PLAY system also participated in passive-aggression. When he and I were in the standoff phase, he enjoyed toying with me. He would, for example, state his intention to clean his room, but a week later, he would say that he and his mother had argued about its squalid conditions. When I reminded him of his previously stated intention, a sly smile would creep across his face.

When Lewis criticized him so harshly, Colin was ready to abandon his friends and become ever more embittered and alone. At that moment of crisis, I acted like a coach rather than a traditional therapist. A coach points out a player's weakness, and I confronted Colin with his hostile demanding behavior toward Lewis. A coach encourages players to improve on their weakness, and I advised him to apologize and man up. A coach sets an example for his players. I joked that I had never been a fuckwit, indicating that if I could recover from my stupid mistakes, so could he.

This conversation gave Colin hope and put his SEEKING system on a more productive path. He saw the consequences of his passive-aggressive behavior, and the risk of change was better than continuing to behave in covertly hostile ways. Once he had hope that he could succeed in life, he no longer needed to pamper himself and he could CARE about other people. He was also no longer as FEARful of failure. As a consequence, his GRIEF system was assuaged by improved friendships and by winning the love of his girlfriend.

Mitchell

Nine-year-old Mitchell suffered from many fears. Newsreels of urban riots and lootings upset him, reports of knifings being a particular worry. School lessons dealing with health hazards like drugs and traffic accidents preyed on his mind. Over the past year, he had dropped out of athletics and stopped playing field hockey, at which he excelled. Recently, he had opted to remain indoors when his classmates went outside for free play after lunch. He had also begun to show signs of an incipient school phobia, feigning illness, and begging his parents to allow him to stay home.

Mitchell was a lanky boy with even facial features, like his pretty mother. We met only three times, the first two sessions being a week apart. Then the summer holidays intervened, and we did not meet again for more than a month. Mother attended all sessions, and it was she who related the litany of her son's fears. This was the summer of 2002, almost a year after the fall of the twin towers in New York, and Mitchell had had heard about the possibility of anthrax poisoning by terrorists.

The current focus of his worries was a classmate named Rashad who lived with his English mother, his Pakistani father having returned home. Rashad boasted that his father was a member of Al-Qaeda and said that when he grew up, he would go to Pakistan and join their ranks. Rashad did not single out Mitchell as a target. In fact, the boys hardly knew each other, but Mitchell worried that Rashad would secretly sprinkle anthrax on his lunch. He consulted the Internet to find out symptoms of anthrax poisoning, which included dizziness, nausea, and coughing, all of which he periodically experienced, probably due to anxiety and hyperventilation. He stopped eating lunch at school and lost a couple of kilos.

His parents and his teacher searched in vain for ways to reassure him. His teacher offered to lock his lunchbox in her desk, but he worried that Rashad could steal the key. Mother recommended that he drape a thread across his lunchbox in the morning. If the thread was in place at lunchtime, he would know that nobody had tampered with his food. But Mitchell suspected that Rashad might remove and replace the thread.

He had always enjoyed good health, save from phimosis (tight foreskin) at age four, which caused an infection due to trapped urine. Over the course of several hospital visits spanning about a month, medical professionals tried nonsurgical attempts to manipulate and stretch the foreskin. These were painful, distressing, and unsuccessful. The problem was resolved by an eventual circumcision from which he recovered well physically. However, Mother said that thereafter, he became reserved and was never again the outgoing boy that he had been. Nevertheless, during the early years of childhood, he was not especially fearful and aside from his reserve, he developed well. Around age eight, obsessive fears came to the fore. As soon as one abated, another took its place, and he was in a chronic state of dread.

It is likely that Mitchell had been fearful throughout his childhood, but when he was little, his fears were manageable because young boys play under the supervision of adults, and their games are generally tame. When boys get older, they enjoy more independence and are apt to play and speak in ways that are rebellious and rough. That was when Mitchell's fears proliferated.

As Mother spoke about Mitchell's fears, he sat passively and gazed despondently into the middle distance. No doubt he had heard it all before, and he did not seem to expect much from another discussion. I asked him for a firsthand account of his worries. In addition to the topics that his mother mentioned, he said that he could not go on a climbing frame because he was afraid of falling. He could not submerge his face in water when he went swimming. He had dropped out of field hockey after a teammate's elbow had grazed his cheek. He worried that next time, an elbow, or a stick might put out his eye. On a recent family outing to an amusement park, he was embarrassed to be the largest child on rides for little children. His brother and sister wanted him to join them on the roller coaster, but he was afraid of being thrown off. He especially hated free play after lunch because there were no rules, and you never knew what might happen.

I asked what he would want if I could grant his most important wish. He said that he would want me to make his life completely safe, but he knew that I could not do that. I nodded, saying I could not even do that for myself. Nobody is completely safe, but most people are not tormented by worries as he is. It seemed to me that the lack of complete safety was not his problem. His problem was fear. He looked up, interested for the first time.

Mother agreed that fear was the problem, rather than the things that he feared. If he ever got over his fear of Rashad, there were other Asian children in his class, and probably, he would become frightened of them. In any case, he would find something new to fear. Mitchell hung his head, saying that he knew he was stupid to be so frightened. His parents and teachers were right when they told him there was nothing to fear, and he knew that they were getting fed up with him. But when he worries, he forgets everything that they said. Later, when he feels better, he promises himself that he will change, but he never does.

I said that I did not think he was stupid. Nobody is scared without reason, and nobody wants to be scared. If he is frightened, then something must have frightened him. A scary experience can sometimes leave you in a bad way and fear spreads so that you can become afraid of almost anything. I related a true story about a colleague at work whose handbag was snatched by a mugger who raced by on a bicycle and knocked her down. She was not hurt, but she was badly shaken, and for several weeks, she was easily startled, and she could not watch her favorite crime drama on TV. She also worried when she walked down the street, even though she knew that she would probably never get mugged again.

He seemed to be suffering from the same kind of worry. Something bad happened, and now he is frightened by many things. The lady at work was an adult when she was mugged, so she could remember it, and she knew why she was so fearful. His bad experience seems to have happened when he was very young and endured those hospital appointments. Maybe he cannot remember them, but they must have frightened him very badly. Because he cannot remember, the reason for his worries is hidden. Maybe that is why they seem stupid.

I asked how he would feel if he had a lunchbox with a padlock. He could keep the key, perhaps in a zipped pocket, or on a lariat worn around his neck. Without hesitation, he said that would be fine. Mother said that she would implement the plan immediately, which she did. Thereafter, he ate lunch at school and stopped losing weight.

I related another true story, this time from my childhood. I attended a swimming class, and the teacher wanted us to learn how to dive. The first step was to kneel by the side of the pool and fall headfirst into the water. Hard as I tried, I could not bring myself to take the plunge, and finally, the teacher put her foot on my bottom and pushed me in. I was shocked and incensed, but once I hit the water, I was not at all frightened. It felt weird and entirely different from any other experience. I was not sure if I liked it, but I wanted to try it again. By the end of the summer, I was diving off quite a high board, and I loved it.

Mitchell laughed hard when I spoke of my surprise and consternation at being pushed in the water. During the course of this first meeting, he became uncommonly fond of me, leaning toward me, and smiling with raised brows. When he and his mother left, he returned to the door two or three times to wave goodbye yet again.

In the week between the first two sessions, I pondered on his remarks about the chaotic atmosphere on the playground after lunch where there were no rules. This fear of malicious and capricious behavior seemed to lie at the heart of all his fears: Rashad would surreptitiously poison him; a stray elbow, or hockey stick would blind him; he would fall from the bars of a climbing frame; he would be engulfed by water while swimming; and he would be catapulted off a roller coaster. I thought that this sense of chaos and danger must reflect his impressions of the medical interventions early in his life.

At the start of our second meeting, I asked his permission to have a frank conversation with him, adding that some of the topics I would raise might appear rude, or impolite. I did not wish to seem ill mannered, but I did want to speak openly, so would he agree to an honest discussion? He nodded, and I said that I had been thinking about the hospital visits in his early childhood. He was very young and could not have understood much about the world. He could not read, or write, or do any math. Probably, he did not even know many words. However, even children of four understand some things very well. They know that their willies (a British term for penis that Mother used) feel different from other parts of their bodies. He looked down and smiled. I repeated that I was not trying to embarrass him, and besides, willies are supposed to feel good. I continued that even little boys know that they should not play with their willies in public. Young children also know that they are not supposed to hurt each other.

Of course, sometimes children openly play with their willies and hurt each other. After all, they are just children. But a young child never expects to see an adult playing with his willy, or hurting somebody on purpose. Yet when he went to hospital, grown-up doctors and nurses fooled around with his willy, and they sometimes hurt him. Maybe he thought that the hospital was a terrible place with no rules where doctors and nurses were allowed to play bad games with his willy.

He listened with mute attention. In a quiet voice, he said that when he was in hospital, he saw a long knife, something that he had never seen before, and he thought that the doctors were going to cut him. I doubt that this memory was accurate. The hippocampus continues to develop throughout childhood and adolescence (Riggins et al. 2018). At age four, memories are apt to contain only a kernel of reality. Perhaps he saw a scalpel that took on an exaggerated appearance over time, or he might have remembered a bad dream. I commiserated and said that this entire scary experience must lie at the root of his worries—the fear that anything bad might happen and that anyone might behave in dangerous unexpected ways.

We spoke about overcoming his fears in practical ways. Mother regretted his giving up field hockey. He had been a good player, and his teammates wanted him to come back. Mitchell too felt bad about letting them down. I said that hockey is an energetic sport, and it is possible to get a bruise, or even a black eye. But he would not go blind. I asked if he might start to fight his fears in small ways. For example, he could go into a swimming pool with one of his parents and hold hands while he put his face in the water for just a second to see what it feels like. Or he might try climbing on the lower bars of a climbing frame so that he could become sure of his footing. Probably, it would be best if Mum, or Dad spotted him at first. We all agreed that the upcoming holiday would be a golden opportunity for Mitchell to try doing some of the things he feared. We made an appointment to meet again following the summer break.

Over the summer, Mitchell's parents helped him to overcome his fears. He learned to swim under water and enjoyed scuba diving. He could now reach the top of the climbing frame, and he went on a roller coaster with his older brother. He no longer needed a lock on his lunchbox. He had rejoined the hockey team and again went out for free play. He had even spoken with Rashad on a few occasions without becoming upset.

Mitchell's parents were concerned that his worries might reemerge and asked me to continue seeing him. I dissuaded them, saying that there is no need to fix something that is no longer broken. Instead, I offered to keep his file open for a year. That way, if problems arose, his parents need not go through the lengthy referral process that usually occurs in the British National Health Service. They agreed to this plan. A week later, Mitchell sent me a thank-you card, which he made himself. In it, he wrote that he had enjoyed meeting me because I made him laugh. A year later, when I was about to close his file, I called his mother to ask how he was getting on. His fears were no longer a problem, and all was well.

Discussion of Mitchell

My work with Mitchell was a therapeutic intervention rather than a course of psychotherapy, but I wanted to write about him because he presented a vivid instance of FEAR sensitization. As we noted above, there are two types of anxiety, one stemming from the FEAR system and the other from GRIEF. One might speculate that the medical interventions, to which his parents consented, had undermined his trust in them. This would have indicated that his GRIEF system had been sensitized. However, there were no indications that Mitchell suffered from an attachment disorder. He dearly loved his parents, his extended family, and his teachers, and they loved him. He got on well with his older brother and younger sister, and in spite of his reserve, he was popular with peers. He was a good student, and until recently, he had loved school. His brother and sister were well-adjusted, high-achieving, likable children, indicating that Mitchell had good parents. This allowed me to rule out an attachment disorder.

On the other hand, Mitchell had endured a series of frightening medical interventions when he was very young. His subsequent reserve and the recent expansion of his fears indicated that his FEAR system had become sensitized by these experiences. The sense of chaos must have resulted from the cognitive dissonance that he endured (Festinger 1957). As a little boy, he believed in the rules of conduct that his parents had prescribed. Then he had hospital appointments where adults behaved in ways that contravened everything that he had ever been taught about decent behavior. It is no wonder that he thought the world had gone mad.

Mitchell was primarily troubled by fears that proliferated on a regular basis, one replacing another with equal force. His love of learning indicated that his SEEKING system was operative, but it was compromised by his worries, and he resisted taking any risks that might result in physical injury. Other emotional systems seemed to be intact. As we just noted, his GRIEF system did not appear to be a problem. He exhibited a capacity to CARE for his family and teachers. Mitchell's LUST system appeared normal. He did not have an excessive interest in sex, but his shy smile when I mentioned his willy indicated that he enjoyed good sexual feelings. His enjoyment of PLAY had been recently mitigated by his fears, but he was able to enjoy safe games. It is possible that he passively expressed RAGE when he exasperated other people who tried to help him, but it was more likely that his inability to trust was an expression of fears that he could not control.

Classically trained therapists like me believe that Freud was right in claiming that small children have nascent sexual feelings that they direct the toward their parents—the people they love best. I might have assumed that when Mitchell endured an assault on his penis, he saw it as a punishment for oedipal wishes. However, Mitchell displayed no signs of oedipal pathology. He was not inordinately attached to his mother, nor was he especially rivalrous, or submissive to his father. Furthermore, most children weather the Oedipus complex, and it does not usually result in neurosis or mental illness.

Even if Mitchell had suffered from oedipal pathology, his excessive fears contraindicated a classical approach. If I had spoken to him about unacceptable sexual thoughts and fears of retribution, my remarks might have upset him, further sensitizing his FEAR system. He might have become afraid of me and that would have derailed therapy. Because I knew that the FEAR system exists and because I knew that it can become sensitized by experience, I interpreted nothing about oedipal conflicts and instead acted like a coach in helping him overcome his fears.

Like a coach, I identified fear as the weak area that needed to improve. His willingness to keep the key to his lunchbox was a good sign because it indicated that his SEEKING system was functioning and that he felt capable of looking after himself. I encouraged the use of the SEEKING system in combatting his fears and advised him to take small risks, like briefly putting his face in the water and climbing on the low bars of a climbing frame. When I told him about my fear of diving in childhood, I used myself as an example, indicating that he could overcome his fears as I had overcome mine. I also encouraged his PLAY system by telling him that the thing that I had feared eventually became a source of fun. This, by the way, was an exercise in reframing, which is commonly used in cognitive behavioral therapy (Copeland-Linder 2008).

Everyone, including Mitchell himself, thought that his fears were irrational. He felt warmly toward me because I took his fears seriously and believed that they were legitimate. I identified their origin and offered a way to combat them. In all probability, Mitchell suffered from PTSD (Dyregrov and Yule 2006), and empathy is a necessary component in recovery. Once Mother understood the reason for his fears, she told Father and Mitchell no longer felt so alone. His parents also felt better because they could apply a strategy to help their son. Indeed, it was the parents who did the bulk of the work in effecting a cure.

I discouraged further treatment because fear-extinction experiments indicate that fear circuitry atrophies over time, at least partially. I hoped that in time, some of the neural pathways encoding Mitchell's fears would deteriorate. This deterioration process might be hindered if I continued to talk to him about his worries. In any case, it seemed that by leading a normal life, Mitchell would continue to consolidate the skills that extinguished his fears.

Once Mitchell had hope of overcoming his fears, his SEEKING and PLAY systems, which had become increasingly inactive, were freed up, and he was prepared to try and eventually enjoy some of the activities that he feared.

Caveats

In the last chapter, we learned that neural pathways encoding the conditioned fear response are not erased by extinction. Instead, extinction creates new circuitry that successfully competes with the old. However, the old circuitry can dominate during periods of stress, and fear of the conditioned stimulus can reemerge. Successful therapy helps to create circuitry that extinguishes painful affects, but it cannot eradicate their potential reemergence.

Neither Colin, nor Mitchell was completely cured. Colin could still fall prey to low self-esteem. A poor grade at school, or a carelessly critical comment tended to hurt his feelings more than it should. He typically looked to his girlfriend for reassurance but left to his own devices he was not as resilient as I had hoped. Mitchell also displayed vestiges of fear. After the summer, when he and his mother arrived to tell me about his accomplishments, they were in high spirits. His SEEKING and PLAY systems had transformed his fears into activities that were exciting and fun. But at one point, Mitchell referred to his exploits as acts of courage. The need for courage indicated that his fears still lurked in the background.

Summary

I hope that the discussion of these cases illustrates how neuroscience helped me to make decisions that were scientifically sound. It enabled me to identify GRIEF as the source of Colin's depression and to identify Mitchell's anxiety as a manifestation of FEAR rather than as an attachment disorder. With Colin, I behaved like a traditional therapist most of the time, making remarks that revealed his unconscious motives and defenses. However, when Lewis and his other friends admonished him, I acted like a coach, pointing out his participation in his downfall, offering a way to put things right with Lewis and by offering myself as an example. With Mitchell, I acted like a coach throughout because his fears were pressing and needed immediate attention. Fear-extinction experiments indicated that further treatment for Mitchell was not indicated. My role as a coach mobilized the SEEKING systems of both boys, inducing them to take a proactive stance in getting better.

Concluding Remarks

This book has had the narrow focus of demonstrating that affects are feelings of pleasure and pain that emerge largely from subcortical structures in and around the brainstem. The rest of the book fleshed out this central point by discussing different hypotheses by Damasio and Panksepp, both of which describe how subcortical structures might create affective consciousness. We then considered perplexing issues about the relationship between consciousness and the physical brain and rounded out the discussion by reviewing ways that neuroscience can enhance psychotherapy. It seemed a fairly straightforward enterprise, but there was a surprise in store, at least for me.

The surprise centered around homeostasis and the creation of affects. Damasio's hypothesis states that the purpose of emotional behavior is the restoration, or optimization of homeostasis, something that is not always true. We take risks, and we look after other people, often at our own expense. In other words, there is sometimes a disconnect between homeostasis and affective motivation. If we are not always motivated by homeostatic considerations, what role does homeostasis play in the creation of affects? It was there that the trail went cold.

On the basis of research that I was able to obtain, it is not currently possible to know if homeostasis usually plays a role in the creation of affects as Damasio claims, or if Panksepp is right in proposing that the creation of affects is independent of homeostasis. This is the question that dangles at the end of this book.

This unanswered question has plenty of company. Mind/body mechanisms remain a mystery. We do not know how the physical brain creates consciousness or how immaterial conscious influences the brain. Damasio and Panksepp make informed guesses about the structures that create affects, but we do not know the exact structures involved. Damasio and Panksepp also propose mechanisms for the creation of affective consciousness, but we do not know if either mechanism is correct. Questions abound, and answers are won slowly. In one of his lectures, Panksepp remarked that neuroscience is still in the Dark Ages. I hope that this book has provided a beam of light.

References

Aaronson, S. 2014. *Shtetl-Optimized: The Blog of Scott Aaronson.* http://www.scottaaronson.com/blog/?p=1799.

Abe, K. 2001. "Modulation of hippocampal long-term potentiation by the amygdala: a synaptic mechanism linking emotion and memory." *Jpn J Pharmacol.* 86(1):18-22. http://www.ncbi.nlm. nih.gov/pubmed/11430468.

Abrams, L., (2013). "Study: Spayed and Neutered Dogs Live Longer." *The Atlantic.* https://www.theatlantic.com/health/archive/2013/04/ study-spayed-and-neutered-dogs-live-longer/275121/.

Abrams, MH. (2012). *A Glossary of Literary Terms.* Boston MA: Wadsworth.

Adamec, R., Berton, O., and Razek, WA. (2009). "Viral Vector Induction of CREB Expression in the Periaqueductal Gray Induces a Predator Stress-Like Pattern of Changes in pCREB Expression, Neuroplasticity, and Anxiety in Rodents." *Neural Plasticity,* Volume 2009. https://www.ncbi.nlm.nih.gov/pmc/ articles/PMC2664642/.

Adolphs, R. 2008. "Fear, Faces, and the Human Amygdala." *Curr. Opin. Neurobiolol.,* 1(2): 166-172. https://www.ncbi.nlm.nih. gov/pmc/articles/PMC2580742/.

Adolphs, R. 2017. "How should neuroscience study emotions? By distinguishing emotion states, concepts, and experiences." *Soc Cogn Affect Neurosci.*:12(1): 24–31. https://www.ncbi.nlm.nih. gov/pmc/articles/PMC5390692/.

Ahrens, S., Wu, M., Furlan, A., Hwang, G-R., Raehum, P., Li, H., Penzol, M.A., Tollkuhn, J.v, and Li, B. (2018). "A central extended amygdala circuit that modulates anxiety." *The Journal of Neuroscience*: 705-18. http://www.jneurosci.org/content/jneuro/early/2018/05/29/JNEUROSCI.0705-18.2018.full.pdf.

Ainsworth MD. 1962. "The effects of maternal deprivation: a review of findings and controversy in the context of research strategy." *Public Health Pap.* 14:97-165.

Aisa, B., Tordera, R., Lasheras, B., Del Rı´o, J. and Ramı´rez, MJ.. 2007. "Cognitive impairment associated to HPA axis hyperactivity after maternal separation in rats." *Psychoneuroendocrinology.* https://www.cns.nyu.edu/ledoux/pdf/HPA2007.pdf.

Aitkin, L.M.; Dickhaus, H., Schult, W., and Zimmerman, M. 1978. "External nucleus of inferior colliculus: auditory and spinal somatosensory afferents and their interactions." *Journal of Neurophysiology.* vol. 41 no. 4: 837-847.

Akpan, N. 2015. "8 things you didn't know about Orville Wright." *Science.* https://www.pbs.org/newshour/science/8-things-didnt-know-orville-wright.

Alcedo, J., Maier, W., and Ch'ng, Q. 2009. "Sensory Influence on Homeostasis and Lifespan: Molecules and Circuits." *Madame Curie Bioscience Database* [Internet]. https://www.ncbi.nlm.nih.gov/books/NBK25445/.

Amano, T., Unal, C.T., and Paré, D. (2010). "SYNAPTIC CORRELATES OF FEAR EXTINCTION IN THE AMYGDALA." *Nat. Neurosci.* 13(4):489-94. https://www.ncbi.nlm.nih.gov/pmc/articles/PMC2847017/.

American Psychological Association (2018). "Stress Effects on the Body." https://www.apa.org/topics/stress-bod.

Anaesthetist.com (2006). "The Anatomy and Physiology of Pain." http://www.anaesthetist.com/icu/pain/Findex.htm#pain3.htm.

Antoniadis, E.A, Winslow, J.T, Davis, M., and Amaral, D.G. (2009). "THE NON-HUMAN PRIMATE AMYGDALA IS NECESSARY FOR THE ACQUISITION BUT NOT THE RETENTION OF FEAR-POTENTIATED STARTLE." *Biol Psychiatry.* 65(3): 241–248.

Arciniegas, D.B. 2013. "Emotion." In *Behavioral Neurology & Neuropsychiatry* (Behavioral Neurology & Neuropsychiatry

(DB. Archiniegas, CA Anderson & Filley, CM eds.). New York: Cambridge University Press.

Arnsten, AFT. 2009. "Stress signaling pathways that impair prefrontal cortex structure and function." *Nat Rev Neurosci.* 10 (6):410-22. https://www.ncbi.nlm.nih.gov/pubmed/19455173.

Arnsten, A.F.T. 2018. "The Neurobiology of the Prefrontal Cortex and its Role in Mental Disorders." https://www.youtube.com/watch?v=DEtnoiKGDwI.

Audiopedia, 2017. "What is Nervous Laughter?" https://www.youtube.com/watch?v=nXs5U96bSiE.

Austin, J.H. 2003. "Your Self, Your Brain and Zen." *Cerebrum.* http://www.dana.org/Cerebrum/2003/Your_Self, _Your_Brain,_and_Zen/.

Auvray, M., Myin, E., and Spence, C. 2010. "The sensory-discriminative and affective-motivational aspects of pain." *Neuroscience and Biobehavioral Reviews,* 34: 214–223 http://www.nstu.net/malika-auvray/files/malika-auvray-auvray-myin_spence_nbr_2010.pdf.

Ayala, F.J. 2010. "Religion has nothing to do with science – and vice versa." *The Guardian.* https://www.theguardian.com/science/blog/2010/may/28/religion-science-richard-dawkins.

Babaev, O., Chatain, C.P., and Krueger-Burg, D. 2018. "Inhibition in the amygdala anxiety circuitry." *Exp. Mol. Med* 50(4):18. https://www.ncbi.nlm.nih.gov/pmc/articles/PMC5938054/.

Bader, M. 2009. "The Difference Between Coaching and Therapy Is Greatly Overstated." *Psychology Today.*

Bailey, P. and Davis, E.W. 1942. "Effects of lesions of the periaqueductal gray matter in the cat." *Proceedings of the Society for Experimental Biology and Medicine,* 351, 305–306.

Bailey, P. and Davis, E.W. 1943. "Effects of lesions of the periaqueductal gray matter on the Macaca Mulatta." *J. Neuropathol. Exp. Neurol.* 3, 69–72.

Bailey, R. 2018. "The Amygdala's Location and function in the Brain." *ThoughtCo.* https://www.thoughtco.com/amygdala-anatomy-373211.

Balderston, N.L., Schultz, D.H., and Helmstetter, F.J. 2011. "The human amygdala plays a stimulus specific role in the detection of novelty." *Neuroimage.*, 55(4):1889-1898. https://www.ncbi.nlm.nih.gov/pmc/articles/PMC3062695/.

Bandler, R. and Keay, K.A. 1996 "Columnar organization in the midbrain periaqueductal gray and the integration of emotional expression." *Progress in Brain Research* 107:285–300.

Barbey, AK., Colom, & Grafman, R. (2012). Dorsolateral prefrontal contributions to human intelligence. *Neuropsychologia.* https://decisionneurosciencelab.org/pdfs/Barbey_et_al_in_press.pdf.

Barrett, L.F 2006. "Solving the emotion paradox: Categorization and the experience of emotion." *Personality and Social Psychology Review,* 10, 20-46. https://www.affective-science.org/pubs/2006/Barrett2006paradox.pdf.

Barrett, L.F 2008. "The Science of Emotion." In *Human Behavior in Military Contexts.* Blascovich, J.J & Hartel, C.R. (eds.) Washington D.C.:National Academies Press.

Barrett, L.F. 2011. "Was Darwin Wrong About Emotinal Expressions?" *Current Directions in Psychological Science* 20(6):400-406 https://www.affective-science.org/pubs/2011/current-directions-was-darwin-wrong.pdf.

Barrett, LF. (2012). Emotions Are Real. *Emotion, Vol. 12, No. 3*:413–429. https://www.affective-science.org/pubs/2012/emotions-are-real.pdf.

Barrett, L.F 2017a. *How Emotions Are Made.* New York:Houghton Mifflin Harcourt Publishing Company.

Barrett, L.F 2017b. "The Mental Inference Fallacy." https://lisafeldmanbarrett.com/2017/05/24/mental-inference-fallacy/.

Barrett, L.F., Mesquita, B., and Gendron, M. 2011. "Context in Emotion Perception." *Current Directions in Psychological Science.* https://www.affective-science.org/pubs/2011/CD_face_in_context_2011.pdf.

Bartels, A., and Zeki, S. 2004. "The neural correlates of maternal and romantic love". *Neurolmage,* vol 21, issue 3:1155-1166. http://www.sciencedirect.com/science/article/pii/S1053811903007237.

Bateman, A. and Fonagy, P. 2010. "Mentalization based treatment for borderline personality disorder." *World Psychiatry,* 9(1): 11–15. http://www.ncbi.nlm.nih.gov/pmc/articles/PMC2816926/.

Bechara, A. 2015. *Dr. Antoine Bechara talks about the IOWA Gambling Task.* https://www.youtube.com/watch?v=wBdwzToxQPU.

Bechara, A., Damasio, A.R., Damasio, H., and Anderson, S.W. 1994. "Insensitivity to future consequences following damage to human prefrontal cortex." *Cognition,* 50(1-3), 7-15.

Bechara. A., Damasio. H., Tranel, D., Damasio, A.R. 1997. "Deciding Advantageously Before Knowing the Advantageous Strategy." *Science,* 275(5304):1293-5.

Bechara, A. and Damasio, A,R. 2005. "The Somatic marker hypothesis: A neural theory of economic decision." *Games and Economic Behavior,* 52:336-372. www.docdroid.net/xi0j/05-12-07-theoretical-research-bechara-damasio-2005.pdf.html.

Bechara, A., Damasio, H., Tranel, D., and Damasio, A.R. 2005. "The Iowa Gambling Task and the somatic marker hypothesis: some questions and answers." *TRENDS in Cognitive Sciences* Vol.9 No.4: 159-162. http://citeseerx.ist.psu.edu/viewdoc/download?doi=10.1.1.137.6124&rep=rep1&type=pdf.

Bechtel, W. and Williamson, R.C. 1998. E Craig (ed.). "Vitalism." *Routledge Encyclopedia of Philosophy.* London:Routledge.

Behbehani,M.M. 1995. "Functional characteristics of the midbrain periaqueductal gray." *Progress in Neurobiology* 46:575–605. http://www.ncbi.nlm.nih.gov/pubmed/8545545.

Bekoff, M., Byers J.A. 1998. *Animal Play: Evolutionary, Comparative, and Ecological Perspectives.* Cambridge: Cambridge University Press.

Bergman, M.S. 1982. "Platonic love, transference love, and love in real life." *J. Am. Psychoanal. Assoc.* 30(1):87-111. https://pubmed.ncbi.nlm.nih.gov/6926999/.

Bernard, C. 1974 "Lectures on the phenomena common to animals and plants." Trans Hoff HE, Guillemin R, Guillemin L., Springfield (IL): Charles C Thomas.

Bernard, J.F., Peschanski, M., Besson, J.M. 1989. "A possible spino (trigemino)-ponto-amygdaloid pathway for pain." *Neuroscience*

Letters, Vol 100, Issues 1-3:83-88. http://www.sciencedirect. com/science/article/pii/0304394089906642.

Bernardi, M., Genedani, S., Tagliavini, S., Bertolini, A. 1986. "Effects on long-term sensitivity to pain and morphine of stress induced in the newborn rat by pain or manipulation." *Physiol Behav*;37:827-31.

Berridge, K.C. 2003. "Pleasures of the Brain." *Brain Cogn.*52 (1):106-28.

Berridge, K.C. 2007. "The debate over dopamine's role in reward: the case for incentive salience." *Psychopharmacology,* 191:391-431. http://citeseerx.ist.psu.edu/viewdoc/ download?doi=10.1.1.122.4519&rep=rep1&type=pdf.

Berridge, K.C. 2009. "'Liking' and 'wanting' food rewards: Brain substrates and roles in eating disorders." *Physiol Behav.* 97(5):537–550. https://www.ncbi.nlm.nih.gov/pmc/articles/ PMC2717031/.

Berridge, K.C. and Kringelbach, M.L. 2008. "Affective neuroscience of pleasure: reward in humans and animals." *Psychopharmacology* (Berl.) 199(3):457-480. https://www.ncbi.nlm.nih.gov/pmc/ articles/PMC3004012/#S12title.

Berridge, K.C. and Kringelbach, M.L. 2011. "Building a neuroscience of pleasure and well-being." *SpringerOpen.* https://psywb. springeropen.com/articles/10.1186/2211-1522-1-3.

Berridge, K.C. and Kringelbach, M.L. 2015. "Pleasure Systems in the Brain." *Neuron* 86.

Black, A.E. 2019. "Treating Insecure Attachment in Group Therapy: Attachment Theory Meets Modern Psychoanalytic Technique." *International Journal of Group Psychotherapy.*
Volume 69, 2019 - Issue 3. https://www.tandfonline.com/doi/abs/1 0.1080/00207284.2019.1588073.

Blackford, J.U., Buckholtz, J.W., Avery. S.N., and Zald, D.H. 2010. "A unique role for the human amygdala in novelty detection." NeurIoimage., 50(3): 1188-1193. https://www.ncbi.nlm.nih. gov/pmc/articles/PMC2830341/.

Block, N. 1995. "On a confusion about a function of consciousness." *Behavioral and Brain Sciences* 18:227–87.

Boeree, C.G. 2002. "Early Medicine and Physiology." https://web-space.ship.edu/cgboer/neurophysio.html.

Bourtchouladze, R. 2004. "Memories Are Made of This: How Memory Works in Humans and Animals." New York: Columbia University Press.

Bouton, M.E. 2020. "Conditioning and learning." In R. Biswas-Diener & E. Diener (Eds), *Noba textbook series: Psychology.* Champaign, IL: DEF publishers. Retrieved from http://noba. to/ajxhcqdr.

Bowlby, J. 1951. "Maternal Care and Mental Health." *Geneva: World Health Organisation.*

Bowlby, J. 1960. "Grief and Mourning in Infancy and Early Childhood." *Psychoanalytic Study of the Child* 15: 9-52.

Bowlby, J. 1969. *Attachment and Loss, Vol. 1: Attachment.* London: Hogarth Press and the Institute of Psycho-Analysis.

Bowlby, J. 1988. *A Secure Base: Clinical Applications of Attachment Theory.* Bristol: Arrowsmith.

Bozarth, M.A. 1994. "Pleasure systems in the brain." In D.M. Warburton (ed.), *Pleasure: The politics and the reality.* New York: John Wiley & Sons. (pp. 5-14 + refs). http://wings.buffalo.edu/ aru/ARUreport01.htm.

Bramlet, K. 2013. *What makes cancer patients and caregivers smile on their toughest days.* University of Texas MD Anderson Cancer Center. https://www.mdanderson.org/cancerwise/what-makes-cancer-patients-and-caregivers-smile.h00-158832801.html.

Bottom of Form.

Brass, M. and Haggard, P. 2008. "The what, when, whether model of intentional action." *Neuroscientist* 14(4):319-325.

Breiter, H.C., Etcoff, N.E., Whalen, P.J., Kennedy, W.A., Rauch, S..L., Buckner, RL., Srauss, M.M., Hyman, S.E., Rosen, B.R. 1996. "Response and Habituation of the Human Amygdala during Visual Processing of Facial Expression." *Neuron 17:* 875–887. https://www.sciencedirect.com/science/article/pii/ S0896627300802196.

Brenner, C. 1955. *An Elementary Textbook of Psychoanalysis.* New York: International Universities Press, Inc.

Brenner, C. 1982. *The Mind in Conflict.* New York: International Universities Press.

Brooks, J.C., Nurmikko, T.J., Bimson, W.E, Singh, K.D., and Roberts, N. 2002. "fMRI of thermal pain: effects of stimulus laterality and attention." *Neuroimage.*, 15(2):293-301. http://www.ncbi.nlm.nih.gov/pubmed/11798266.

Brosnan S.F. 2006. "Nonhuman species' reactions to inequity and their implications for fairness." *Soc. Just. Res.*19: 153–18510. http://www.uib.no/insuhc/files/cognitive_emotional_sensitization.pdf.

Buirski, P. and Haglund, P. 2001. *Making sense together: the intersubjective approach to psychotherapy.* Northvale, NJ: Jason Aronson.

Bush, G., Luu, P., and Posner, M.I. 2000. "Cognitive and emotional influences in anterior cingulate cortex." *Trends in Cognitive Sciences,* Vol. 4, No. 6. http://www.georgebushmd.com/GBMD-Website/Research_&_Publications_files/Bush_2000_TICS_CingReview.pdf.

Cabanac, M. (1979). Sensory Pleasure Q Rev, Biol, 54: 1-29.

Cabanac, M. 1992. "Pleasure: The common currency." *Journal of Theoretical Biology* 155:173–200.

Cannon, W.B. 1927. "The James-Lange theory of emotions: A critical examination and an alternative theory." *American Journal of Psychology* 39: 106-124.

Cannon, W.B. 1932. *The Wisdom of the Body.* New York: Norton.

Ceunen, E., Vlaeyen, J.W.S., and Van Diest, I. 2016. "On the Origin of Interoception." *Front Psychol.* 7:743. https://www.ncbi.nlm.nih.gov/pmc/articles/PMC4876111/.

Chalmers, D.J. 1995. "Facing up to the problem of consciousness." *J. of Consciousness Studies* 2(3): 200-219.

Chalmers, D.J. 1996. *The conscious mind: In search of a fundamental theory.* New York, Oxford: Oxford University Press.

Chang, C-h, Knapska, E., Orsini, CA., Rabinak, CA., Zimmerman, JA, and Maren, S. 2009. "Fear Extinction in Rodents." *Curr Protoc Neurosci.*, Unit 8.23 https://www.ncbi.nlm.nih.gov/pmc/articles/PMC2756523/.

Chen, S.W.C., Shemyakin, A., and Wiedenmayer, C.P. 2006. "The Role of the Amygdala and Olfaction in Unconditioned Fear in Developing Rats." *Journal of Neuroscience*: 26 (1) 233-240. http://www.jneurosci.org/content/26/1/233.

Cherry, K. 2019. "What Is Operant Conditioning and How Does It Work? How Reinforcement and Punishment Modify Behavior." https://www.verywellmind.com/operant-conditioning-a2-2794863.

Ciompi, L. and Panksepp, J. 2005. "Energetic effect of emotions on cognitions: complementary psychobiological and psychosocial findings." In *Consciousness and Emotion: Agency, conscious choice, and selective perception*. (R. Ellis & N Newton, eds.) John Benjamins North America: Philadelphia.

Cirulli, F., Francia, N., Berry, A., Aloe, L., Alleva, E. and Suomi, S.J. 2009. "Early life stress as a risk factor for mental health: role of neurotrophins from rodents to non-human primates." *Neuroscience and Biobehavioral Reviews*. 33,573-85.

Clasen, M. 2017. "How Evolution Designed Your Fear: The universal grip of Stephen King's personal terrors." *Nautilus*. http://nautil.us/issue/53/monsters/how-evolution-designed-your-fear.

Cochrane, T.I. and Williams, M.A. 2015. "Disorders of Consciousness: Brain Death, Coma, Vegetative and Minimally Conscious States." *Dana Foundation*. https://dana.org/article/disorders-of-consciousness-brain-death-coma-and-the-vegetative-and-minimally-conscious-states/.

Complexity labs. 2016. "Emergence Theory 5: Strong and Weak." https://www.youtube.com/watch?v=66p9qlpnzzY.

Cooney, R.E., Atlas, L.Y., Fanny, E., Gotlib, and I.H. 2006. "Amygdala activation in the processing of neutral faces in social anxiety disorder: Is neutral really neutral?" *Psychiatry Research: Neuroimaging* 148:55–59. https://web.stanford.edu/group/mood/gotlib_pdfs/cooney_gotlib_2006.pdf.

Copeland-Linder, N. PhD, M.P.H. 2008. "Posttraumatic Stress Disorder Posttraumatic Stress Disorder." *PEDIATRICS IN REVIEW* Vol. 29 No. 3: pp. 103 -104.

Copleston, F. 1963. *A History of Philosophy,* vol 4 Modern Philosophy: Descartes to Leibniz. Garden City, NY: IMAGE BOOKS, a Division of Doubleday & Company Inc.

Corradini A, O'Connor T. (editors). 2010 *Emergence in Science and Philosophy.* Routledge.

Cowey, A. 2004. "The 30th Sir Frederick Bartlett lecture. Fact, artefact, and myth about blindsight." *Quarterly Journal of Experimental Psychology A,* 57: 577-609.

Craig, A.D. 2002. "How do you feel? Interoception: The sense of the physiological condition of the body." *Nature Reviews Neuroscience,* 3, 655-666. http://www.nature.com/nrn/journal/v3/n8/abs/nrn894.html.

Craig, A.D., Chen, K., Bandy, D., and Reiman, E.M. 2000. "Thermosensory activation of insular cortex." *Nature Neuroscience* 3: 184 – 190. http://www.nature.com/neuro/journal/v3/n2/full/nn0200_184.html.

Craig, A.D. 2003. "A new view of pain as homeostatic emotion." *Trends Neurosci.* 26: 303-307. http://sunburst.usd.edu/~cliff/Courses/Advanced%20Seminars%20in%20Neuroendocrinology/Pain/Craig03.pdf.

Crick, F. and Koch, C. 1990. "Toward a neurobiological theory of consciousness." *Seminars in Neuroscience 2*: 263-275. http://papers.klab.caltech.edu/22/1/148.pdf.

Crivellato, E. and Ribatti, D. 2007. "Soul, mind, brain: Greek philosophy and the birth of neurosciences." *Brain Research Bulletin,* 71, 327-336.

Culler, E., and Mettler, F.A. 1934. "Conditioned behavior in a decorticate dog." *Journal of Comparative Psychology,* 18(3), 291-303. http://psycnet.apa.org/record/1935-01728-001.

Damasio, A.R., 1994. *Descartes' Error. Emotion, Reason and the Human Brain.* Avon Books: New York.

Damasio, AR. 1996. "The Somatic marker hypothesis and the possible functions of the prefrontal cortex." *Phil. Trans. R. Soc. Lon. B,* 351: 1413-1420. http://www.iee.unibe.ch/unibe/philnat/biology/zoologie/content/e7493/e7854/e8920/e8926/DamasioPhilTransRSocB96.pdf.

Damasio, A.R., 1999. *The Feeling of What Happens: Body and Emotion in the Making of Consciousness.* Harcourt Brace: New York.

Damasio, A.R., 2003. *Looking for Spinoza: Joy, Sorrow and the Feeling Brain.* Harcourt: Orlando.

Damasio, A.R. 2004. "Emotions and Feelings: A Neurobiological Perspective." In *Feelings and Emotions: The Amsterdam Symposium.* (ASP. Manstead, N. Frijda & A. Fisher eds.). Cambridge UK: Cambridge University Press.

Damasio, A.R. 2005. "Feeling our Emotions." *Scientific American.* http://www.scientificamerican.com/article/feeling-our-emotions/?page=2.

Damasio, A.R. 2010. *Self comes to mind: Constructing the conscious brain.* New York: Pantheon Books.

Damaso, A.R. 2011. "The Neural Basis of Emotions." *Scholarpedia,* 6(3):1804. http://www.scholarpedia.org/article/Neural_basis_of_emotions.

Damasio, A.R. 2018. *The Strange Order of Things: Homeostasis, Feeling, and the Making of Cultures.* New York: Vintage Books.

Damasio, A.R 2020. "Feelings and Consciousness." https://www.youtube.com/watch?v=ilrelFkDYls&t=98s.

Damasio, A.R.; Everitt, B. J.; Bishop, D. 1996. "The Somatic marker hypothesis and the possible functions of the prefrontal cortex". Phil. Trans. R. Soc. Lond. B 351 (1346): 1413–20.

Damasio. A.R., Grabowski, T.J., Bechara, A., Damasio, H., Ponto, L.L.B., Parvizi, J. and Hichwa, R.D. 2000. "Subcortical and cortical brain activity during the feeling of self-generated emotions." *Nature Neuroscinence* 3:1049-1056. http://www.nature.com/neuro/journal/v3/n10/full/nn1000_1049.html.

Damasio, A.R and Hutsvedt, S. 2011. "A Neurological Basis for Free Will." https://www.youtube.com/watch?v=18tPNgru25s.

Damasio, A.R., Damasio, H., and Tranel, D. 2012. "Persistence of feeling and sentience after bilateral damage of the insula." *Cerebral Cortex.* 23 (4): 833–846. http://www.ncbi.nlm.nih.gov/pmc/articles/PMC3657385/.

Damasio, A.R. and Damasio, H.R. 2016. "Exploring the concept of homeostasis and considering its implications for economics."

Journal of Economic Behavior & Organization. Vol 126, Part B: 125-29. http://www.sciencedirect.com/science/article/pii/S016726811500325X.

Dana, J.N. and Whirledge, S. 2017. "Stress and the HPA Axis: Balancing Homeostasis and Fertility." *Int J. Mol. Sci.*, 18(10):2224. https://www.ncbi.nlm.nih.gov/pmc/articles/PMC5666903/.

Daniels, W.M., Pieetersen, C.Y., Carstens, M.E., and Stein, D.J. 2004. "Maternal separation in rats leads to anxiety-like behavior and a blunted ACTH response and altered neurotransmitter levels in response to a subsequent stressor." *Metab. Brain Dis.*, 19(1-2):3-14. https://www.ncbi.nlm.nih.gov/pubmed/15214501.

Dantzer, R., O'Connor, J.C., Freund, G.G., Johnson, R.W. and Kelley, K.W. 2008. "From inflammation to sickness and depression: when the immune system subjugates the brain." *Nature Reviews Neuroscience*, 6, 46-57. https://www.ncbi.nlm.nih.gov/pmc/articles/PMC2919277/.

Davidson, R.J., Putnam, K.M., and Larson, C.L. 2000. "Dysfunction in the neural circuitry of emotion regulation--a possible prelude to violence." *Science*, 289(547):591-4. https://pubmed.ncbi.nlm.nih.gov/10915615/.

Decety, J., Michalska, K., Kalina, J., Akitsuki,Y and Lahey, B.B. 2008. "Atypical empathic responses in adolescents with aggressive conduct disorder: A functional MRI investigation." *Biol. Psychol.* xxx-xxx: 1-9. https://pdfs.semanticscholar.org/a39f/7cfffb2242e4ed780d86eb7742cfc01ef727.pdf.

de Gelder, B., Vroomen, J., Pourtois, G., and Weiskrantz, L. 2000. "Affective blindsight: are we blindly led by emotions?Response to Heywood and Kentridge". *Trends in Cognitive Sciences*, 4: 126-127.

de Gelder, B., and Hadjikhani, N. 2006. "Non-conscious recognition of emotional body language." *Neuroreport*, 17: 583-586.

DeHaven, E. 2014. "5 Qualities of a Great Coach." https://www.youtube.com/watch?v=ZjqYGkNh5KA.

DeLeo, L. 2018. "Reasons to Laugh." *Ted Talks*. https://www.youtube.com/watch?v=Q7cz-yXkUgk.

Delgado, MR., Olsson, A., and Phelps, EA. 2006. "Extending animal models of fear conditioning to humans." *Biological Psychology* 73:39–48. http://citeseerx.ist.psu.edu/viewdoc/ download?doi=10.1.1.325.1043&rep=rep1&type=pdf.

Delgado, M.R., Beer, J.S., Fellows, L.K., Huettel, S.A., Platt, M.L., Quirk, G.J., and Schiller, D. 2016. "Viewpoints: Dialogues on the functional role of the ventromedial prefrontal cortex." *Nature Neuroscience, 19*(12), 1545–1552. https://psycnet. apa.org/record/2017-20202-001.

Dennen, J.M.G.V.D. 2005. "Theories of Aggression: Psychoanalytic theories of aggression." *Default journal.* https://www.rug.nl/ research/portal/files/2888993/a-panal.pdf.

Dennett, D. 2003a. "Explaining the 'Magic' of Consciousness." *Journal of Cultural and Evolutionary Psychology*, 1(1), pp. 7-19.

Dennett, D. (2003b). "The Illusion of Consciousness." *TED: ideas worth spreading.* https://www.ted.com/talks/dan_dennett_on_ our_consciousness.

Denny, B.T., Fan, J., Fels, S., Galitzer, H., Schiller, D., and Koenigsberg, H.W. 2018. "Sensitization of the Neural Salience Network to Repeated Emotional Stimuli Following Initial Habituation in Patients With Borderline Personality Disorder." *American Journal of Psychiatry.* https://ajp.psychiatryonline.org/ doi/10.1176/appi.ajp.2018.17030367y.

Depaulis, A. and Bandler, R. (eds.) 1991. *The midbrain periaqueductal gray matter: Functional anatomical and neurochemical organization.* New York: Plenum Press.

Derrow, C. 2019. "Why Taking Risks Can Be Good for Your Mental Health." *ENTREPRENEURSHIP LIFE.* https:// www.entrepreneurshiplife.com/why-taking-risks-can- be-good-for-your-mental-health/.

De Souza Santos, A.M., Ferraz, M.R., Teixeira, V.C., Sampaio, F.J., and da Fonte Ramos, C. 2004. "Effects of undernutrition on serum and testicular testosterone levels and sexual function in adult rats." *Horm. Metab. Res.* 36(1): 27-33. https://pubmed. ncbi.nlm.nih.gov/14983403/.

Dickerson, B. (2003). "A child's life shows folly of adults." *Detroit Free Press*. http://law.gsu.edu/ccunningham/PR/JessicaUpdates.htm.

Dieleman, GC., Huizink, AC., Tulenc, JHM., Utens, E.M.W.J., Creemers, H.E., van der Endea, J., and Verhulst, FC. 2015. "Alterations in HPA-axis and autonomic nervous system functioning in childhood anxiety disorders point to a chronic stress hypothesis." *Psychoneuroendocrinology*, 51:135-150.

Dimatelis, J.J., Stein, D.J., and Russell, V.A. 2012. "Behavioral changes after maternal separation are reversed by chronic constant light treatment." *Brain Res. https://pubmed.ncbi.nlm.nih.gov/22975437/*.

Dollard, J.C. and Miller, N.E., 1950. *Personality and Psychoptherapy.* New York: McGraw-Hill.

Donahue, C.J., Glasser, M.F., Preuss, T.M., Rilling, J.K. and Van Essen, D.C. 2018. Quantitative assessment of prefrontal cortex in humans relative to nonhuman primates." *PNAS,* 115 (22): 183-192. *https://www.pnas.org/content/115/22/E5183*.

Drolet, G., Dumont, E.C., Gosselin, I., Kinkead, R., Laforest, S., Trottier, J-F 2001. "Regulation of endogenous opioid system in the regulation of the stress response." *Progress in Neuro-Psychopharmacology and Biological Psychiatry*. Volume 25, Issue 4:729-41. https://www.sciencedirect.com/science/article/abs/pii/S0278584601001610#!

Dunn, B.D., Dalgleish, T., and Lawrence, A.D. 2006. "The somatic marker hypothesis: A critical evaluation." *Neuroscience and Biobehavioral Reviews*, 30, 239-271. http://cel.huji.ac.il/courses/structureandprocesses/Bibliography/Somatic_Marker_%20 2006.pdf.

Durrayappah-Harrison, A, 2010. "What Science Has to Say about Genuine vs. Fake Smiles." https://www.psychology-today.com/blog/thriving101/201001/what-science-has-say-about-genuine-vs-fake-smiles.

Duvarci, S., Popa, D., and Paré, D. 2011. "Central Amygdala Activity during Fear Conditioning." *J. Neurosci. 31(1):*289-294. https://www.ncbi.nlm.nih.gov/pmc/articles/PMC3080118.

Dyregrov, A. and Yule, W. 2006. "A Review of PTSD in Children." *Child and Adolescent Mental Health* Volume 11, No. 4:176-84.

Eagle, M. N. 1984. *Recent developments in psychoanalysis: A critical evaluation.* Harvard University Press.

Eagle, M. 2011. *From Classical To Contemporary Psychoanalysis.* New York: Routledge.

Ebert, R. 1977. "Star Wars." http://www.rogerebert.com/reviews/star-wars-1977.

Ekkekakis, P. 2013. The measurement of affect, mood, and emotion: A guide for health-behavioral research. Cambridge University Press. https://doi.org/10.1017/CBO9780511820724.

Ekman, P. 1992. "An argument for basic emotions." *Cognition and Emotion*, 6, 169-200. http://www.paulekman.com/wp-content/uploads/2013/07/An-Argument-For-Basic-Emotions.pdf.

Ekman, P. 2014. "Darwin's Claim of Universals in Facial Expression Not Challenged." *Paul Ekman Group.* https://www.paulekman.com/blog/darwins-claim-universals-facial-expression-challenged/.

Ekman, P. and Friesen, W.V. 1971. "Constants across cultures in the face and emotion." *Journal of Personality and Social Psychology.* 17: 124–129. http://psycnet.apa.org/buy/1971-07999-001.

Ekman, P., Friesen, W.V., O'Sullivan, M., Chan, A., Diacoyanni-Tarlatzis, I., Heider, K., Krause, R., LeCompte, W.A., Pitcairn, T., Ricci-Bitti, P.E., Scherer, K., Tomita, M., and Tzavaras, A. 1987. "Universals and cultural differences in the judgments of facial expressions of emotion." *Journal of Personality and Social Psychology,* 53(4), 712–717.

Elliott, R. 2003. "Executive functions and their disorders." *British Medical Bulletin,* (65); 49–59.

Engelhaupt, E. 2014. "Schadenfreude Starts Young." *ScienceNews.* https://www.sciencenews.org/blog/gory-details/schadenfreude-starts-young.

Etherington, L. (2020). "Melanie Klein and Object Relations Theory." *SimplyPsychology.* https://www.simplypsychology.org/Melanie-Klein.html.

Fairbairn, W.R.D. 1952. *An Object Relations Study of the Personality.* New York: Basic Books.

Feinstein, J.S., Buzza., Hurlemann, R., Follmer, R.L., Dahdaleh, NS., Coryell, W.H., Welsh, M.J. , Tranel, D. and Wemmie. J.A. 2013. "Fear and panic in humans with bilateral amygdala damage." *Nature Neuroscience* volume16:270–272. https://www.nature.com/articles/nn.3323.

Ferris, C.F., Cai, X., Qiao, J., Switzer, B., Baun, J., Morrison, T., Iriah, S., Madularu, D., Sinkevicius, KW and Kulkarni, P. 2019. "Life without a brain: Neuroradiological and behavioral evidence of neuroplasticity necessary to sustain brain function in the face of severe hydrocephalus." *Scientific Reports* 9,#16479. https://www.nature.com/articles/s41598-019-53042-3.

Festinger, L. 1957. *A Theory of Cognitive Dissonance.* California: Stanford University Press.

Finkbiner, A.C.F. III, Bregstein, N.J., and Snitzer, P.D. 1993. "MOTION OF CONCERNED ACADEMICS FOR LEAVE TO SUBMIT BRIEF AMICI CURIAE AND BRIEF AMICI CURIAE IN SUPPORT OF STAY APPLICATION OF PETITIONER JESSICA DeBOER." https://fieldcenteratpenn.org/wp-content/uploads/2013/05/Amicus-Brief-Jessica-DeBoer-.pdf.

Fivush, R., and Hamond, N.R. 1990. "Autobiographical memory across the preschool years: toward reconceptualizing childhood amnesia." In: R. Fivush & J.A. Hudson (Eds.), *Knowing and remembering in young children.* New York: Cambridge University Press. (pp. 223-248).

Fonagy, P. 2001. *Attachment Theory and Psychoanalysis.* New York: Other Press.

Formica, M.J. 2009. "Ego, Insecurity, and the Destructive Narcissist: The bully is always the weakest kid on the playground." *Psychology Today.* https://www.psychologytoday.com/us/blog/enlightened-living/200911/ego-insecurity-and-the-destructive-narcissist.

Fotopoulou, A. and Tsakiris, M. 2017. "Mentalizing homeostasis: The social origins of interoceptive inference." *Neuropsychoanalysis, Vol 19, issue 1. https://www.tandfonline.com/doi/full/10.1080/15294145.2017.1294031.*

Frank, S., Kullmann, S., and Veit, R. 2013. "Food related processes in the insular cortex." *Front Hum Neurosci.* 7: 499. http://www.ncbi.nlm.nih.gov/pmc/articles/PMC3750209/.

Frederici, A.D., Mueller, J.L., Sehm, B., and Ragert, P. 2013. "Language learning without control: the role of the PFC." *J. Cog. Neurosci.*, 25(5):814-21. https://pubmed.ncbi.nlm.nih.gov/23281779/.

Freeman, W.J., 2000. *How Brains Make Up Their Minds.* New York: Columbia University Press.

Freud, A. 1936. *The Ego and the Mechanisms of Defense.* New York: I.U.P.

Freud, S., 1900. *The Interpretation of Dreams.* Standard Edition 3&4. London: Hogarth Press, 1968.

Freud, S., 1905. *Three essays on the theory of sexuality.* Standard Edition 7. London: Hogarth Press, 1968.

Freud, S. 1926. *Inhibitions, Symptoms and Anxiety.* Standard Edition 20.

Freud, S., 1933. *New Introductory Lectures on Psychoanalysis.* Standard Edition 23: 144-207.

Friedkin, N. 2015. "The Problem of Social Control and Coordination of Complex Systems in Sociology." *IEEE CONTROL SYSTEMS MAGAZINE.*

Gandhi, N.J and Katnani, H.A. 2011. "Motor Functions of the Superior Colliculus." *Annu Rev Neurosci.*, 34:205-231. https://www.ncbi.nlm.nih.gov/pmc/articles/PMC3641825/#!po=1.31579.

Garde, M. and Cowey, A. 2000. "Deaf Hearing: Unacknowledged Detection of Auditory Stimuli in a Patient with Cerebral Deafness." *Cortex* 36 (1): 71–79.

Garrison, F.H. 1966. *History of Medicine.* Philadelphia: W.B. Saunders Company.

Gazzaniga, M.S., 1995 "Consciousness and the Cerebral Hemispheres." In Gazzaniga, Michael S. (editor-in-Chief). *The Cognitive Neurosciences Cambridge.* Mass:The MIT Press. 1391-1400.

Gazzaniga, M.S. 2000. "Cerebral specialization and interhemispheric communication: does the corpus callosum enable the human condition?" *Brain.* 123, 1293-326. http://brain.oxfordjournals. org/content/123/7/1293.

Gazzaniga, M.S. 2009. Gifford Lecture 3. *The Interpreter.* https://www.youtube.com/results?search_query=michael+gazzaniga+the+interpreter+gifford+lecture.

Gazzaniga, M.S. 2012. *Who's In Charge.* London: Constable & Robinson Ltd.

Gelso, C.J., and Kanninen, K.M. 2017. "Neutrality revisited: On the value of being neutral within an empathic atmosphere." Journal of Psychotherapy Integration, 27(3), 330–341. https://doi. org/10.1037/int0000072.

Gendron, M., Robertson, D., van der Vyer, J.M., Barrett, L.F. 2014. "Perceptions of Emotion from Facial Expressions are Not Culturally Universal: Evidence from a Remote Culture." *Emotion,* 14(2):251-262. https://www.ncbi.nlm.nih.gov/pmc/ articles/PMC4752367/.

Gendron, M., Crivelli, C. and Barrett, L.F. 2018. "Universality Reconsidered: Diversity in Making Meaning of Facial Expressions." *ASSOCIATION FOR PSYCHOLOGICAL SCIENCE, Vol. 27(4):* 211–219. https://journals.sagepub.com/ doi/pdf/10.1177/0963721417746794.

Ghashghaei, H.T, Hilgetag, C.C, and Barbas, H. 2007. "Sequence of information processing for emotions based on the anatomic dialogue between prefrontal cortex and amygdala." *Neuroimage,* 34(3):905-923. https://www.ncbi.nlm.nih.gov/pmc/articles/ PMC2045074/.

Gibson E.J. and Walk R.D. "The 'visual cliff'" *Scientific American.* 1960;202:64–71.

Gill, N.S. 2019. "Hippocratic Method and the Four Humors." *ThoughtCo.* https://www.thoughtco.com/four-humors-112072.

Gillaspy, R. 2015. Animal Behavior: Innate vs. Learned:" *Chapter 19/Lesson 3. Life Science: Middle School/ Science Courses.* http://study.com/academy/lesson/animal-behavior-innate-vs-learned. html.

Gillispie, C.C. 1997. *Pierre-Simon Laplace 1749-1827: A Life in Exact Science.* New Jersey: Princeton University Press.

Gizowski, C., Bourque, C. 2017. "The neural basis of homeostatic and anticipatory thirst." *Nat Rev Nephrol* 14, 11–25. https://www.nature.com/articles/nrneph.2017.149.

Gjerstad, J.K., Lightman, S.L, and Spiga, F. 2015. "Role of glucocorticoid negative feedback in the regulation of HPA axis pulsatility." *Stress*, 21(5):403-416. https://www.ncbi.nlm.nih.gov/pmc/articles/PMC6220752/.

Glassman, N.S., and Anderson, S.M. 1999. "Transference in Social Cognition: Persistence and Exacerbation of Significant-Other-Based Inferences over Time." *Cognitive Therapy and Research* vol 23:75-91. https://link.springer.com/article/10.1023/A:1018762724798.

Glassman, R.B. 1987. "An hypothesis about redundancy and reliability in the brains of higher species: analogies with genes, internal organs, and engineering systems." *Neurosci. Biobehav. Rev.*, 11(3):275-85. https://www.ncbi.nlm.nih.gov/pubmed/3684057.

Gleitman, H., Fridlund, A., Reisberg, D. 2007. *Psychology* (7 ed.). New York: W. W. Norton & Company.

Glita, P. 2010. "Usefulness of the concepts of deficit and defect in the psychotherapeutic process". *Archives of Psychiatry and Psychotherapy*, 2:51–59. http://www.archivespp.pl/uploads/images/2010_12_2/GlitaAPP2010i2p51.pdf.

Goel, V. and Dolan, R.J. 2003. "Reciprocal neural response within lateral and ventral medial prefrontal cortex during hot and cold reasoning." *Neuroimage*, 20: 4, 2314-232. 1http://www.nature.com/nature/journal/v322/n6078/abs/322419a0.html.

Golland, Y., Bentin, S., Gelbard, H., Benjamini, Y., Heller, R., Nir, Y., Hasson, U., and Malach, R. 2007. "Extrinsic and Intrinsic Systems in the Posterior Cortex of the Human Brain Revealed during Natural Sensory Stimulation." Cerebral Cortex, Volume 17, Issue 4, April 2007, Pages 766–777, https://doi.org/10.1093/cercor/bhk030.

Goosens, K.A. and Maren, S. 2001. "Contextual and Auditory Fear Conditioning are Mediated by the Lateral, Basal, and Central

Amygdaloid Nuclei in Rats." Learn Mem. 8(3): 148–155. https://www.ncbi.nlm.nih.gov/pmc/articles/PMC311374/.

Goosens, K.A., Hobin, J.A., Maren, S. 2003. "Auditory-evoked spike firing in the lateral amygdala and Pavlovian fear conditioning: mnemonic code or fear bias?" *Neuron.* 40(5):1013-22. http://www.ncbi.nlm.nih.gov/pubmed/14659099.

Gopnik, A. 2010. "How Weird Is Consciousness?" *Books:Reading Between the Lines.* http://www.slate.com/articles/arts/books/2010/11/how_weird_is_consciousness.htmls.

Gosselin, N., Peretz, I. Johnsen, E. and Adolphs, R. 2007. "Amygdala damage impairs emotion recognition from music." *Neuropsychologia,* 28(45):236-44. https://www.ncbi.nlm.nih.gov/pubmed/16970965/.

Gottfredson, L.S. 1997. "Mainstream science on intelligence: An editorial with 52 signatories, history and bibliography." *Intelligence,* 24(1), 13–23.

Gottlieb, J. and Oudeyer, P-Y. 2018. "Towards a neuroscience of active sampling and curiosity." *Nat. Rev. Neurosci., 12:*p 758-770. https://pubmed.ncbi.nlm.nih.gov/30397322/.

Graeff, F.G. 2004. "Serotonin, the periaqueductal gray and panic." *Neuroscience & Biobehavioral Reviews,* 28, 239-59.

Greene, B. 2020. *Until the end of Time.* New York: Alfred A Knope.

Greenfield, S.A. 2000. *The private life of the brain.* Pergamon Press.

Greenspan, R.J. and Baars, B.J. 2005. "Consciousness eclipsed: Jacques Loeb, Ivan P. Pavlov, and the rise of reductionsistic biology after 1900." *Consciousness and Cognition,* 14: 219-230.

Gross-Isseroff, R., Biegon, A., voet, H., and Wezman, A. 1998. "The suicide brain: a review of postmortem receptor/transporter binding studies." *Neuroscience & Biobehavioral Reviews,* 22, 653-661.

Grossman, K.E. 1995. "The Evolution and History of Attachment Research and Theory." In *Attachment Theory: Social, Developmental and Clinical Perspectives.* Susal Goldberg, Roy Muir & John Kerr (eds.). Hillsdale NJ: The analytic Press Inc.

Guyton, A.C. and Hall, J.E. 2006. *Textbook of Medical Physiology.* Philadelphia PA: Saunders Elsevier.

Haidt, J. and Keltner, D. 1999. "Culture and Facial Expression: Open-ended Methods Find More Expressions and a Gradient of Recognition." *Cognition and Emotion, 13(3):*225-266. http://citeseerx.ist.psu.edu/viewdoc/download?doi=10.1.1.477.5237&rep=rep1&type=pdf.

Hamann, S.B., Ely, T.D., Hoffman, J.M., and Kilts, C.D. 2002. "Ecstasy and Agony: Activation of the Human Amygdala in Positive and Negative Emotion." *Psychological Science.* https://journals.sagepub.com/doi/abs/10.1111/1467-9280.00425.

Harlow, H.F. 1958. "The nature of love." *Am Psychol.* 13:673-685.

Harro, J., and Oreland, L. 2001. "Depression as a spreading adjustment disorder of monoamin- ergic neurons: A case for primary implications of the locus coeruleus." *Brain Research Reviews,* 38, 79-128.

Hartmann, H., Kris, E., and Loewenstein, R. 1949. "Notes on the Theory of Aggression." *Psychoanalytic Study of the Child* 3:9- 34.

Hartney, E. 2020. "An Overview of Methamphetamine (Meth) Withdrawal." *verywellmind.* https://www.verywellmind.com/what-to-expect-from-meth-withdrawal-22358.

Harvard Medical School 2020. "Understanding the stress response." *Harvard Health Publishing.* https://www.health.harvard.edu/staying-healthy/understanding-the-stress-response.

Heath, R. G. 1975. "Brain function and behavior: I. Emotion and sensory phenomena in psychotic patients and in experimental animals." *Journal of Nervous and Mental Disease* 160:159–75.

Herry, C, Bach, D.R., Esposito, F., Di Salle, F., Perrig, W.J., Scheffler. K., Lüthi, A., and Seifritz, E. 2007. "Processing of temporal unpredictability in human and animal amygdala." *J. Neurosci.,* 27(22):5958-66. https://www.ncbi.nlm.nih.gov/pubmed/17537966.

Holstege, G.R., Bandler, R., and Saper, C. B. 1996. "The emotional motor system." In G. Holstege, R. Bandler, and C.B. Saper (Eds.), *Progress in brain research*: Vol 170. (pp. 3-6). Amsterdam: Elsevier.

Hoopes, L. 2008. "Gene Expression and Regulation." *Scitable*. https://www.nature.com/scitable/topic/gene-expression-and-regulation-15/

Horgan, J. 2015. "Can Integrated Information Theory Explain Consciousness?" *SCIENTIFIC AMERICAN*. https://blogs.scientificamerican.com/cross-check/can-integrated-information-theory-explain-consciousness/.

Hountondji, P.J. 1996. *African Philosophy, Myth and Reality: Second Edition*. Bloomington, IN : Indiana University Press.

Howard, K., Martin, A., Berlin, LJ., and Brooks-Gunn, J. 2011. "Early Mother-Child Separation, Parenting, and Child Well-Being in Early Head Start Families." *Attach Hum Dev.*, 13(1):5-26. https://www.ncbi.nlm.nih.gov/pmc/articles/PMC3115616/.

Hughes, J.R. 1958. "Post-tetanic Potentiation".*Physiological Reviews* 38 (1): 91–113.

Ikemoto, S., 2010. "Brain reward circuitry beyond the mesolimbic dopamine system: A neurobiological theory." *Neuroscience & Biobehavioral Reviews*, 35, 129-150.

Inglis-Arkell, E., 2013. "Why do we smile and laugh when we're terrified?" *GIZMODO*. https://io9.gizmodo.com/why-do-we-smile-and-laugh-when-were-terrified-1441046376.

Ingrassia, M. and Springen, K. 1994. "She's Not Baby Jessica Anymore." *Newsweek*. Vol. CXXIII, No. 12, p 60-66.

Jaffe, E. 2010. "The Psychological Study of Smiling." *Association for Psychological Science*. https://www.psychologicalscience.org/observer/the-psychological-study-of-smiling.

Jamero, D., Borghol, A., Vo, N., and Hawawini, F. 2011. "The Emerging Role of NMDA Antagonists in Pain Management." *US Pharmacist*. http://www.medscape.com/viewarticle/744071.

James, W., (1884). "What is an Emotion?" In M. Arnold, ed., *The Nature of Emotion*. Baltimore: Penguin 1968.

Jenck, F., Moreau, J-L, and Martin, JR. 1995. "Dorsal periaqueductal gray-induced aversion as a simulation of panic anxiety: Elements of face and predictive validity." *Psychiatry Research*, Volume 57, Issue 2: 181-191. http://www.psy-journal.com/article/0165-1781(95)02673-K/abstract.

Jenkins, Stephen. 1997. "The Many Body Problem and Density Functional Theory." http://newton.ex.ac.uk/research/qsystems/people/jenkins/mbody/mbody3.htm.

Johansen, J.P., Cain, C.K., Ostroff, L.E and LeDoux, J.E. 2011. "MOLECULAR MECHANISMS OF FEAR LEARNING AND MEMORY." *Cell, 147(3):509-524. https://www.ncbi.nlm.nih.gov/pmc/articles/PMC3215943/.*

Jordão, EMA., Onishi, BKA., and Xavier, GF. 2015. "Pre-Training Reversible Inactivation of the Basal Amygdala (BA) Disrupts Contextual, but Not Auditory, Fear Conditioning, in Rats." *PLOSONE.* https://journals.plos.org/plosone/article/related?id=10.1371/journal.pone.0125489.

Khan Academy 2013. "Emotions: limbic system." https://www.youtube.com/watch?v=GDlDirzOSI8.

Kalamara. M., Spacapan, M., Mandic-Mulec, I., and Stanley-Wall, NR. 2018. "Social behaviours by Bacillus subtilis: quorum sensing, kin discrimination and beyond." *Mol. Microbiol.,* 110(6):863-878. https://www.ncbi.nlm.nih.gov/pmc/articles/PMC6334282/.

Kalin, N.H., Shelton, S.E and Davidson, J. 2004. "The Role of the Central Nucleus of the Amygdala in Mediating Fear and Anxiety in the Primate." *Journal of Neuroscience,* 24 (24) 5506-5515. https://centerhealthyminds.org/assets/files-publications/KalinRoleNeuroscience.pdf.

Kaluzeviciute, G 2020. "The role of empathy in psychoanalytic psychotherapy: A historical exploration." *CLINICAL PSYCHOLOGY & NEUROPSYCHOLOGY | REVIEW ARTICLE.* https://www.tandfonline.com/doi/full/10.1080/23311908.2020.1748792.

Kandel, E. 2006. *In Search of Memory - The Emergence of a New Science of Mind.* WW Norton & Company, New York.

Katsouni, E., Sakkas, P., Zarros, A., Skandali, N., and Liapi, C. 2009. "The Involvement of Substance P in the Induction of Aggressive Behavior." *PubMed* https://pubmed.ncbi.nlm.nih.gov/19442694/.

Kawkabani, S. 2018. "Preserved Consciousness in the Absence of a Cerebral Cortex, the Legal and Ethical Implications of Redefining Consciousness and Its Neural Correlates: A Case for a Subcortical System Generating Affective Consciousness." The University of Akron. https://ideaexchange.uakron.edu/honors_research_projects/734/.

Keesey, R.E. and Powley, T.L. 2008. "Body energy homeostasis." *Appetite 51(3):*442-5. https://pubmed.ncbi.nlm.nih.gov/18647629/.

Keifer, O.P. Jr.., Hurt, R.C., Ressler, K.J., and Marvar, P.J. 2015. "The Physiology of Fear: Reconceptualizing the Role of the Central Amygdala in Fear Learning." *PHYSIOLOGY* 30: 389 – 401. http://www.resslerlab.com/uploads/7/4/9/1/74915911/keifer_marvar_2015_physiology.pdf.

Kelly, A. and Berridge, K.C. 2002. "The Neuroscience of Natural Rewards: Relevance to Addictive Drugs." *Journal of Neuroscience,* 22(9):3306-3311). https://www.jneurosci.org/content/22/9/3306.

Kelly, F.C. 1989. The Wright Brothers: A Biography. New York:Dover Publications.

Keltner D., Horberg E.J., Oveis C. 2006. "Emotional intuitions and moral play." *Soc. Justice Res.* 19: 208–217.

Kennedy, S.E., Koeppe, R.A., Young, E.A. and Zubieta, J.K. 2006. "Dysregulation of endogenous opioid emotion regulation circuitry in major depression in women." *Archives of General Psychiatry.* 63. 1199-1208.

Kernberg, O.F. 2016. "The four basic components of psychoanalytic technique and derived psychoanalytic psychotherapies." *World Psychiatry.* https://www.ncbi.nlm.nih.gov/pmc/articles/PMC5032492/.

Killingmo, B. 1985. "Problems in contemporary psychoanalytic theory: 1. Controversial issues." *Scandinavian J of Psychology*, vol 26, issue 1. https://onlinelibrary.wiley.com/doi/abs/10.1111/j.1467-9450.1985.tb01141.x.

Killingmo, B. 1989. "Conflict and deficit: implications for technique" *Int J Psychoanal.* 70 (Pt 1):65-79 https://pubmed.ncbi.nlm.nih.gov/2737831/.

Kim, E.J., Kin, E.S, Covey, E., and Kim, J.J. 2010. "The Role of 22-kHz Ultrasonic Distress Vocalization." *PLoS One*, 5(12):e15077. https://www.ncbi.nlm.nih.gov/pmc/articles/PMC2995742/.

Kim, EJ., Horovitz, O., Pellman, BA., Tan, LM., Li, Q., Richter-Levin, G., & Kin, JJ. (2013). Dorsal periaqueductal gray-amygdala pathway conveys both innate and learned fear responses in rats. *Proc, Natl. Adad. Sci. USA., 110(36)*:14795-800. https://www.ncbi.nlm.nih.gov/pubmed/23959880.

Kim, J., Pignatelli, M., Sangyu, X., Shigeyoshi, I., and Tonegawa, S. 2016. "Antagonistic negative and positive neurons of the basolateral amygdala." *Nature Neuroscience.* https://tonegawalab.mit.edu/research/publications/.

Kim, J., Zhang, X., Muralidhar, S., LeBlanc, SA. & Tonegawa, S. 2017. "Basolateral to Central Amygdala Neural Circuits for Appetitive Behaviors." Neuron. https://www.cell.com/neuron/fulltext/S0896-6273(17)30142-3.

Klein D.F. 1964. "Delineation of two drug-responsive anxiety syndromes." *Psychopharmacologia*, 5:397-408.

Kluver, H., and Bucy, P.C., (1939). "Preliminary analysis of the functions of the temporal lobes in monkeys." *Arch. Neuro. Psychiatry*, 42, 979-1000.

Koch, C. 2009. "A 'Complex' Theory of Consciousness: Is complexity the secret to sentience, to a panpsychic view of consciousness?" *Scientific American Mind.* http://www.scientificamerican.com/article.cfm?id=a-theory-of-consciousness.

Koch C. 2012a. "The Nature of Consciousness: How the Internet Could Learn to Feel." Inerview by Steve Paulson. *The Atlantic.* https://www.theatlantic.com/health/archive/2012/08/the-nature-of-consciousness-how-the-internet-could-learn-to-feel/261397/.

Koch, C., PhD. 2012b. "Interview with Author of Consciousness: Confessions of a Romantic Reductionist." *Brain Science Podcast* (Ginger Campbell MD, interviewer). Episode #84 http://www.brainsciencepodcast.com/bsp/update-on-consciousness-research-with-christof-koch-bsp-84.html.

Koch, C. 2014. "Ubiquitous Minds." *Scientific American Mind.* http://www.klab.caltech.edu/koch/CR/CR-Panpsychism-14.pdf.

Koh, N.B. and Wong, J.S. 2015. "Survival of the Fittest and the Sexiest: Evolutionary Origins of Adolescent Bullying." *Journal of Interpersonal Violence.* https://journals.sagepub.com/doi/abs/10.1177/0886260515593546.

Kohler-Dauner, F., Roder, E., Krausr, S., Buchheim, A., Gundel, H., Fegert, J. M., Ziegeenhain, U., and Waller, C. 2019. "Reduced caregiving quality measured during the strange situation procedure increases child's autonomic nervous system stress response." *Child Adolesc. Psychiatry Ment. Health.* 13:41 https://pubmed.ncbi.nlm.nih.gov/31695745/.

Kohut, H. (1971) The Analysis of the Self. New York:Int. Univ. Press.

Kolb, B., and Wishaw, I. Q. 2009. *Fundamentals of Human Neuropsychology: Sixth Edition.* New York: Worth Publishers.

Kosten, T.R., and George, T.P. 2002. "The Neurobiology of Opioid Dependence: Implications for Treatment." *Sci Pract Perspect.,* 1(1): 13–20. http://www.ncbi.nlm.nih.gov/pmc/articles/PMC2851054/.

Koutsikou, S., Watson, T.C., Crook, J.J., Leith J.L., Lawrenson,C., Apps, L. and Lumb, B. 2015. "The Periaqueductal Gray Orchestrates Sensory and Motor Circuits at Multiple Levels of the Neuraxis." *J. Neurosci.* 35(42):14132–14147.

Kringelbach, M. L. 2010. "The Neuroscience of Happiness and Pleasure." *Soc Res* (New York), 77(2): 659–678. https://www.ncbi.nlm.nih.gov/pmc/articles/PMC3008658.

Kringelbach, M. L., and Berridge, K. 2009. "Towards a functional neuroanatomy of pleasure and happiness." *Trends Cogn Sci.,* 13(11):479–487. http://www.ncbi.nlm.nih.gov/pmc/articles/PMC2767390/.

Kringelbach, M. L., O'Doherty, J., Rolls, E. T., and Andrews, C. 2003. "Activation of the human orbitofrontal cortex to a liquid food stimulus in correlated with its subjective pleasantness." *Cereb. Cortex* 13: 1064–1071.

Kupers, RC., Gybels, JM., and Gjedde, A. 2000. Positron emission tomography study of a chronic pain patient successfully treated with somatosensory thalamic stimulation. *Pain*, 87(3): 295-302. http://www.ncbi.nlm.nih.gov/pubmed/10963909/.

Lambert, M. 2007. "What we have learned from a decade of research aimed at improving psychotherapy outcome in routine care." *Psychotherapy Research*, 17, 1–14. https://www.researchgate.net/publication/254439590_Presidential_Address_What_we_have_learned_from_a_decade_of_research_aimed_at_improving_psychotherapy_outcome_in_routine_care.

Lamm, C. and Singer, T. 2010. "The Role of the Anterior Insula in Social Emotions." *Brain Struct. Funct.*, 214:579-591. http://www.researchgate.net/profile/Claus_Lamm/publication/43352852_The_role_of_anterior_insular_cortex_in_social_emotions/links/54be2bb20cf218da9391da2c.pdf.

Land, B.B., Bruchas, M.R., Melief, E., Xu, M., Lemos, J. and Chavkin, C. 2008. 'The dysphoric component of stress is encoded by activation of the dynorphine-kappa opioid system." *Journal of Neuroscience*, 28, 407-414.

Landa, A. PhD, Peterson, B.S., MD, and Fallon. B.A. MPH. (2012). "Somatoform Pain: A Developmental Theory and Translational Research Review." *Psychosomatic Medicine* 74: 717-727.

Lange, C., (1885). *Om Sindsbevaegelser et Psyco. Studie*. Copenhagen: Kronar.

Lashley, KS. (1923). "The Behavioristic Interpretation of Consciousness I." *The Psychological Review*, vol.30, no. 4:237-272. https://pure.mpg.de/rest/items/item_2352616/component/file_2352615/content.

Lawrence, N. 1993. "The Untold Story Of Baby Jessica's Heartache." *Midwest Today*. http://www.midtod.com/bestof/babyjess.phtml.

Lebow, MA., and Chen, A. 2016. "Overshadowed by the amygdala: the bed nucleus of the stria terminalis emerges as key to psychiatric disorders." *Molecular Psychiatry*, volume21: pages 450–463. https://www.nature.com/articles/mp20161.

LeDoux, J.E, 1996. *The Emotional Brain: The Mysterious Underpinnings of Emotional Life*. New York: Simon and Schuster.

LeDoux, J.E. 1999. "Psychoanalytic theory: Clues from the brain." *Neuropsychoanalyis*, 1: 44–49.

LeDoux, J.E. 2000. "Emotion circuits in the brain." *Annual Review of Neuroscience*, 23, 155-184. http://www.cns.nyu.edu/ledoux/pdf/155.pdf.

LeDoux, J.E., 2002. *The Synaptic Self: How Our Brains Become Who We Are.* New York: Penguin Books.

LeDoux, J.E. 2008. "Amygdala". *Scholarpedia* 3(4):2698 http://www.scholarpedia.org/article/Amygdala.

LeDoux, J.E. 2011. "Our Emotional Brains" *(2011 Copernicus Centre Lecture)* https://www.youtube.com/results?search_query=joseph+ledoux+memory.

LeDoux, J.E. 2014. "Coming to terms with fear." *PNAS. 111(8):*2871-2878. https://www.pnas.org/content/111/8/2871.

LeDoux, J.E. 2015. "Feelings: What Are They & How Does the Brain Make Them?" *American Academy of Arts & Sciences* https://www.cns.nyu.edu/ledoux/pdf/daed_LeDoux_2015.pdf.

LeDoux, J.E. 2016. The Amygdala: Beyond fear. *Neuroscientifically Challenged.* https://www.neuroscientificallychallenged.com/blog/amygdala-beyond-fear.

Lee, A.C.H., Yeung, L.K., and Barense, M.D. 2012. "The Hippocampus and visual perception." *Frontiers in Human Neuroscience*, 6: 91. https://www.ncbi.nlm.nih.gov/pmc/articles/PMC3328126/.

Lee, J., Lakha, S.F., Mailis, A. 2015". Efficacy of Low-Dose Oral Liquid Morphine for Elderly Patients with Chronic Non-Cancer Pain: Retrospective Chart Review." *Drugs Real World Outcomes*, 2(4):369-376. https://www.ncbi.nlm.nih.gov/pmc/articles/PMC4674530/.

Lee, J. and Zhang, L. 2015. "The hierarchy quorum sensing network in Pseudomonas aeruginosa." *Protein Cell*, 6(1):26-41. https://www.ncbi.nlm.nih.gov/pmc/articles/PMC4286720/.

Leknes, S. and Tracey, I. 2008. "A common neurobiology for pain and pleasure." *Perspectives, volume 9:*314-20. https://demystifyingmedicine.od.nih.gov/dm18/m04d17/reading01.pdf.

Lenzen, M. 2005. "Feeling our Emotions." *Mind Brain* http://www.scientificamerican.com/article.cfm?id=feeling-our-emotions.

Leonard, B.E. 2010. "The concept of depression as a dysfunction of the immune system." *Curr. Immunol. Rev.* 6(3): 205–212. https://www.ncbi.nlm.nih.gov/pmc/articles/PMC3002174/.

Lewis, M.B. and Bowler, P.J. 2009. "Botulinum toxin cosmetic therapy correlates with a more positive mood." *Journal of Cosmetic Dermatology* 8 (1) , pp. 24-26. http://orca.cf.ac.uk/30821/.

Li, Y-H and Tian, X. 2012. "Quorum Sensing and Bacterial Social Interactions in Biofilms." *Sensors.* https://www.ncbi.nlm.nih.gov/pmc/articles/PMC3376616/.

Libet, B., Wright, E.W., Jr., Feinstein, B. and Pearl, D.K. (1979) 'Subjective referral of the timing for a conscious sensory experience: A functional role for the somatosensory specific projection system in man." *Brain* 102:193–224.

Liotti, M. and Panksepp, J. 2004. "Imaging human emotions and affective feelings: Implications for biological psychiatry." In J. Panksepp (Ed.), *Textbook of Biological Psychiatry*, (pp. 33-74). Hoboken, NJ: Wiley.

Little, D. 2012. "Emergence. Understanding Society." https://understandingsociety.blogspot.com/2012/01/emergence.html.

Lloyd 2019 "What is information." https://www.youtube.com/watch?v=u8VdPW8tCWY.

Lodato S., and Arlotta P. 2015. "Generating neuronal diversity in the mammalian cerebral cortex." *Annual Review of Cell and Developmental Biology.* 31 (1): 699–720.

Lodge, G., Walsh, J.A. and Kramer, M. 2003. "A TRILINEAR THREE-BODY PROBLEM." *International Journal of Bifurcation and Chaos,* Vol. 13, No. 8: 2141-2155 http://math.bu.edu/people/mak/three_body_trilinear.pdf.

Lopez-Duran, N.L., McGinnis, E., Kuhlman, K., Geiss, E., Vargas, I. and Mayer, S. 2015. "HPA-axis stress reactivity in youth depression: evidence of impaired regulatory processes in depressed boys." *Stress,* 18(5):545-553. https://www.ncbi.nlm.nih.gov/pmc/articles/PMC5403248/.

Lorberbaum, J.P., Newman, J.D., Horwitz, A.R., Dubno, J.R., Lydiard, R.B., Hamner, M.B., Bohning, D.E., and George, M.S. 2002. "A potential role for thalamocingulate circuitry in human maternal behavior." *Biological Psychiatry*, 51, 431-45.

Lorenz, K. 1935. "Der Kumpan in der Umwelt des Vogels." *J. Ornithologie*, 83, 137-213.

Loria, A.S., Brands, M.W., Pollack, D.M., and Pollack J.S. 2013. "Early life stress sensitimezes the renal and systemic sympathetic system in rats." *Arican Journal of Physiology*. https://journals.physiology.org/doi/full/10.1152/ajprenal.00008.2013.

Lui, J.H., Hansen, D.V., and Kriegstein, A.R. 2011. "Development and evolution of the human neocortex." *Cell*, 145(1):18-36. https://www.ncbi.nlm.nih.gov/pubmed/21729779.

Maken, D.S., Weinberg, J., Cool, D.R., and Hennessy, M.B., 2016. "An Investigation of the Effects of Maternal Separation and Novelty on Central Mechanisms Mediating Pituitary-Adrenal Activity in Infant Guinea Pigs (Cavia porcellus)." *Behav Neurosci.*, 124(6):800-809.https://www.ncbi.nlm.nih.gov/pmc/articles/PMC4833454/#!po=69.4030.

Marcus, G. 2013. "How Much Consciousness Does an iPhone Have?" *The New Yorker*.

Maren, S. 2001. "NEUROBIOLOGY OF PAVLOVIAN FEAR CONDITIONING." *Annu. Rev. Neurosci.*, 24:897–931 http://deepblue.lib.umich.edu/bitstream/handle/2027.42/61939/marenARN01.pdf?sequence=1.

Matsumoto, D., and Willingham, B. 2009. "Spontaneous facial expressions of emotion of congenitally and non-congenitally blind individuals." *Journal of Personality and Social Psychology*, 96(1), 1-10.

Matsumoto, D. and Hwang, H.S. 2011. "Reading facial expressions of emotions." *American Psychological Association*. http://www.apa.org/science/about/psa/2011/05/facial-expressions.aspx.

Maynz, M. 2019. "Why Birds Form Flocks: How Flocks Help (and sometimes hurt) Birds." *The Spruce*.

Mayr, E. 1988. *Toward A New Philosophy of Biology: Observations of an Evolutionist*. USA: Library of Congress.

McClurem. M. 2011. "Stanford psychologists find that jokes help us cope with horrifying images." *Stanford News*. https://news.stanford.edu/news/2011/august/humor-coping-horror-080111.html.

McCormick W.C and Schreiner, R.L. 2001. "Diagnosis and treatment of opiate-resistant pain in advanced AIDS." *West J Med.* 175(6): 408–411. http://www.ncbi.nlm.nih.gov/pmc/articles/PMC1275976/.

McEwen, B.S. and Sapolsky, R.M. 1995. "Stress and Cognitive Function." *Curr. Opin. Neurobiol.,* 5:205-16.

McGinn, C. 1989. "Can we solve the mind-body problem?" *Mind* 98:349-66.

McLean, J. 2007. "Psychotherapy with a Narcissistic Patient Using Kohut's Self Psychology Model." *Psychiatry,* 4(10):40-47. https://www.ncbi.nlm.nih.gov/pmc/articles/PMC2860525/.

McLeod, S. 2017. "Behaviorist Approach." *Simply Psychology.* https://www.simplypsychology.org/behaviorism.html.

McNaughton, B.L., Barnes, C.A., Gerrard, J.L., Gothard, K., Jung, M.W., Knierim, J.J., Kurimoti, H., Qin, Y., Skaggs, W.E., Suster, M., and Weaver, K.L. (1996). "DECIPHERING THE HIPPOCAMPAL POLYGLOT: THE HIPPOCAMPUS AS A PATH INTEGRATION SYSTEM." *The Journal of Experimental Biology* 199:173–185. http://citeseerx.ist.psu.edu/viewdoc/download?doi=10.1.1.130.4332&rep=rep1&type=pdf.

Melzack, R. and Casey, K.L. 1968. "Sensory, Motivational and Central Control of Determinants of Pain." In *The Skin Senses*: Procedings of the First International Symposium on the Skin Senses Held at The Florida State University at Tallahassee, Florida. (Dan R. Shalo PhD. Ed.). Charles C. Thomas:Springfield Ill. Chapter 20, p423-439.

Merker, B. 1997. The common denominator of conscious states: Implications for the biology of consciousness. Cogprints Electronic Archive: Biology; Theoretical biology. [Archives preprint.] Available at: (http://cogprints.soton.ac.uk).

Merker, B. 2004 "The local and the global in cortical phylogeny and function. Reply to Finlay and Lamme." *Cortex* 40:582–83.

Merker, B. 2007. "Consciousness without a cerebral cortex: A challenge for neuroscience and medicine." *Behavioural and Brain Sciences* 30, 63-134. http://www.willamette.edu/~levenick/cs448/Merker.pdf.

Mesulam, M-M. MD and Geula. C. PhD., 1988". "Acetylcholinesterase-rich pyramidal neurons in the human neocortex and hippocampus: Absence at birth, development during the life span, and dissolution in Alzheimer's disease." *Annals of Neurology*. Volume 24, Issue 6: 765–773.

Milad, M.R., Rauch, S.L., Pitman, R.K., and Quirk, G.J. 2006. "Fear extinction in rats: Implications for human brain imaging and anxiety disorders." *Biological* Psychology 73:61–71. http://www.md.rcm.upr.edu/wp-content/uploads/sites/52/2016/07/Milad-et-al.-2006.pdf.

Milad, M.R. and Quirk, G.J. 2016. "Fear Extinction as a Model for Translational Neuroscience: Ten Years of Progress." *Annu Rev Psychol*. 2012; 63: 129–151. https://www.ncbi.nlm.nih.gov/pmc/articles/PMC4942586/.

Miles, O. and Maren, S. 2019. "Role of the Bed Nucleus of the Stria Terminalis in PTSD: Insights From Preclinical Models." *Front. Behav. Neurosci. https://www.frontiersin.org/articles/10.3389/fnbeh.2019.00068/full.*

Miller, A.H., Maletic, V. and Raison, C.L. 2009. "Inflammation and its discontents: The role of cytokines in the pathophysiology of major depression." *Biological Psychiatry*, 65, 732-741.

Miller, E.K, Freedman, D.J. and Wallis, J.D. 2002. "The prefrontal cortex: categories, concepts and cognition." *Philos Trans R Soc Lond B Biol Sci.*,357(1424): 1123–1136. https://www.ncbi.nlm.nih.gov/pmc/articles/PMC1693009/.

Mills, J. 2004. "Clarifications on Trieb: Freud's Theory of Motivation Reinstated." *Psychoanalytic Psychology,* 21(4), 673–677.

Morelli, S., Ranesibm L.T. and Lieberman, M.D. 2014. "The neural components of empathy: Predicting daily prosocial behavior." *Soc Cogn Affect Neurosci.* 9(1):39-47. https://www.ncbi.nlm.nih.gov/pmc/articles/PMC3871722/.

Morgenson, G.J. and Kucharczyk, J. 1978. "Central Neural Pathways for Angiotensin-Induced Thirst." *Fed Proc.*,37(13):2683-8. https://pubmed.ncbi.nlm.nih.gov/213317/.

Morris, J.S., Frith, C.D., Perrett, D.I., Rowland, D., Young, A.W., Calder, A.J. and Dolan, R.J. 1996. "A differential neural response in the human amygdala to fearful and happy facial expressions." *Nature*, Vol 383. http://library.mpib-berlin.mpg.de/ft/ext/rd/RD_Differential_1996.pdf.

Morris, R.W., Sparks, A., Mitchell, P.B., Weickert, C.S, and Green, M.J. 2012. "Lack of cortico-limbic coupling in bipolar disorder and schizophrenia during emotion regulation." *Translational Psychiatry.* https://www.nature.com/articles/tp201216

Moruzzi, G. and Magoun, H.W. 1949. "Brain stem reticular formation and activation of the EEG." *Electroencephalography and Clinical Neurophysiology* 1: 455–73. http://www.ncbi.nlm.nih.gov/pubmed/18421835.

Muller, D. 2019. "The Science Behind the Butterfly Effect." *Veritasium.* https://www.veritasium.com/videos/2019/12/6/the-science-of-the-butterfly-effect-.

Murphy, G. 2002. *The Big Book of Concepts.* Massachusetts Institute of Technology.

Mutschler, H., Gebhardt, M., Shoeman, R.L., and Meinhart, A. 2011. "A Novel Mechanism of Programmed Cell Death in Bacteria by Toxin–Antitoxin Systems Corrupts Peptidoglycan Synthesis." *PLOS.* https://journals.plos.org/plosbiology/article?id=10.1371/journal.pbio.1001033.

Myers, K.M. and Davis, M. 2007. "Mechanisms of fear extinction." *Molecular Psychiatry* 12: 120–150. http://www.nature.com/mp/journal/v12/n2/full/4001939a.html.

Nagera, H. 2018. "The Psychoanalytic Theory of Conflicts." https://www.youtube.com/watch?v=ZEfNmEA09ho.

Nashold B.S., Wilson W.P., and Slaughter G. 1969. "Sensations evoked by stimulation of the midbrain of man." *Journal of Neurosurgery.* 30: 14–24.

Nelson, D. 2013. *The Mystery of Pain.* Singing Dragon: London.

Neuman, F. 2015. "Standard Interpretations in Psychotherapy." *Psychology Today.* https://www.psychologytoday.com/us/blog/fighting-fear/201511/standard-interpretations-in-psychother-apy.

Newcombe, N., Drummey, A., Fox N., Lai E., and Ottinger-Alberts, W. 2000. "Rembering Early Childhood: How Much, How, and Why (or Why Not)". *Current Directions in Psychological Science* 9 (2): 55–58.

NIMH 2019. "Post-Traumatic Stress Disorder." https://www.nimh.nih.gov/health/topics/post-traumatic-stress-disorder-ptsd/index.shtml.

Noori, S. 2016. "What happens when a bee stings you?" *Science Curiosity.* http://explorecuriocity.org/Explore/ArticleId/5094/what-happens-when-a-bee-stings-you.aspx.

Northoff, G., Schneider, F., Rotte, M., Matthiae, C., Tempelmann, C., Wiebking, C., Bermpohl, F., Heinzel, A., Danos, P., Heinze, H.J., Bogerts, B., Walter, M., and Panksepp, J. 2009. "Differential parametric modulation of self-relatedness and emotions in different brain regions." *Human Brain Mapping,* 30, 369-382.

Nummenmaa, L., Glereana, E., Harib, R., and Hietanend, J.K. 2013. "Bodily maps of emotions." http://www.pnas.org/content/111/2/646.full.pdf.

Oakley, DA. 1980. "Improved instrumental learning in neodecorticate rats." *Physiology & Behavior,* Vol 24, Issue 2, p 357-366. https://www.sciencedirect.com/science/article/abs/pii/0031938480900992

Odendaal, J.S. and Meintjes, R.A. 2003. "Neurophysiological correlates of affiliative behaviour between humans and dogs." *Veterinary Journal,* 165(3(:296-301. https://www.sciencedirect.com/science/article/pii/S109002330200237X?via%3Dihub.

Olds, J., 1977. *Drives and Reinforcement,* New York: Raven.

Olds, J. and Milner, P. 1954. "Positive reinforcement produced by electrical stimulation of septal area and other regions of rat brain." *J Comp Physiol Psychol.* 1954 Dec;47(6):419-27.

Olmstead, M.C. and Franklin, K.B.J. 1997. "The development of conditioned place preference to morphine: Effects of microinjections into various CNS sites." *Behavioral neuroscience*, 111 (6), pp.1324-34.

Oostra, B.A and Nelson, D.L. 2006. "Animal Models of Fragile X Syndrome: Mice and Flies." In *Genetic Instabilities and Neurological Diseases (Second Edition)*, (Robert D.Wells & Tetsuo Ashizawa (eds.). UK:Academic Press. https://www.sciencedirect.com/topics/veterinary-science-and-veterinary-medicine/freezing-behavior.

Oremland, J.D., Blacker, K.H., and Norman, H.F. 1975. "Incompleteness in 'Successful' psychoanalyses: A follow-up study." *Journal of the American Psychoanalytic Association*, 23, 819-844. https://psycnet.apa.org/record/1976-22572-001.

Oza, N. 2014. "The Importance of Homeostasis in the Human Body: Keeping Us Alive." *Bright Hub* http://www.brighthub.com/science/medical/articles/111342.aspx.

Panksepp, J. 1981. "Brain opioids: A neurochemical substrate for narcotic and social dependence." In *Progress in theory in psychopharmacology*. S. Cooper (Ed.). London: Academic Press, 149-175.

Panksepp, J. 1992. "Oxytocin effects on emotional processes: separation distress, social bonding, and relationships to psychiatric disorders." *Annual of the New York Academy of Sciences*, 652,243-252.

Panksepp, J., 1995. "The Emotional Sources of 'Chills' Induced by Music." *Music Perception*. Vol. 13, No. 2, 171-207.

Panksepp, J., 1998a. *Affective Neuroscience: The Foundations of Human and Animal Emotions*. New York: Oxford University Press.

Panksepp, J. 1998b. "The periconscious substrates of consciousness: Affective states and the evolutionary origins of the SELF." *Journal of Consciousness Studies*, 5: 566-582.

Panksepp, J. 2005. "Affective consciousness: Core emotional feelings in animals and humans." *Consciousness and Cognition*, 14,

30-80. http://cmapspublic2.ihmc.us/rid=1GQXCR08F-1VH-0C1J-GB5/affective%20consciousness.pdf.

Panksepp, J. 2011a. "The basic emotional circuits of mammalian brains: Do animals have affective lives?" *Neuroscience and Biobehavioral Reviews* 35:1791–1804. https://library.allan-schore.com/docs/Panksepp11.pdf

Panksepp, J. 2011b. "Cross-Species Affective Neuroscience Decoding of the Primal Affective Experiences of Humans and Related Animals." *PLOS ONE* 6(8). http://journals.plos.org/plosone/article?id=10.1371/journal.pone.0021236.

Panksepp, J. 2015. "Affective Preclinical Modeling of Psychiatric Disorders: taking imbalanced primal emotional feelings of animals seriously in our search for novel anti-depressants." *Dialogues Clin Neurosci.*, 17(4):363-79. https://www.ncbi.nlm.nih.gov/pmc/articles/PMC4734875/.

Panksepp, J., Normansell, L.A., Cox, J.F. and Siviy, S. 1994. "Effects of neonatal decortication on the social play of juvenile rats." *Physiology & Behavior*, 56, 429-443 https://pubmed.ncbi.nlm.nih.gov/7972392/.

Panksepp, J. and Bernatzky, G. 2002. "Emotional sounds and the brain: the neuro-affective foundations of musical appreciation." *Behavioural Processes,* 60: 133-155.

Panksepp, J. and Northoff, G. 2009. "The trans-species core self: the emergence of active cultural and neuro-ecological agents through self related processing within subcortical-cortical mid-line networks." *Consciousness & Cognition*, 18, 193-215.

Panksepp, J., and Trevarthen, C. 2009. "Psychobiology of music: Motive impulses and emotions in expressions of musicality and in sympathetic emotional response to music." In S. Malloch and C. Trevarthen (Eds.), *Communicative musicality* (pp. 105–146). Cambridge, UK: Cambridge University Press.

Panksepp, and J Biven L. 2012. *The Archaeology of the Mind: Neuroevolutionary Origins of Human Emotions.* New York:Norton.

Papiasvili, E.D. 1995. "Conflict in psychoanalysis and in life." *International Forum of Psychoanalysis.* Volume 4, Issue 4.

https://www.tandfonline.com/doi/abs/10.1080/08037069 508409551?journalCode=spsy20.

Papple, D. 2017. "Innate Fears: Even Babies Get Stressed When They See Spiders And Snakes." *Inquisitr.* https://www.inquisitr. com/4556275/babies-stressed-spiders-and-snakes//.

Paré, D., Quirk, G.J., and LeDoux, J. 2004. "New Vistas on Amygdala Newtorks in Conditioned Fear." *Journal of Neurophysiology* 92: 1-9 http://www.ncbi.nlm.nih.gov/pubmed/15212433.

Paris, J. 2005. "Borderline Personality Disorder." *CAMJ*, 172(12): 1579–1583. https://www.ncbi.nlm.nih.gov/pmc/articles/PMC 558173/.

Parvizi, J. and Damasio AR. 2001. "Consciousness and the Brainstem." *Cognition*, 79 :135-159. http://citeseerx.ist.psu.edu/viewdoc/ download?doi=10.1.1.851.8108&rep=rep1&type=pdf.

Paul, E.S., Sher, S., Tamietto, M., Winkielman, P., and Mendl, M.T. 2020. "Towards a comparative science of emotion: Affect and consciousness in humans and animals." *Neuroscience & Behavioral Reviews*, vol 108:749-770. https://www.sciencedi- rect.com/science/article/pii/S0149763419303677

http://www.theatlantic.com/health/archive/2012/08/the-nature-of- consciousness-how-the-internet-could-learn-to-feel/261397/.

Paulus, M.P. 2007. "Neural basis of reward and craving--a homeo- static point of view." *Dialogues Clin Neurosci.* 2007;9(4):379-87. http://www.ncbi.nlm.nih.gov/pmc/articles/PMC3202500/.

Pellow, S., Chopin, P., File, S.E., and Briley, M. 1985. "Validation of open:closed arm entries in an elevated plus-maze as a mea- sure of anxiety in the rat." *Journal of Neuroscience*, vol 14, issue 3:149-167. https://www.ncbi.nlm.nih.gov/pubmed/2864480.

Penfield, W. and Jasper, H.H. 1954 *Epilepsy and the functional anat- omy of the human brain*. Little, Brown.

Pessoa, L. 2005. "To what extent are emotional visual stimuli pro- cessed without attention and awareness?" *Current Opinion in Neurobiology*, 15: 188-196.

Pessoa, L. 2010. "Emotion and Cognition and the Amygdala: From 'what is it?' to 'what's to be done?'" *Neuropsychologia*, 48

(12): 3416-3429. http://www.ncbi.nlm.nih.gov/pmc/articles/PMC2949460/.

Peters-Golden, H. 2012. *Cultural Sketches: Case Studies in Anthropology.* Dubuque, Iowa:The McGraw https://zodml.org/sites/default/files/%5BHolly_Peters-Golden%5D_Culture_Sketches_Case_Studi.pdf.

Peterson, J. 2018. "The Big IQ Controversy." https://www.youtube.com/watch?v=h02w5E7FGlY.

Peterson,J.2019a."TheMeaningandRealityofIndividualSovereignty." https://www.youtube.com/watch?v=JpA5iDpnrbw.

Peterson, J. 2019b. "Why You Cannot Be Yourself In Society." https://www.youtube.com/watch?v=d3wtxYmkr2o.

Pfeffer, AZ., 1963. "The meaning of the analyst after analysis – A contribution to the theory of therapeutic results." *Journal of the American Psychoanalytic Association,* 11:229-244. http://www.pep-web.org/document.php?id=apa.011.0229a&type=hitlist&num=14&query=zo.

Phan, K.L., Wager, T., Taylor, S.F., and Liberzon, I. 2002. "Functional neuroanatomy of emotion: A meta-analysis of emotion activation studies in PET and fMRI." *Neuroimage,* 16, 331-348. http://www.sciencedirect.com/science/article/pii/S1053811902910876.

Phelps, E.A., O'Connor, K.J., Gatenby, C., Gore, JC., Grillon, C., and Davis, M. 2001. "Activation of the left amygdala to a cognitive representation of fear." *Nature Publishing Group.* https://www.researchgate.net/profile/Chris_Gatenby/publication/12057625_Activation_of_the_left_amygdala_to_a_cognitive_representation_of_fear/links/09e4150a28d32f03b5000000.pdf.

Ploj, K., Roman, E., and Nylander, I. 2003. "Long-term effects of short and long periods of maternal separation on brain opioid peptide levels in male Wistar rats." *Neuropeptides* 37:149–156.

Popkin. B.M., D'Anci, K.E; and Rosenberg, I.H. 2010. "Water, Hydration and Health." *Nutr Rev.,* 68(8): 439–458. http://www.ncbi.nlm.nih.gov/pmc/articles/PMC2908954/.

Popova, M. 2019. "An Evolutionary Anatomy of Affect: Neuroscientist Antonio Damasio on How and Why We Feel What We Feel." *brainpickings* https://www.brainpickings.org/2018/02/22/antonio-damasio-the-strange-order-of-things/.

Preston, A.R. and Eichenbaum, H. 2013. "Interplay of hippocampus and prefrontal cortex in memory." *Curr. Biol.,* 23(17). 764-773. https://www.ncbi.nlm.nih.gov/pmc/articles/PMC3789138/.

Purandare, M. 2018. "Psychological Foundations." https://www.youtube.com/watch?v=9-aRP9xQNmU.

Purves, D., Augustine, G.J., Fitzpatrick, D., Katz, L.C., LaMantia, A-S., McNamara, J.O., Williams, S.M. 2001. "Physiological Changes Associated with Emotion." *Neuroscience, 2nd edition.* Sinauer Associates: Sunderland (MA). https://www.ncbi.nlm.nih.gov/books/NBK10829/.

Rakic, P. 2009. "Evolution of the neocortex: Perspective from developmental biology". *Nat. Rev. Neurosci.,* 10 (10): 724-735. http://www.ncbi.nlm.nih.gov/pmc/articles/PMC2913577/.

Ramachandran, V. S. 2009. *SELF AWARENESS: THE LAST FRONTIER: An Edge Original Essay.* http://edge.org/conversation/self-awareness-the-last-frontier.

Ray Li, C-s., and Sinha, R. 2009. "Inhibitory Control and Emotional Stress Regulation: Neuroimaging Evidence for Frontal-Limbic Dysfunction in Psycho-stimulant Addiction." *Neurosci. Biobehav. Rev.* https://www.ncbi.nlm.nih.gov/pmc/articles/PMC2263143.

Redgrave, P., McHaffie, J.G., and Stein, B.E. 1996. "Nociceptive neurons in rat superior colliculus I: Antidromic activation from the contralateral predorsal bundle." *Experimental Brain Research* 109:185–96.

Rees, G., Kreiman, G. and Koch, C. 2002. "Neural correlates of consciousness in humans." *Nature Reviews Neuroscience* 3(4):261–70. http://www.nature.com/nrn/journal/v3/n4/full/nrn783.html.

Reid, R. 2017. "Bad news guys – celibacy probably makes you live longer." *Metro.* https://metro.co.uk/2017/01/17/bad-news-guys-celibacy-probably-makes-you-live-longer-6385873/.

Reynolds, C.W. 1987. "Flocks, Herds, and Schools: A Distributed Behavioral Model." *Computer Graphics*, 21(4): 25-34. http://www.cs.toronto.edu/~dt/siggraph97-course/cwr87/.

Riggins, T., Geng, F., Botdorf, M., Canada, K., Cox, L., and Hancock, G.R. 2018. "Protracted hippocampal development is associated with age-related improvements in memory during early childhood." *Neuroimag. 174*:127-37. https://www.ncbi.nlm.nih.gov/pmc/articles/PMC5949262/.

Rizzolatti, G., Fadiga, L., Gallese, V., and Fogassi, L. 1996. "Premotor cortex and the recognition of motor actions." *Cognitive Brain Research*, 3(2):131-141.

Roberts, A.C., and Clarke, H.C. 2019. "Why we need nonhuman primates to study the role of ventromedial prefrontal cortex in the regulation of threat- and reward-elicited responses." *PNAS*, 116 (52): 26297–26304. https://www. pnas.org/content/116/52/26297.

Robertson, J. and Robertson, J. 1967 Film: "Kate, Aged Two Years Five Months, in Foster Care for Twenty-seven Days." 16 mm, 33 minutes, in English, French and Danish. *Young Children in Brief Separation Film Series.* Concord Video and Film Council.

Robertson, J. and Robertson, J. 1968. Film: "Jane, Aged Seventeen Months, in Foster Care for Ten Days." 16 mm, 39 minutes, in English, Danish, French, German and Swedish. *Young Children in Brief Separation Film Series.* Concord Video and Film Council.

Robertson, J. and Robertson, J. 1971. Film: "Thomas, Aged Two Years Four Months, in Foster Care for Ten Days". 16 mm, 38 minutes, in English. *Young Children in Brief Separation Film Series.* Concord Video and Film Council.

Rodrigues, S.M., Schaffe, G.E., and LeDoux, J.E. 2001. "Intra-Amygdala Blockade of the NR2B Subunit of the NMDA Receptor Disrupts the Acquisition But Not the Expression of Fear Conditioning." *J. of Neuroscience.* 21(17): 6889-6896. http://www.jneurosci.org/content/21/17/6889.short.

Roelofs, K. 2017. "Freeze for action: neurobiological mechanisms in animal and human freezing." *Philos. Trans. R. Soc. Lond.*

B. Biol. Sci., 372(1718). https://www.ncbi.nlm.nih.gov/pmc/articles/PMC5332864/.

Rolls, E.T. 2000. "Neurophysiology and functions of the primate amygdale, and the neural basis for emotion." In *The Aamygdala* (Aggleton JP ed.) Oxford: Oxfore University Press.

Rolls, E.T. 2005. *Emotions.* Oxford: Oxford University Press.

Ronningstam, E. 2016. "New Insights Into Narcissistic Personality Disorder." *Psychiatric Times.* https://www.psychiatrictimes.com/view/new-insights-narcissistic-personality-disorder.

Rorty, R. 1991. "Blunder around for a while." *London Review of Books.* Vol. 13, No. 22.21:3-6. https://www.lrb.co.uk/v13/n22/richard-rorty/blunder-around-for-a-while.

Rosen, J.B. 2004. "The Neurobiology of Conditioned and Unconditioned Fear: A Neurobehavioral System Analysis of the Amygdala." *Behavioral and Cognitive Neuroscience Reviews.* http://www.ask-force.org/web/Ethics/Rosen-Neurobiology-Conditioned-Unconditioned-Fear.pdf.

Rosenblatt, J.S., Factor, E.M and Mayer, A.D. 1994. "Relationship between maternal aggression and maternal care in the rat." *Wiley Online Library.* https://onlinelibrary.wiley.com/doi/abs/10.1002/1098-2337(1994)20:3%3C243::AID-AB2480200311%3E3.0.CO;2-L.

Rossetti, Y., Rode, G., and Boisson, D. 1995. "Implicit processing of somaesthetic information: a dissociation between where and how?" *NeuroReport,* 6: 506-510.

Rotenberg, S and McGrath, J.J. 2016. "Inter-relation between autonomic and JOA axis activity in children and adolescents." *Biol. Psychol.* ncbi.nim.nih.gov/pmc/articles/PMC5731846/.

Rutherford, S.T and Bassler, B.L 2012. "Bacterial Quorum Sensing: Its Role in Virulence and Possibilities for Its Control." *Cold Spring Harb Perspect Med.,* 2 (11). https://www.ncbi.nlm.nih.gov/pmc/articles/PMC3543102/.

Ryczko, D. and Dubuc, R. 2013. "The multifunctional mesencephalic locomotor region." *Curr. Pharm. Des.* 19(24): 4448-70. http://www.ncbi.nlm.nih.gov/pubmed/23360276.

Salzman, C.D. and Fusi, S. 2010. "Emotion, Cognition, and Mental State Representation in Amygdala and Prefrontal Cortex." *Annu Rev Neurosci.*, 33:173-202. https://www.ncbi.nlm.nih.gov/pmc/articles/PMC3108339/.

Samson, R.D. and Paré, D. 2005. "Activity-Dependent Synaptic Plasticity in the Central Nucleus of the Amygdala. *J. Neurosci.* 16:25(7):1847-55. https://pubmed.ncbi.nlm.nih.gov-/15716421/J. Neurosci.

Samuel, L. 2011. "The three parts of the brainstem and their function." *Interactive Biology*: Making Biology Fun. https://www.youtube.com/watch?v=yQetOVB_VZo.

Sanfey, A.G., Rilling J.K., Aronson, J.A., Nystrom, L.E., Cohen, J,D. (2003). "The neural basis of economic decision-making in the Ultimatum Game". *Science*, 300, (5626): 1755–8. http://www.sciencemag.org/content/300/5626/1755.

Santolaria-Fernández, F.J., Gómez-Sirvent, J.L., González-Reimers, C.E., Batista-López, J.N., Jorge-Hernández, J.A., Rodríguez-Moreno, F., Martínez-Riera, A., Hernández-García, M.T. 1995. "Nutritional assessment of drug addicts." *Drug Alcohol Depend.*, 38(1):11-8. http://www.ncbi.nlm.nih.gov/pubmed/7648992.

Sapolsky, R.M. 1992. *Stress, the Aging Brain and the Mechanisms of Neuron Death*. MIT Press: Cambridge MA.

Saplosky, R.M. 2010. "Chaos and Reductionism." http://www.youtube.com/watch?v=_njf8jwEGRo.

Sargis, R.M. 2015. "An Overview of the Hypothalamus:The Endocrine System's Link to the Nervous System." http://www.endocrineweb.com/endocrinology/overview-hypothalamus.

Sarwari, K. 2019. "You Think You Can Read Facial Expressions? You're Wrong." *News@Northeastern* https://news.northeastern.edu/2019/07/19/northeastern-university-professor-says-we-cant-gauge-emotions-from-facial-expressions-alone/.

Satputea, A.B., Wagerb, T.D , Cohen-Adadc, J., Bianciardid, M., Choid, J-K., Buhlee, J.T., Waldd, L.L. , and Barrett, L.F. 2013. "Identification of discrete functional subregions of the human periaqueductal gray." *PNAS*, vol. 110, no. 42:17101–17106. https://www.pnas.org/content/pnas/110/42/17101.full.pdf.

Schafer, R. 1983. *The Analytic Attitude*. New York: Basic Books.

Schiff, N.D. 2007. "Global disorders of consciousness." In M. Velmans M. and S. Schneider (Eds.) *The Blackwell Companion to Consciousness*. (pp. 589-604) Oxford, UK: Blackwell Publishing.

Schmid, M.C., Mrowka, S.W., Turchi, J., Saunders, R.C., Wilke, M., Peters, A.J., Ye, F.Q., and Leopold, D.A. 2010. "Blindsight depends on the lateral geniculate nucleus." *Nature* 466: 373–377.

Schmitter, A.M. 2010. "17th and 18th century theories of emotions." In: *The Stanford Encyclopedia of Philosophy*, (Zalta EN editor). http://plato.stanford.edu/archives/win2010/entries/emotions-17th, 18th/.

Schore, A.N. 2001. "Effects of a secure attachment relationship on right brain development, affect regulation and infant mental health." *Infant Mental Health Journal*, Vol 22 (1-2): 7-66 http://www.allanschore.com/pdf/SchoreIMHJAttachment.pdf.

Schubert, A. and Schmidt, N. 2018. "Most Nazis escaped justice. Now Germany is racing to convict those who got away https://www.cnn.com/2018/12/14/europe/germany-nazi-war-trials-grm-intl/index.html.

Scott, E. 2020. "The Health Benefits of Laughter. *Verywellmind*. https://www.verywellmind.com/the-stress-management-and-health-benefits-of-laughter-3145084

Scott-Phillips, 2015. "Infections of the mind: why anti-vaxxers just 'know' they're right." *The Conversation. https://theconversation. com/us.*

Seamans, J.K., Lapish, C.C., and Durstenwitz, D., 2008. "Comparing the Prefrontal Cortex of Rats and Primates: Insights from Electrophysiology." *Neurotoxicity Research, VOL. 14(2,3)* 249-262.

Sedwick, C. 2011. "PezT: A Bacterial Suicide Gene." *PLoS Biol* 9(3). https://doi.org/10.1371/journal.pbio.1001036.

Sevenster, D., Visser, R.M., and D'Hooge, R. 2018. "A translational perspective on neural circuits of fear extinction: Current promises and challenges." *Neurobiol Learn Mem.*, 155:113-126. https://www.ncbi.nlm.nih.gov/pmc/articles/PMC6805216/.

Shafer, R. 1982. *The Analytic Attitutude.* London:Karnac Books

Sharma, K., LeBlanc, R., Haque, M., Nishimori, K., Reid, M.M., Teruyama, R. 2019. "Sexually dimorphic oxytocin receptor-expressing neurons in the preoptic area of the mouse brain." *PLOS ONE.* https://journals.plos.org/plosone/article?id=10.1371/journal.pone.0219784.

Shewmon, D.A., Holmes, D.A. and Byrne, P.A. 1999. "Consciousness in congenitally decorticate children: developmental vegetate state as a self-fulfilling prophecy." *Developmental Medicine and Child Neurology.* 41: 6, 364-374.

Shik, M.L., Severin, F.V., and Orlovskii, G.N. 1966. "Control of walking and running by means of electric stimulation of the midbrain." *Biofizka*, 11(4): 659-66. http://www.ncbi.nlm.nih.gov/pubmed/6000625.

Shostak, M. 1983. *Nisa: The Life and Words of a !Kung Woman.* New York:Vintage.

Shrand, J. A. 2017. "The Science of Schadenfreude." *Psychology Today.* https://www.psychologytoday.com/us/blog/the-i-m-approach/201703/the-science-schadenfreude.

Siebert, M., Markowitsch, H.J., Bartel, P. 2003. "Amygdala, affect and cognition: evidence from 10 patients with Urbach±Wiethe disease." *Brain*, 126.

Silbersweig, D., Clarkin, J.F., Goldstein, M. Kernberg, O.F., Tuescher, O, Levy, K.N., Brendel, G., Pan, H., Beutel, M., Pavony, M.T., Epstein, J., Lenzenweger, M.F., Thomas, K.M., Posner, M.I., and Stern, E. 2008. "Failure of Frontolimbic Inhibitory Function in the Context of Negative Emotion in Borderline Personality Disorder. *Pennstate.* *https://pennstate.pure.elsevier.com/en/publications/failure-of-frontolimbic-inhibitory-function-in-the-context-of-neg.*

Simon, G.E. 2001. "Treating depression in patients with chronic disease." *West J. Med.* 175(5):292-293 https://www.ncbi.nlm.nih.gov/pmc/articles/PMC1071593/.

Simon-Thomas. M.R. 2017. "Are Emotions Born or Made?" *Greater Good Magazine: Science-Based Insights for a Meaningful Life.* https://greatergood.berkeley.edu/article/item/are_emotions_born_or_made.

Skinner, B.F. 1953. *Science and Human Behavior.* New Jersey: Simon&Schuster. http://www.bfskinner.org/bfskinner/Society_files/Science_and_Human_Behavior.pdf.

Smith, K., 2018. "Substance Abuse and Depression." *PSYCOM.* https://www.psycom.net/depression-substance-abuse.

Smith, W.D. 1979. *Hippocratic Tradition.* Ithaca :Cornell University Press.

Solano, C., Echeverz, M., and Inigo, L. 2014. "Biofilm dispersion and quorum sensing." *Current Opinion in Microbiology,* vol 18:96-104. https://www.sciencedirect.com/science/article/abs/pii/S1369527414000290.

Solms, M. 2013. "The Conscious Id." *Neuropsychoanalysis,*15 (1):5-19. http://www.tandfonline.com/doi/pdf/10.1080/15294145.2013.10773711.

Solms, M. and Turnbull, O. 2002. *The Brain and the Inner World: An Introduction to the Neuroscience of Subjective Experience.* London: H. Karnac (Books) Ltd.

Solms, M., and Panksepp, J. 2012. "The 'Id' Knows More than the 'Ego' Admits: Neuropsychoanalytic and Primal Consciousness Perspectives on the Interface Between Affective and Cognitive Neuroscience." *Brain Sci.,* 2(2): 147-15. https://www.ncbi.nlm.nih.gov/pmc/articles/PMC4061793/.

Sotres-Bayon, F., Bush, D.E.A. and LeDoux, J.E. 2004. "Emotional Perseveration: An Update on Prefrontal–Amygdala Interactions in Fear Extinction." *Cold Spring Harbor Laboratory Press ISSN:* 11:525–535 http://citeseerx.ist.psu.edu/viewdoc/download?doi=10.1.1.829.1682&rep=rep1&type=pdf.

Sparks, D.L. 1988. "Neural cartography: Sensory and motor maps in the superior colliculus." *Brain Behav. Evol.* 31: 49-56.

Sperry, R.W. 1969. "A Modified Concept of Consciousness." *Psychological Review,* vol. 76, no. 6:532-536. http://people.uncw.edu/puente/sperry/sperrypapers/60s/147-1969.pdf.

Spitz, R.A. 1945 "Hospitalism." *Psychoanalytic Study of the Child,* 1: 53-74.

Spitz, R.A. 1946. "Anaclitic depression." *Psychoanalytic Study of the Child,* 2, 313-342.

Stevens, F.L., Hurley, R.A., Taber, K.H., and Hayman, L.A. 2001. "Anterior Cingulate Cortex: Unique Role in Cognition and Emotion." *Neuropsychiatry.* https://neuro.psychiatryonline.org/doi/full/10.1176/jnp.23.2.jnp121.

Stephens, M.A.C., and Wand, G. 2012. "Stress and the HPA axis: Role of glucocorticoids in alcohol dependence." *Alcohol Research: Current Reviews,* 34(4), 468–483.

Sternberg, R.J. 2003. "Contemporary theories of intelligence." In W.M. Reynolds amd G.E. Miller (Eds.), *Handbook of psychology: Educational psychology* (Vol. 7, pp. 23–45). Hoboken, NJ: John Wiley & Sons

Stewart, I. 1997. *Does God Play Dice?* The New Mathematics of Chaos. London: Penguin Books.

Stratford, M. 2014. "What Are Two Examples of Responses Organisms Display to Maintain Homeostasis?" http://classroom.synonym.com/two-examples-responses-organisms-display-maintain-homeostasis-15560.html.

Strominger N.L., Demarest R.J., and Laemle L.B., 2012. "Cerebral Cortex." In: Noback's *Human Nervous System, Seventh Edition.* Humana Press, Totowa, NJ. https://link.springer.com/chapter/10.1007/978-1-61779-779-8_25#citeas

Stuber, G.D. and Wise, R.A. 2016. "Lateral Hypothalamic Circuits for Feeding and Reward." *Nat. Neurosci.,* 19(2):198-205. https://www.ncbi.nlm.nih.gov/pmc/articles/PMC4927193/.

Sugarman, A. 1995. "Psychoanalysis: Treatment of conflict or deficit?" *Psychoanalytic Psychology,* 12(1), 55–70. https://doi.org/10.1037/h0079605.

Sukel, K. 2011. "The Synapse – A Primer." http://www.dana.org/News/Details.aspx?id=43512.

Suttie I 1935. *The origins of love and hate.* London: Penguin.

Swain, J.E, Lorberbaum, J.P, Korse, S, and Strathearn, L. 2007. "Brain basis of early parent-infant interactions: psychology, physiology, and in vivo function neuroimaging studies." *Journal of Child and Adolescent Psychiatry*, 48: 262-287.

Swenson, R.S., 2006. "REVIEW OF CLINICAL AND FUNCTIONAL NEUROSCIENCE." http://www.dartmouth.edu/~rswenson/NeuroSci/chapter_11.html.

Terbeck, S., Savulescu, J., Chesterman, L.P., and Cowen, P.J. 2016. "Noradrenaline effects on social behaviour, intergroup relations, and moral decisions." *Neurosci. Biobehav. Rev.* 66:54-60. https://www.ncbi.nlm.nih.gov/pmc/articles/PMC4899514/.

Tershner, S.A., and Helmstetter, F.J. 2000. "Antinociception produced by mu opioid receptor activation in the amygdala is partly dependent on activation of mu opioid and neurotensin receptors in the ventral periaqueductal gray." *Brain Research* 865: 17–26. file:///Users/barriebiven/Downloads/00b49535fe5edac90e000000.pdf.

Thompson, J. 2011. "Is Nonverbal Communication a Numbers Game?" *Psychology Today.* https://www.psychologytoday.com/us/blog/beyond-words/201109/is-nonverbal-communication-numbers-game

Thornton, S.P. 1995-present. "Sigmund Freud (1856—1939)." *Internet Encyclopedia of Philosophy.* http://www.iep.utm.edu/freud/.

Tinbergen, N. 1951. *The study of instinct.* New York & London, Oxford University Press.

Tonneau, F. 2008. "THE CONCEPT OF REINFORCEMENT: EXPLANATORY OR DESCRIPTIVE?" *Behavior and Philosophy*, 36: 87-96 (2008). http://escola.psi.uminho.pt/unidades/lca/artigos/philosophy/Tonneau2008.pdf.

Tononi, G. 2004. "An information integration theory of consciousness." *BMC Neuroscience* 5(1):42.

Toronchuk, J.A., and Ellis, G.F.R. 2012. "Affective Neuronal Selection: The Nature of the Primordial Emotion Systems." *Front Psychol.* 3: 589. http://www.ncbi.nlm.nih.gov/pmc/articles/PMC3540967/.

Travagli, R.A. 2007. "The nucleus tractus solitarius: an integrative centre with 'task-matching' capabilities." *J Physiol.*,582:471. http://www.ncbi.nlm.nih.gov/pmc/articles/PMC2075317/.

Travers, J.B. and Norgren, R. 1986. "Electromyographic analysis of the ingestion and rejection of sapid stimuli in the rat". *Behavioral Neuroscience.* 100 (4): 544–555. https://pubmed.ncbi.nlm.nih.gov/3741605/.

Trimble, M.R., Mendez, M.F., and Cummings, J.L. 1997. "Neuropsychiatric Symptoms From the Temporolimbic Lobes." In *The Neuropsychiatric of Limbic and Subcortical Disorders.* Stephen Salloway, Paul Malloy & Jeffery L. Cummings (eds.). Washington DC: American Psychiatric Press Inc.

Tyng, C.M., Amin, H.U., Saad, M.N.N., and Malik, A.S. 2017. "The Influences of Emotion on Learning and Memory." *Front. Psychol.* https://www.frontiersin.org/articles/10.3389/fpsyg.2017.01454/full.

Tzschentke, T.M. 2007. "Measuring reward with the conditioned place preference (CPP) paradigm: update of the last decade." *Addiction Biology*, 12, 227-462.

United States Department for Veterans Affairs: *National Centre for PTSD* 2007. http://www.ptsd.va.gov/public/pages/ptsd-and-re-lationships.asp.

Uttal, W.R. 2011. *Mind and Brain: A Critical Appraisal of Cognitive Neuroscience.* MA.: MIT Press.

Vacek, M. 2002. "High on Fidelity: What can voles teach us about monogamy." *American Scientist.* http://www.americanscientist.org/template/AssetDetail/assetid/14756.

Valenstein, E.S., Cox, V.C., and Kakolwski, V.C. 1970. "Reexamination of the role of the hypothalamus in motivated behaviour." *Psych. Rev.* 77: 16-31.

Van Der Horst, F.C.P. and Van Der Veer, R. 2009. "Separation and Divergence: The Untold Story of James Robertson's and John Bowlby's Theoretical Dispute On Mother-Child Separation." *Journal of the History of Behavioral Sciences,* Volume 45(3):236-252.

van der Westhuizen, D. and Solms, M. 2015. "Basic emotional foundations of social dominance in relation to Panksepp's affective taxonomy." *Neuropsychoanalysis*, vol. 17, issue 1: 19-37. http://www.tandfonline.com/doi/full/10.1080/15294145.2015.1021 371?scroll=top&needAccess=true.

van Furth, W.R; Wolterink, G., and van Ree, J.M. 1995. "Regulation of masculine sexual behavior: involvement of brain opioids and dopamine." *Brain Research Reviews* 21: 162-184.

Van Melderen, L. and Saavedra De Bast, M. 2009. "Bacterial Toxin–Antitoxin Systems: More Than Selfish Entities?" *PLoS Genet*, 5(3). https://www.ncbi.nlm.nih.gov/pmc/articles/PMC2654758/.

van Steenbergen, H., Eikemo, M. and Leknes, S. 2019. "The role of the opioid system in decision making and cognitive control: A review." *Cogn Affect Behav Neurosci* 19, 435–458 (2019). https://doi.org/10.3758/s13415-019-00710-6.

Veening, J-W., Igoshin, O.A., Eijlander, R.T, Nijland, R., Hamoen, L.W., and Kuipers, O.P. 2008. "Transient heterogeneity in extracellular protease production by Bacillus subtilis." *Molecular Systems Biology* 4, 184. https://igoshin.rice.edu/papers/Veening%282008%29MSB.pdf.

Velasco, M., Velasco, F., Machado, J. and Olvera, A. 1972. "Effects of Novelty, Habituation, Attention and Distraction on the Amplitude of the Various Components of the Somatic Evoked Responses." *International Journal of Neuroscience* Vol. 5, Issue 3. https://www.tandfonline.com/doi/abs/10.3109/00207457309149461.

Velmans, M. 1995. "Modern Dualism: David Chalmers." http://webspace.webring.com/people/nj/jwschmidt/books/Chalmers.html.

Vemuri, V. 1978. *Modeling of Complex Systems: An Introduction*. New York: Academic Press.

Walker, D.L. and Davis, M. 2008. "Role of the extended amygdala in short-duration versus sustained fear: a tribute to Dr. Lennart Heimer." *Brain Struct Funct.*, 213(1-2):29-42. https://www.ncbi.nlm.nih.gov/pubmed/18528706.

Wargo, E. 2010. "Understanding the Interactions Between Emotion and Cognition." *Association for Psychological Science.* https://www.psychologicalscience.org/observer/understanding-the-interactions-between-emotion-and-cognition.

Waska, R.T. 2001. "Schizoid Anxiety: A Reappraisal of the Manic Defense and the Depressive Position." *AMERICAN JOURNAL OF PSYCHOTHERAPY,* Vol. 55, No. 1. https://psychotherapy.psychiatryonline.org/doi/pdf/10.1176/appi.psychotherapy.2001.55.1.105.

Watson, T.C., Cerminara, N.L., Lumb, B.M., and Apps, R. 2016. "Neural Correlates of Fear In the Periaqueductal Gray." *Journal of Neuroscience* 36 (50:) 12707-12719. https://www.jneurosci.org/content/36/50/12707.

Watt, D.F. 2017. "Reflections on the neuroscientific legacy of Jaak Panksepp (1943–2017)." *Neuropsychoanalysis* Vol 19, issue 2. https://www.tandfonline.com/doi/full/10.1080/15294145.2017.1376549.

Watt, D.F. and Pincus, D.I. 2004. "Neural substrates of consciousness: Implications for clinical psychiatry." In *Textbook of Biological Psychiatry*, J.Panksepp (ed.). Hoboken NJ: Wiley.

Watt, D. amd Panksepp, J. 2009. "Depression: An Evolutionarily Conserved Mechanism to Terminate Separation Distress? A Review of Aminergic, Peptergic and Neural Networks Perspectives." *Neuropsychoanalysis* Vol 11 No. 1: 7-51

Weierich, M.R., Wright. C.I., Negreira, A., Dickerson, B.C., and Barrett, L.F. 2010. "Novelty as a Dimension in the Affective Brain" *Neuroimage.*, 49(3):2871. https://www.ncbi.nlm.nih.gov/pmc/articles/PMC2818231/.

Weiskrantz, L. 1956. "Behavioral Changes Associated with Ablation of the Amygdaloid Complex in Monkeys." *Journal of Comparative Physiology and Psychology*, 49, 381-391

Weiskrantz, L. (1986). Blindsight: A Case Study and Implications. Oxford University Press.

Weiskrantz, L., Warrington, E.K., Sanders, M.D., and Marshall, J. 1974. "Visual capacity in the hemianopic field following a restricted occipital ablation." *Brain*, 97: 709-728.

Whishaw, I.Q. and Kolb, B. 1985. "The mating movements of male decorticate rats: Evidence for subcortically generated movements by the male but regulation of approaches by the female." *Behavioural Brain Research* 17:171–91.

Wicker, B., Keysers, C., Plailly, J., Royet, J. P., Gallese, V., and Rizzolatti, G. 2003. "Both of us disgusted in my insula: The common neural basis of seeing and feeling disgust." *Neuron,* 40(3), 655-664. https://www.ncbi.nlm.nih.gov/pubmed/14642287.

Wilensky A.E, Schafe G.E., Kristensen, M.P., LeDoux, J.E. 2006. "Rethinking the fear circuit: the central nucleus of the amygdala is required for the acquisition, consolidation, and expression of pavlovian fear conditioning." *J Neurosci* 26:12387–12396.

Williams, C.R. and Arrigo, B.A. 2002. *Law Psychology and Justice.* State University of New York: Albany.

Williams, M.A., Morris, A.P., McGlone, F., Abbott, D.F., and Mattingley, J.B. 2004. "Amygdala responses to fearful and happy facial expressions under conditions of binocular suppression." *J. Neurosci.,* 24(12):2898-904. https://www.ncbi.nlm.nih.gov/pubmed/15044528.

Wirsig, C.R. and Grill, H.J. 1982. "Contribution of the rat's neocortex to ingestive control: I. Latent learning for the taste of sodium chloride." *Journal of Comparative and Physiological Psychology.* 96 (4): 615–627.

Wolanin, A., Gross, M., Hong, E.M. 2015. "Depression in Athlete Prevalence and Risk Factors." *Current Sports Medicine Reports.* Vol 14, issue 1:56-60. https://journals.lww.com/acsm-csmr/fulltext/2015/01000/depression_in_athletes__prevalence_and_risk.17.aspx.

Wootton, D. 2006. *Bad Medicine: Doctors doing more harm than good since Hippocrates.* Oxford, New York: Oxford University Press.

Wright, J., and Panksepp, J. 2011. "Toward affective circuit-based preclinical models of depression: Sensitizing dorsal PAG arousal leads to sustained suppression of positive affect in rats." *Neuroscience & Biobehavioral Reviews.*

Wright, P., He, G., Shapira, N.A., Goodman, W.K., Liu, Y. 2004. "Disgust and the insula: fMRI responses to pictures of mutilation and contamination". *NeuroReport* 15 (15): 2347–51.

Wright, R. and Barrett, L.F 2017. *The Wright Show.* https://www.youtube.com/watch?v=Ax8PShRiA5Q.

Yang, Q.E. and Walsh, T.R. 2017. "Toxin–antitoxin systems and their role in disseminating and maintaining antimicrobial resistance." *FEMS Microbiol Rev.,* 41(3): 343-353. https://www.ncbi.nlm.nih.gov/pmc/articles/PMC5812544/.

Yates, D. 2015. "Feeling anxious? Check your orbitofrontal cortex, cultivate your optimism." *ScienceDaily.* https://www.sciencedaily.com/releases/2015/09/150922115819.htm.

Yeo, S.S., Chang, P.H., and Jang, S.H. 2013. "The Ascending Reticular Activating System from Pontine Reticular Formation to the Thalamus in the Human Brain." *Front. Hum. Neurosci.,*7:416. https://www.ncbi.nlm.nih.gov/pmc/articles/PMC3722571/.

Young, P.T. 1959. "The role of affective processes in learning and motivation." *Psychological Review,* Vol 66(2): 104-125.

Young, R.F., and Rinaldi, P.C. 1997. "Brain stimulation." In R. B. North & R. M. Levy (Eds.), *Neurosurgical management of pain* (pp. 228–290) New York, NY: Springer.

Zeevalk, G.D. 2010. "Nervous System and Behavioral Toxicology" In *Comprehensive Toxicology (Second Edition)* Volume 13:*3-27.*

Zeithamova, D., Mack, M.L., Braunlich, K., Davis, T., Seger, C.A., van Kesteren, M.T.R. and Wutz, A. 2019. "Brain Mechanisms of Concept Learning." *The Journal of Neuroscience, 39(42):*8259 – 8266. https://www.jneurosci.org/content/jneuro/39/42/8259.full.pdf.

Zimmerman, J.M., Rabinak, C.A., McLachlan, I.G and Maren, S. 2007. "The central nucleus of the amygdala is essential for acquiring and expressing conditional fear after overtraining." *Learning and Memory,* 14(9):634-644. https://www.ncbi.nlm.nih.gov/pmc/articles/PMC1994080/.

Zubieta, J.K, Ketter, T.A., Bueller, J.A., Xu Y, Kilbourn MR, Young EA, and Koeppe RA. 2003. "Regulation of human affective responses by anterior cingulate and limbic mu-opioid neuro-transmission." *Archives of General Psychiatry*, 60, 1145-1153.

Zuckerberg, M. 2017. "Mark Zuckerberg on taking risks and finding talented people. https://www.youtube.com/watch?v=VAUt2j6juHU.

About the Author

Lucy Biven is a US citizen who trained at the Anna Freud National Centre for Children and Families in England. She became interested in neuroscience twenty-five years ago and subsequently coauthored *The Archaeology of the Mind* with Jaak Panksepp in 2012. She has practiced psychotherapy in the United States, South Africa, and England. Most recently, she was head of child and adolescent psychotherapy child at the Leicestershire Partnership NHS Trust in the UK. After many years of living in the UK, she returned to the United States and currently lives in Maryland.